Book Yourself Solid

ILLUSTRATED

The Fastest, Easiest, and Most Reliable System
for Getting MORE Clients Than You Can Handle
Even if You Hate Marketing and Selling

MICHAEL PORT

with visual strategist
JOCELYN WALLACE

WILEY

For general information on our other products and services or for technical support, please contact our Customer Care Department within the United States at (800) 762-2974, outside the United States at (317) 572-3993 or fax (317) 572-4002.

Wiley also publishes its books in a variety of electronic formats. Some content that appears in print may not be available in electronic books. For more information about Wiley products, visit our web site at www.wiley.com.

Library of Congress Cataloging-in-Publication Data:

Port, Michael, 1970–

 Book yourself solid: the fastest, easiest, and most reliable system for getting more clients than you can handle even if you hate marketing and selling / Michael Port—.
  p. cm.
 ISBN 978-1-118-49542-1 (pbk.), ISBN 978-1-118-61135-7 (ebk); 978-1-118-61149-4 (ebk); 978-1-118-62992-5 (ebk)
  1. Selling. 2. Marketing. 3. Strategic planning. I. Title.
 HF5438.25.P67 2010
 658.8—dc22   2010024728

Printed in the United States of America
10 9 8 7 6 5 4 3 2 1

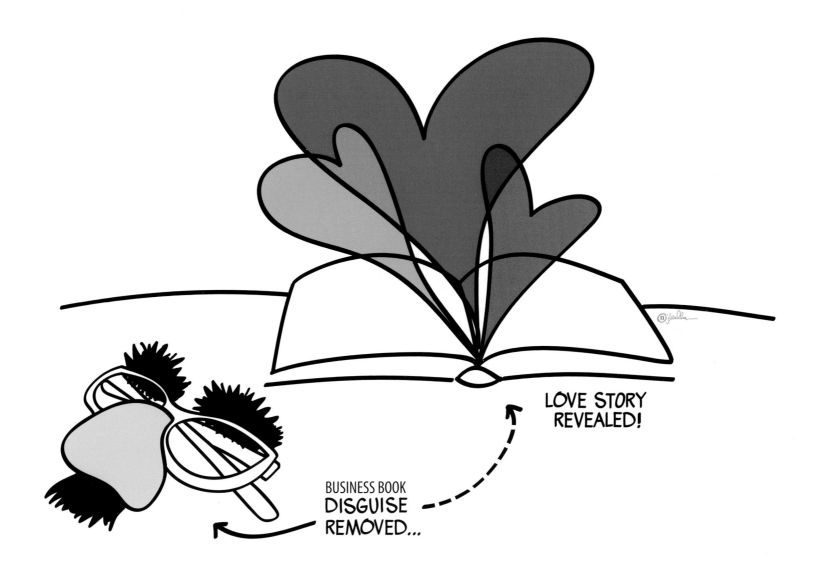

BUSINESS BOOK DISGUISE REMOVED...

LOVE STORY REVEALED!

Contents

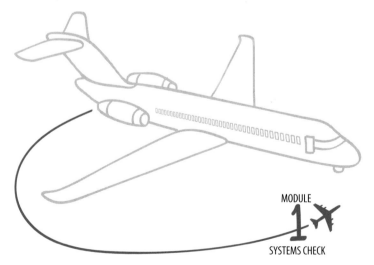

MODULE
1
SYSTEMS CHECK

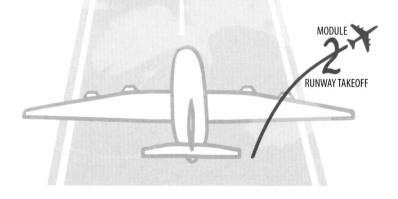

MODULE
2
RUNWAY TAKEOFF

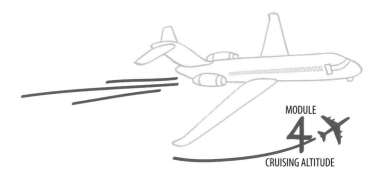

MODULE
3✈
FULL THROTTLE

MODULE
4✈
CRUISING ALTITUDE

Acknowledgments

The first line of the acknowledgments section in virtually every book goes something like this: To list everyone I want to thank for their contributions to this book would be a book in itself. You really don't know how true that is until you write your own book.

Book Yourself Solid Illustrated is the third in the Book Yourself Solid line of books and I think it's the best. I wish I could take credit for it but the book is better than my original because of the contributions of Jocelyn Wallace. Her talent is immeasurable and her work ethic is, frankly, astonishing.

My agent, Stephen Hanselman, is the coolest cat in town. My right-hand man, Matthew Kimberley, is the most trustworthy and capable business partner a guy can have. My ops team, lead by Jaimie and Dan VanSickle, allow me to live the life of my dreams. My partner, Petra Kolber, is a beacon in a sea of mediocrity. My son, Jake, makes me a better person. In all of these relationships, I'm the lucky one.

MICHAEL PORT

New York Times bestselling author...
Book Yourself Solid, Beyond Booked Solid,
The Contrarian Effect, and *The Think Big Manifesto*

thanks

Michael is right as usual—I can't thank everyone who played a role in making this book possible. But there are a few who get me choked up. Head nods, fist bumps, and high-fives:

To my morning reading companion. Thanks for the gift. I hope it makes you smile.

To my rock star husband, Andy. You cooked, cleaned, and transported kids while I worked late nights and weekends on this book. What husband would do that? Not many. Love is a verb, and you showed it. Thank you.

To my brilliant son, Adam. You gave it to me straight when my ideas weren't working. And when I was discouraged, you told me not to sweat it, and that I could do it, keep trying. "Give it your VERY best, Mom!" … Ahh, those words sound familiar.

To my beautiful daughter, Lauren. I'm so glad you are still young enough to want hugs every day—they were welcome interruptions. You didn't know it, but many of the visuals and teaching strategies in this book were inspired by you and the things you love. Can you find them?

To Michael Port, you are a genius and I deeply respect your work. Even though the Book Yourself Solid strategies are serious business, you were open to letting me teach the principles in a fun and memorable way. Thanks for the opportunity to help business owners through your work.

j.Wallace

JOCELYN WALLACE

Visual Strategist, Little-Big Cheese at Red Eleven Group, LLC

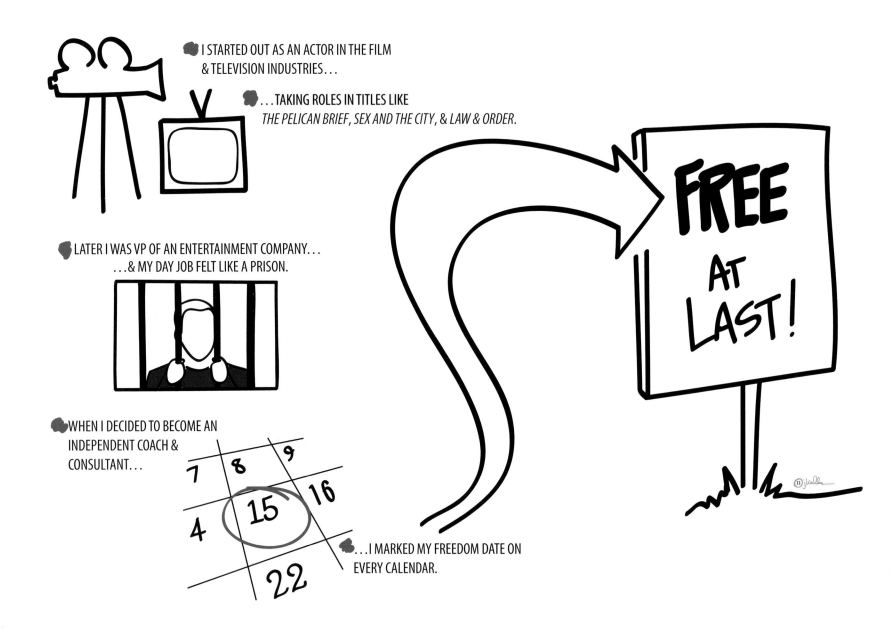

MICHAEL'S STORY: FREE AT LAST

In early 2000 I was utterly dissatisfied and completely disillusioned with my work as the vice president of programming at an entertainment company. The environment felt like a prison—long hours, unresponsive colleagues, and no personal engagement. Sound familiar?

I decided to embark on a new career path as a professional business coach and consultant: a service professional. I secretly passed the time reading, researching, studying, and honing my coaching skills. After much planning, my freedom date was marked on every calendar in my apartment with a huge victorious smiley face. My resignation letter was signed, sealed, and ready for delivery. I could hardly keep my legs from sprinting out the door to follow my heart and head (both of which had checked out long ago).

On that auspicious day, I received the envelope with my bonus inside, ran to the bank, cleared the check, and proudly delivered my letter of resignation. The joy, pride, and satisfaction at that moment was incredible. I floated home and woke up the next day to plunge into my career as a business owner serving others.

NOT SO FAST

I didn't bask for long in the glory, however, before I realized I was in for trouble.

Call me crazy, but I really thought clients were just going to fall into my lap. I expected them to meet me, fall in love with me, and trade their money for my services. Instead, I moped about my very costly New York City apartment, panicking, feeling sorry for myself, and doing trivial busy work that wasn't going to generate a dime of income.

Within six months I was desperate, which heralded a new phase of my life. I was fed up. I'd reached my limit. I was not going to throw in the towel and give up on my career as a business owner. My innate need to support and provide, to serve the people I was meant to serve, kicked into high gear one chilly New York morning.

Rather than dwelling on the cold reality of my financial struggle and the bitter temperature outside, I worked every single day for no less than 16 hours to succeed and pay the bills. I poured myself into more resources and studied everything I could get my hands on about how to attract clients, communicate effectively, sell, market, and promote my services. First and foremost, I wanted to learn how to love marketing and selling by turning it into a meaningful spiritual pursuit.

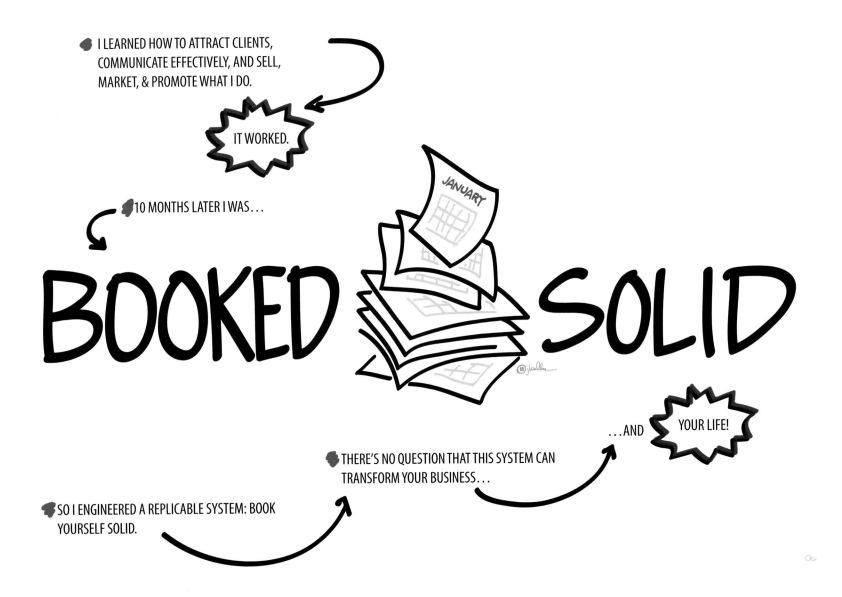

IT WORKED

It worked. Within 10 months I was booked solid with more clients than I could handle. But the personal checks I cashed were not the most valuable part of my business. The real heart of what I was creating was the turnkey system that propelled my business and income every month.

I started sharing my success secrets with a small group of trusted clients, and I watched their success unfold before my eyes. I could hear confidence, pride, and accomplishment in their voices. Their businesses boomed!

I immediately began to engineer a completely replicable system that I could pass on to you. That system is the Book Yourself Solid system, and you're holding it in your hands, the same system I've been teaching to thousands of other service professionals around the world in my live seminars and Book Yourself Solid Intensive Coaching programs. The results are powerful.

Michael Port

Preface

If you have something to say, if there are people you want to serve, then there are people whom you are meant to serve. If you're in the business of serving others, your job is to find them. It will be easy if you do it the Book Yourself Solid way. And 90 percent of those surveyed who have fully implemented the Book Yourself Solid system have increased their revenues by over 40 percent within one year of reading the book. How do you like them apples?

While you'll no doubt get great value just from reading this book, the true value—and your success—lies in your decision to take an active role and to participate fully, learning in action. In doing so, you will begin an evolutionary journey of personal and business development that will empower you to achieve the success you know you're capable of. And now that we've created the illustrated version of *Book Yourself Solid*, it's even easier to learn it, be inspired by it, and apply it.

There may be two simple reasons why you don't serve as many clients as you'd like to today:

1. You don't know what to do to attract and secure more clients.
2. You know what to do, but you're not actually doing it!

The Book Yourself Solid system is designed to help you solve both of these problems. I will give you all the information you need to book even more clients than you can handle; I will give you the strategies, techniques, and tips. If you already know what to do but aren't doing it, I'll inspire you into action and help you stay accountable so you build the business of your dreams and live the life you want to live.

So many talented and inspired service professionals like you run from marketing and sales because they have come to believe that the marketing and selling process is pushy and self-centered and borders on sleazy. This old-school paradigm is not the Book Yourself Solid way; it is the typical client-snagging mentality. And you must never fall into this way of thinking and being. If you do, you'll operate in a mentality of scarcity and shame as opposed to one of abundance and integrity.

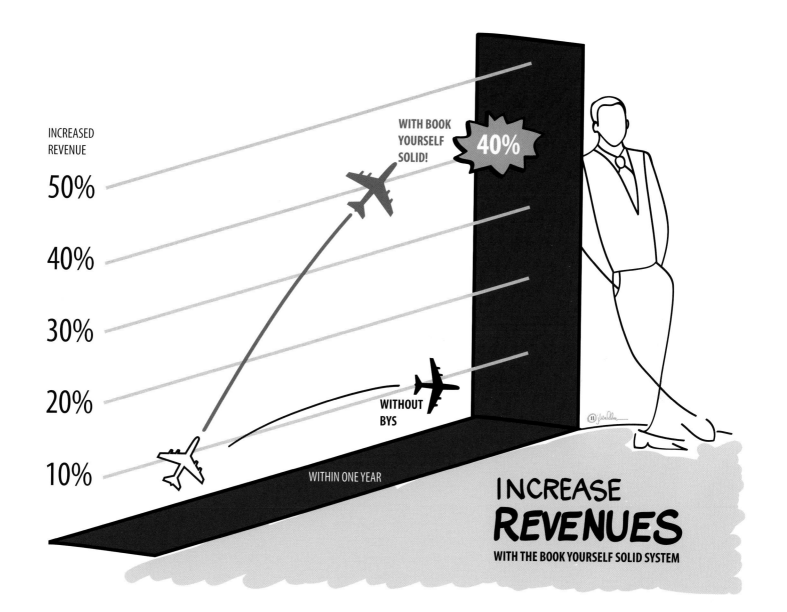

How to Use This Book

The Book Yourself Solid system is organized into four modules:

1. Your Foundation.
2. Building Trust and Credibility.
3. Perfect Pricing and Simple Selling.
4. The Book Yourself Solid 6 Core Self-Promotion Strategies.

In Module One we begin by building a foundation for your service business that is unshakable. If you are truly serious about becoming a super-successful service professional, you must have a steadfast foundation on which to stand.

In Module Two you will then be ready to create and implement a strategy for building trust and credibility. You'll be considered a credible expert in your field and you'll start to earn the trust of the people you'd like to serve.

In Module Three you'll price your offerings in the sweet spot of the customer's desires and you'll know how to have sales conversations of the highest integrity that work.

In Module Four I will teach you how to execute the 6 core self-promotion strategies, thereby creating awareness for the valuable services you offer.

To help you design a service business overflowing with clients who inspire and energize you, this book includes written exercises and Booked Solid Action Steps that will support you in thinking bigger about your business. You have options for doing the exercises: You may either write on the pages of this book, or go to www.BookYourselfSolid.com to download our electronic tools. Step-by-step I walk you through the actions you need to complete on the path to serving as many clients as your heart desires.

If you follow the system, it will work for you. No skipping, jumping, or moving ahead—the Book Yourself Solid 6 Core Self-Promotion Strategies are effectively implemented only after your foundation, credibility-building, pricing, and sales strategies are in place. One of the main reasons that service professionals say they hate marketing and selling is that they're trying to market without these essential elements, which is like eating an egg before it's cooked—of course, you'll hate it. So no matter how compelled you are to skip ahead, I urge you to please follow the system and watch the process unfold.

Ready to get started? Let's do it!

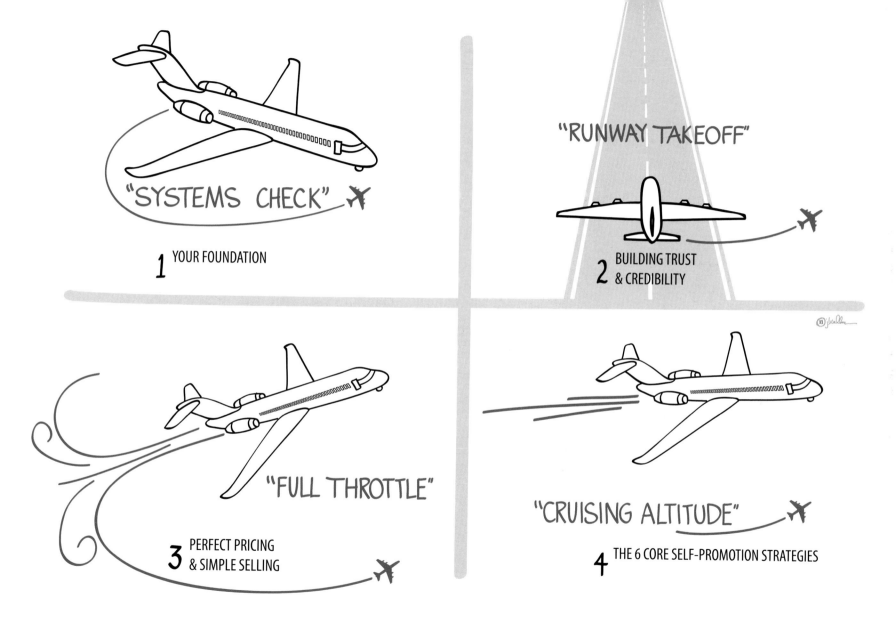

THE SYSTEMS CHECK

Before a pilot confidently and powerfully lifts a plane into the air for a long journey, she charts her flight plan and performs an all systems check while she's on the ground. This takes time and must be done meticulously. Make one mistake and the consequences can be dire.

The same is true when developing your marketing system. Skip the prep work and you won't even get to the jet-way. In the Book Yourself Solid system I refer to this systems check as Your Foundation.

Your Foundation is where most of the heavy lifting is done. Rarely does a new business owner spend enough time laying their foundation. Instead, they think they're meant to start marketing immediately—as if marketing is what gets them clients. It's not.

Surprised? I would think so. Rarely does marketing get you clients. It simply creates awareness for the products and services you offer. The awareness needed to lead potential buyers into your sales cycle.

Think of marketing as the fuel that powers your client-generating engine. If your fuel tank runs empty, you'll take a nosedive. Marketing just gets your sales process moving. It's what you do during the journey that helps you book the business.

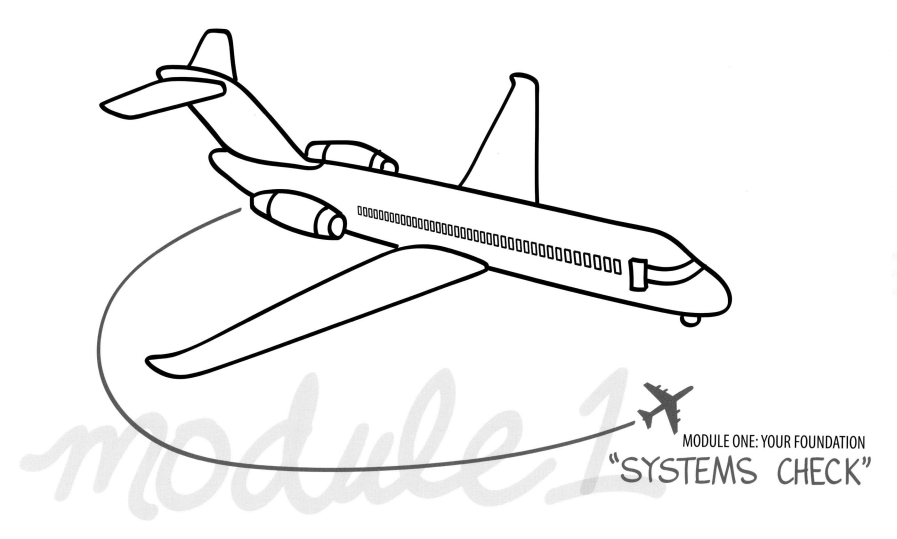

MODULE ONE: YOUR FOUNDATION
"SYSTEMS CHECK"

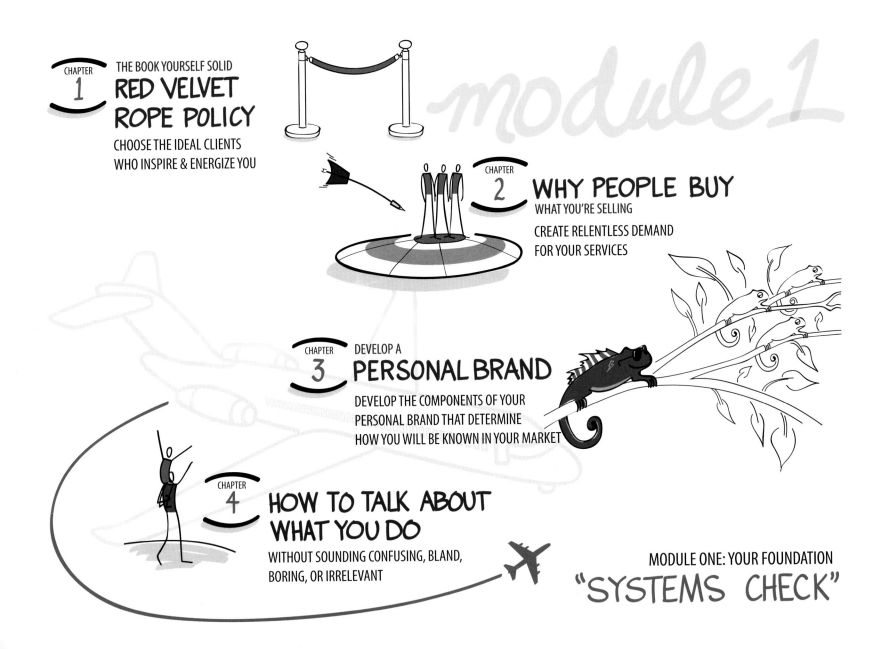

CHAPTER 1 — THE BOOK YOURSELF SOLID
RED VELVET ROPE POLICY
CHOOSE THE IDEAL CLIENTS WHO INSPIRE & ENERGIZE YOU

module 1

CHAPTER 2 — **WHY PEOPLE BUY**
WHAT YOU'RE SELLING
CREATE RELENTLESS DEMAND FOR YOUR SERVICES

CHAPTER 3 — DEVELOP A
PERSONAL BRAND
DEVELOP THE COMPONENTS OF YOUR PERSONAL BRAND THAT DETERMINE HOW YOU WILL BE KNOWN IN YOUR MARKET

CHAPTER 4 — **HOW TO TALK ABOUT WHAT YOU DO**
WITHOUT SOUNDING CONFUSING, BLAND, BORING, OR IRRELEVANT

MODULE ONE: YOUR FOUNDATION
"SYSTEMS CHECK"

Your Foundation

MODULE ONE

To be booked solid requires that you have a solid foundation.

THAT FOUNDATION BEGINS LIKE THIS:

- Choose your ideal clients so you work only with people who inspire and energize you.
- Understand why people buy what you are selling.
- Develop a personal brand so you're memorable and unique.
- Talk about what you do without sounding confusing or bland.

Over the course of Module One, I'll walk you through the process of building your foundation so that you have a platform on which to stand, a perfectly engineered structure that will support all of your business development and marketing, and—dare I add—personal growth. That's because being in business for yourself, especially as someone who stands in the service of others, requires constant personal reflection and spiritual growth.

Building your foundation is a bit like putting a puzzle together. We're going to take it one piece at a time, and when we're done, you'll have laid the foundation for booking yourself solid.

MODULE ONE: YOUR FOUNDATION
"SYSTEMS CHECK"

CHAPTER 1
The Book Yourself Solid
Red Velvet Rope Policy

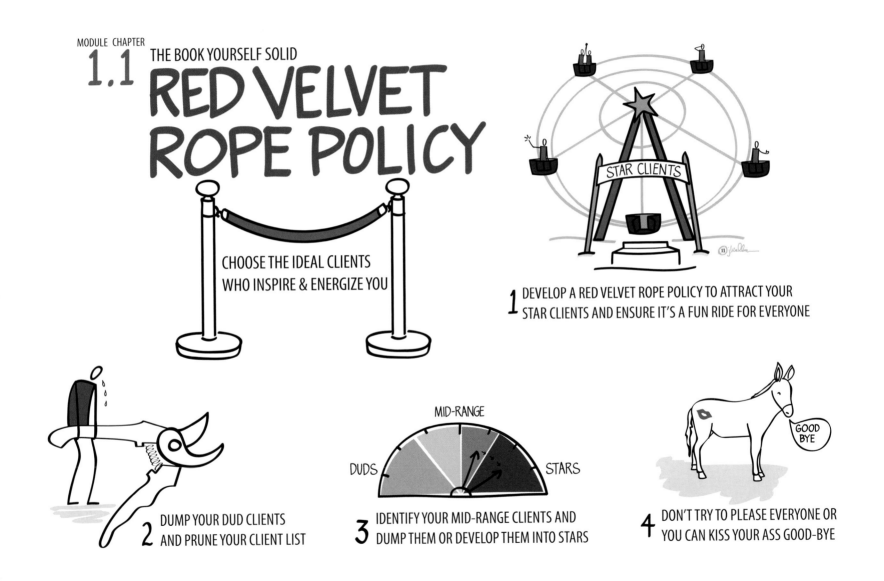

1.1 THE RED VELVET ROPE POLICY

He who trims himself to suit everyone will soon whittle himself away.

— Raymond Hull

Imagine that a friend has invited you to accompany her to an invitation-only special event. You arrive and approach the door, surprised to find a red velvet rope stretched between two shiny brass poles. A nicely dressed man asks your name, checking his invitation list. Finding your name there, he flashes a wide grin and drops one end of the rope, allowing you to pass through and enter the party. You feel like a star.

Do you have your own Red Velvet Rope Policy that allows in only the most ideal clients, the ones who energize and inspire you? If you don't, you will shortly.

The Red Velvet Rope Policy

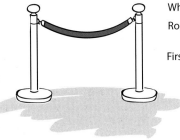

Why should have you have a Red Velvet Rope Policy?

First, because when you work with clients you love, you'll truly enjoy the work you're doing; you'll love every minute of it. And when you love every minute of the work you do, you'll do your best work, which is essential to book yourself solid.

Second, because you are your clients. They are an expression and an extension of you. Do you remember when you were a teenager and your mother or father would give you a hard time about someone you were hanging out with? Your parents may have said that a particular kid reflected badly on you and was a bad influence. As a teen you may have thought about how unfair that felt, but the truth is that you are the company you keep. Let this be the imperative of your business: Choose your clients as carefully as you choose your friends.

The first step in building your foundation is to choose your ideal clients, the individuals or businesses with whom you do your best work, the people or environments that energize and inspire you. I'm going to help you identify specific characteristics of individuals or organizations that would make them ideal to work with. You will then develop a rigorous screening process to find more of them. I'm also going to help you prune your current client list of less-than-ideal clients.

When I began my business I would work with anyone who had a pulse and a checkbook. Then I began to consider what it would mean to choose my clients. What it would mean to work only with clients that were ideal for me. And thank goodness I did. Now I live by what I call the Red Velvet Rope Policy of ideal clients. It increases my productivity and my happiness, it allows me to do my best work, and I have more clients and referrals than I can handle by myself. And so will you.

For maximum joy, prosperity, and abundance, think about the person you are when you are performing optimally, when you are with all the people who inspire and energize you. Now think about all of the frustration, tension, and anxiety you feel when you work with clients who are less than ideal—not so good, right?

Wouldn't it be great to spend every day working with clients who are ideal for you, clients whom you can hardly believe you get paid to work with? This ideal is completely possible once you identify who you want to work with and determine with certainty that you will settle for nothing less. Once you do that, it's just a matter of knowing which of your existing clients qualify and how to acquire more just like them.

LOOK IN THE MIRROR.
YOU ARE YOUR CLIENTS.

Creating Your Red Velvet Rope Policy

Start thinking about what your Red Velvet Rope Policy might look like. Can you picture an ideal client and their qualities and traits? What makes someone move into the star client category for you?

MY STAR CLIENTS HAVE THESE QUALITIES:

- Bright (full of light and easily excitable).
- Resilient (keep coming back).
- Courageous (face their fears).
- Think big (their projects benefit large groups of people).
- Value-oriented (they gain value from relationships with me and others).
- Naturally collaborative (they contribute to and focus on their solutions).
- Rapid responders (talk today, done tomorrow).
- Positive (naturally optimistic).

Your list might look completely different. Maybe you only want to work with certain types of clients. Maybe reliability or long-term goals are important to you. Maybe your top priority is how often a client works with you or how many projects they do with you. The economic status of a client may be one factor, but remember—it's only one of many. In fact, it's often a primary consideration for many service professionals who wind up working with clients who are less than ideal.

So take heed—the economic status of a potential client should be only one of many considerations. Notice that my list considers the quality of my ideal clients first—who they are rather than what they have or the circumstances they're in.

Overall, I want you to envision what your business can be like when you work with ideal clients.

THE BENEFITS OF WORKING WITH STAR CLIENTS ARE MANY:

- You'll have clean energy to do your best work.
- You'll feel invigorated and inspired.
- You'll connect with clients on a deeper level.
- You'll feel successful and confident.
- You'll know your work matters and is changing lives.
- The magic of you will come to life.

It's a pretty fun ride!

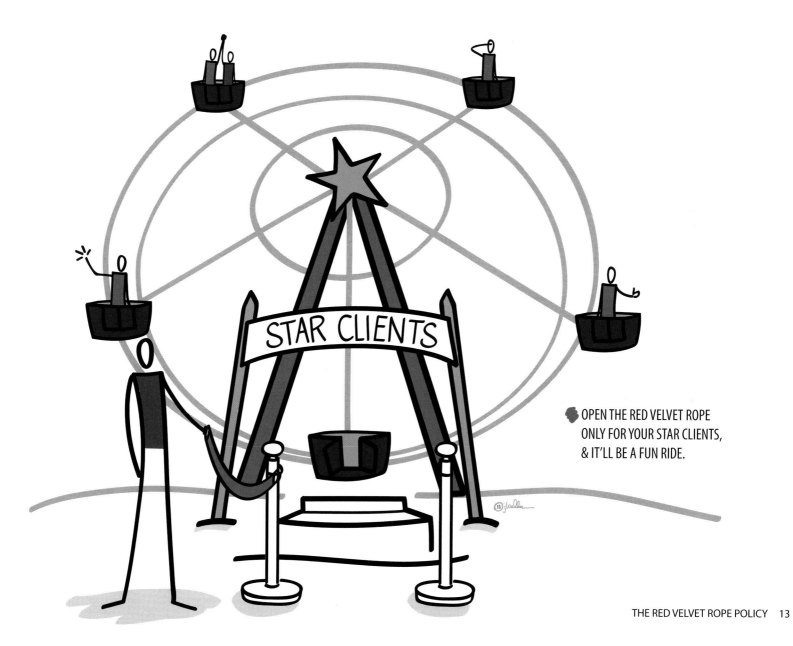

OPEN THE RED VELVET ROPE ONLY FOR YOUR STAR CLIENTS, & IT'LL BE A FUN RIDE.

Written Exercise 1A

WHAT QUALITIES SHOULD YOUR STAR CLIENTS POSSESS?

Use the visual worksheet on the next page for the following exercise.

STEP 1: Think about your ideal potential client, using these questions to prompt you:

- What type of people do you love being around?

- What do they like to do?

- What do they talk about?

- With whom do they associate?

- What ethical standards do they follow?

- How do they learn?

- How do they contribute to society?

- Are they smiling, outgoing, creative?

What kind of environment do you want to create in your life? And who will get past the Red Velvet Rope Policy that protects you?

List the qualities, values, or personal characteristics you'd like your ideal clients to possess.

DEFINE YOUR STAR CLIENTS

LIST THE QUALITIES, VALUES, & PERSONAL CHARACTERISTICS
YOU WOULD LIKE YOUR IDEAL CLIENTS TO POSSESS

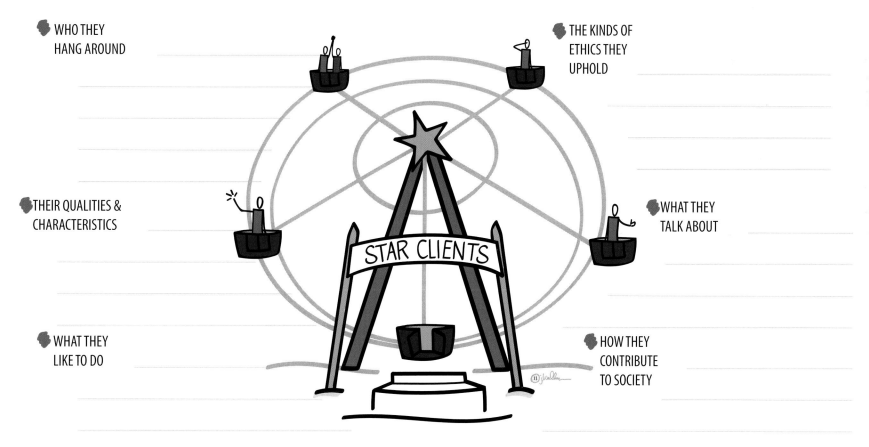

WHO THEY
HANG AROUND

THE KINDS OF
ETHICS THEY
UPHOLD

THEIR QUALITIES &
CHARACTERISTICS

WHAT THEY
TALK ABOUT

STAR CLIENTS

WHAT THEY
LIKE TO DO

HOW THEY
CONTRIBUTE
TO SOCIETY

Written Exercise 1B

YOUR CURRENT IDEAL CLIENTS

Use the visual worksheet on the next page for the following exercise.

STEP 1: Now let's look at your current client base.

- With whom do you love interacting with the most?
- Who do you look forward to seeing?
- Who are the clients who don't feel like work to you?
- Who is it you sometimes just can't believe you get paid to work with?

In the Written Exercise Worksheet on the next page, use the blank space to write down the names of clients, or people you've worked with, whom you love to be around.

STEP 2: Get a clear picture of these people in your head. Write down the top five reasons that you love working with them.

What about working with them turns you on?

YOUR CURRENT IDEAL CLIENTS
IDENTIFY THE CLIENTS YOU LOVE
AND THE TOP FIVE REASONS YOU LOVE THEM

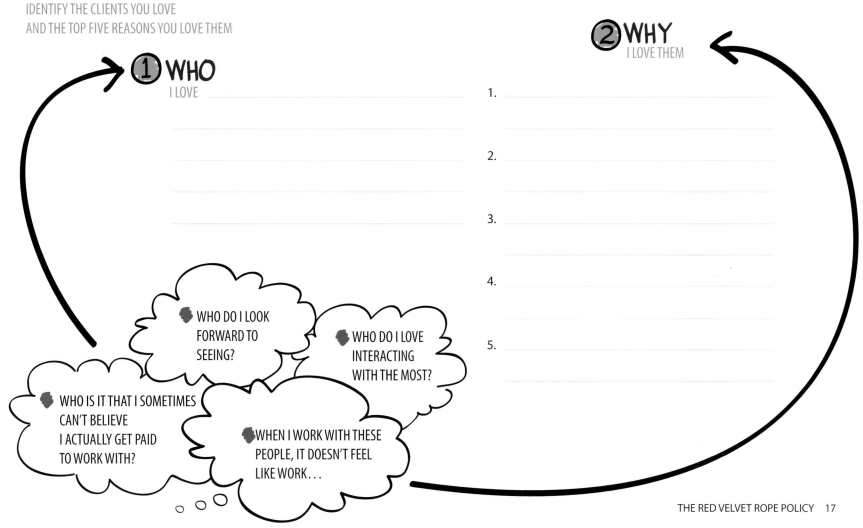

① WHO I LOVE

② WHY I LOVE THEM

1.

2.

3.

4.

5.

WHO DO I LOOK FORWARD TO SEEING?

WHO DO I LOVE INTERACTING WITH THE MOST?

WHO IS IT THAT I SOMETIMES CAN'T BELIEVE I ACTUALLY GET PAID TO WORK WITH?

WHEN I WORK WITH THESE PEOPLE, IT DOESN'T FEEL LIKE WORK...

Written Exercise 1C

THE BEST OF THE BEST

Use the visual worksheet on the next page for the following exercise.

STEP 1: Now go deeper. If you were working only with ideal clients, what qualities would they absolutely need to possess in order for you to do your best work with them?

List what you need in order to be successful with those best of the best clients.

Be honest and don't worry about excluding people. Be selfish. Think about yourself. For this exercise, assume you will work only with the best of the best. Be brave and bold and write without thinking or filtering your thoughts.

STEP 2: When you are with your best clients, you are at your best too. As you are working on Step 1, think about examples of great results for both you and your clients when you are at your best. Write your thoughts down. Let this list spur ideas for the list in Step 1, and vice versa.

THE BEST OF THE BEST

THE QUALITIES YOUR BEST CLIENTS WOULD NEED TO POSSESS
IN ORDER FOR YOU TO DO YOUR BEST WORK WITH THEM

STAR CLIENTS

① TO DO MY BEST
MY CLIENTS MUST HAVE THESE QUALITIES:

② WHEN I'M AT MY BEST
I SEE THESE GREAT RESULTS:

Dump the Duds

Author and business guru Tom Peters takes us a step further. In *Reinventing Work: The Professional Service Firm 50*, he challenges us to dump our dud clients. "Dump my clients?!" you exclaim. I can just hear your shocked protestations and exclamations. " I thought this was a book about getting clients, not dumping them! " But Peters is referring to the dud clients—not all of your clients. It sounds harsh, but think about it. Your dud clients are those you dread interacting with, who drain the life out of you, bore you to tears, frustrate you, or worse, instill in you the desire to do them—or yourself—bodily harm, despite your loving nature.

I'm well aware of the many reasons you think you can't dump your dud clients, and I know this can seem really scary early on, but hang in there with me. Embrace the concept and trust that this is sound advice from a loving teacher and a necessary step on the path to booking yourself solid.

Why have clients, or anyone for that matter, in your life who zap your energy and leave you feeling empty? In the first year of being in business on my own, I cut 10 clients in one week. It wasn't easy. It required a major leap of faith, but the emotional and financial rewards were astonishing. Within three months, I had replaced all 10 and added 6 more. Not only did I increase my revenue, I felt more peaceful and calm than I ever had before, and I enjoyed my clients and my work more.

When I asked myself the question, "Would I rather spend my days working with incredibly amazing, exciting, super cool, awesome people who are both clients and friends, or spend one more agonizing, excruciating minute working with barely tolerable clients who suck the life out me?" I had no choice. I knew the temporary financial loss would be worth the payoff.

Written Exercise 1D

DUMP THE DUDS

Use the visual worksheet on the next page for the following exercise.

STEP 1: To begin to identify the types of clients you don't want, consider which characteristics or behaviors you refuse to tolerate. What turns you off or shuts you down? What kinds of people should not be getting past the red velvet rope that protects you and your business?

STEP 2: Now take a good, hard look at your current clients. Be absolutely honest with yourself. Who among your current clients fits the profile you've just created of people who should not have gotten past the red velvet rope that protects you and your business?

STEP 3: Now take the Booked Solid Action Step listed in the Visual Worksheet.

Taking a Booked Solid Action Step is a bold action and requires courage. And courage is not about being fearless—it's about owning your fear and using it to move you forward, to give you strength. There is no more rewarding feeling than the pride you'll feel once you've moved past the fear to do what you set out to do. Maybe you'll find it easier to take it one step at a time. Start by referring out just one of those dud clients. The feeling of empowerment you'll have once you've done it will motivate you to continue pruning your list of clients until the duds have all been removed.

WHAT TO DO WHEN YOU DON'T (YET) HAVE CLIENTS

But, Michael, what if I just started my business and don't yet have clients, let alone dud clients? Ah, yes, excellent point, my new friend. Consider yourself lucky! You'll never have to worry about dud clients because you'll put your Red Velvet Rope Policy in place on Day One.

In just a moment, you'll begin to create your Red Velvet Rope Policy. If you're starting a new business, and don't yet have many, or any, clients to speak of at this point, as you're working through the exercises, think about current or former co-workers, friends, or even service providers that you've hired in the past. To create your future Red Velvet Rope Policy you'll be able to draw on your past experiences—who inspired you and who made you want to do them bodily harm. Refrain. Rewind. Remember: love and kindness. Love and kindness.

DUMP THE DUDS

IDENTIFY THE TYPES OF
CLIENTS YOU DON'T WANT

 ## CHARACTERISTICS OR BEHAVIORS
I REFUSE TO TOLERATE

 ## OF MY CURRENT CLIENT LIST
THOSE WHO SHOULDN'T GET PAST
MY RED VELVET ROPE

BOOKED SOLID ACTION STEP
DUMP THE DUD CLIENTS
YOU JUST LISTED

Dump the dud clients you just listed. It may be just one client, or you may need another two pages to write them all down. (Did I warn you that I'd push you to step out of your comfort zone? If I didn't before, I am now.) Is your heart pounding? Is your stomach churning at just the thought? Have you broken out in a cold sweat? Or are you jumping up and down with excitement now that you've been given permission to dump your duds? Maybe you're experiencing both sensations at the same time; that's totally normal.

Pruning Your Client List

SNIP SNIP

If you're struggling with the idea of pruning your client list, keep in mind that it's for your client's benefit as much as it is for yours. If you're feeling empty and drained, or frustrated and dreading the interaction with the client, you're giving that client far less than your best, and it's both of you who are suffering for it. You owe it to these clients to refer them to someone who can, and will, do their best work with them. If you are working with people with whom you do not do your best work, you are out of integrity. And as we discussed earlier, you *are* your clients. When your clients go out into the world and speak of you to others, they are representing you.

With whom do you want to be associated—the duds or the ideal clients? It's also the ideal clients, those who are wildly happy with you and your services, who are most likely to go out and talk about you to others, to refer other clients like themselves, more ideal clients. The fewer duds you allow to hang around, the more ideal clients you have room for, the more referrals you'll get, and so on.

Clients are like family to me, so I know this can be hard. I lived through a period of intense and painful negative energy worrying about those challenging client relationships. It exhausted me and took me away from accomplishing the highest good for my clients. It was impossible for me to be productive, effective, or successful when working with less-than-ideal clients.

Let me share a story with you about myself and my former landscaper, when I was the less-than-ideal client. For a variety of reasons, my landscaper and I were just not a good fit for each other. One of them being that every so often I'd cut the grass on a whim and then his guys would show up with nothing to mow. Instead, I'd ask them to do other projects on the property, which I thought was reasonable. Anyhow, the point is, he had issues with me; he knew I wasn't his ideal client, but rather than tell me so, he stayed with me while getting more and more annoyed until he blew up and acted like a jerk, forcing me to let him go. More than likely, he didn't feel comfortable dumping his dud clients, or the idea had never even crossed his mind. Granted, pruning his dud clients wouldn't have been as easy as pruning his clients' trees, but had he not allowed the situation to deteriorate and end on such a bad note, I might have been able to refer other clients to him who would have been ideal for him. His inability to take the Booked Solid Action Step of letting his less-than-ideal clients go left both of us dissatisfied with the situation and jeopardized his reputation.

This is what can happen when you work with clients who are not ideal for you. At some point, you're going to create a conflict, whether intentionally or not, because you're going to be frustrated with those clients. Those clients will think you're not providing them with good service, and they'll be right. It doesn't serve you or the client when you stay in a less-than-ideal situation. Please don't make the same mistake my landscaper did. If you do, you'll have former clients going out into the world telling anyone who will listen that you're the worst person to work with.

There's nothing wrong with your dud clients, of course. They're just not right for you. Clients who are not ideal for you could be ideal for someone else. So keep in mind that you don't need to fire clients; you just need to help them find a better fit. You can be tactful, diplomatic, and loving. You can even attempt, when appropriate, to refer them to a colleague who might be a better fit. Whenever possible, keep it simple. Try, "I'm not the best person to serve you." Or, "I don't think we'd be a good fit."

Are you always going to get a positive response when dumping your dud clients? Probably not. If the first thing that comes to mind is, "I don't want anyone out there thinking badly of me," I'm with you. I want everyone to love me, too. But living life fully requires difficult conversations and you can never please everyone. To even try is an exercise in futility, as the following fable demonstrates.

Written Exercise 1E

IDEAL CLIENTS, THE DUDS, AND EVERYONE ELSE

Use the visual worksheet on the next page for the following exercise.

STEP 1: Divide your clients into Duds, Mid-Range, and Ideal Clients. Don't hold back or leave anyone out.

As if that weren't enough, you may begin to notice that many of your mid-range clients, those who made neither the ideal client nor the dud list, are undergoing a transformation. Why? While you were working with dud clients, you weren't performing at your best. If you think that wasn't affecting your other clients, think again. The renewed energy and the more positive environment you'll create as a result of letting go of the duds will most likely rejuvenate the relationships between you and some of your mid-range clients, turning many of them into ideal clients.

STEP 2: Focus on the Mid-Range Clients for a moment.

From the Mid-Range Client list:

- Which clients need to move to the Duds list? Draw an arrow from these names to the left, under the Duds list.

- Which clients could be moved to the Ideal list? Circle them and draw an arrow toward the Ideal list.

MID-RANGE CLIENTS: DUMP 'EM OR DEVELOP 'EM

Brainstorm your own ideas for developing these mid-range clients into stars. Contemplate the ways in which you may, even inadvertently, have contributed to some of your clients being less than ideal clients.

- Are there ways in which you can light a new fire or elicit greater passion for the work you do together?

- Do you need to set and manage expectations more clearly right from the beginning?

- Can you enrich the dynamics between you by challenging or inspiring your clients in new ways?

Go ahead—turn off your left-brain logical mind for a moment and let your right-brain creativity go wild.

Observe carefully the ways in which your relationships with your clients begin to shift as you embrace the Book Yourself Solid way. Some of your Mid-Range Clients may fall away—and they should move to the Dud List. Others may step up their game and slide into the Ideal Client category.

When you're fully self-expressed, fully demonstrating your values and your views, you'll naturally attract and draw to yourself those you're best suited to work with, and you'll push away those you're not meant to work with.

MID-RANGE CLIENTS

DIVIDE YOUR CLIENTS INTO 3 GROUPS
& THINK ABOUT MOVING UP THE MID-RANGE

MID-RANGE

DUDS

STARS

1 MY DUD CLIENTS:

2 MY MID-RANGE CLIENTS:

3 MY STAR CLIENTS:

The Old Man, the Boy, and the Donkey

An old man, a boy, and a donkey were going to town. The boy rode on the donkey and the old man walked beside him. As they went along they passed some people who remarked it was a shame the old man was walking and the boy was riding. The man and boy thought maybe the critics were right, so they changed positions.

Later, they passed some people who remarked, "What a shame! He makes that little boy walk." They then decided they both would walk.

Soon they passed some more people who thought they were stupid to walk when they had a decent donkey to ride. So they both rode the donkey.

Later, they passed some people who shamed them by saying how awful to put such a load on a poor donkey. The boy and man said they were probably right, so they decided to carry the donkey. As they crossed the bridge, they lost their grip on the animal, and he fell into the river and drowned.

The moral of the story? *If you try to please everyone, you might as well kiss your ass good-bye*.

The point is that you are looking for qualities in a person that you resonate with, so don't limit yourself to just thinking about the clients that you don't yet have. Your Red Velvet Rope Policy is a filtration system that lets in ideal clients. However, you can choose to loosen or tighten the rope at will. I'm not (necessarily) asking you to turn away your very first clients. I understand what you're up against. When you start your business, if you feel that you'd like to keep your red velvet rope a little looser so you can work with more clients, go ahead. Just make sure you know what is ideal and what isn't ideal about the people you're letting into the VIP room. As you become booked solid, you'll tighten your red velvet rope and become even more exclusive so as to work only with those who energize and inspire you—and most important—allow you to do your best work.

A Perpetual Process

The process we've just worked through is one that you must do on a regular basis. Pruning your client list is a perpetual process because all relationships naturally cycle. The positive and dynamic relationships you have now with your ideal clients may at some point reach a plateau, and the time may come to go your separate ways. You'll get more comfortable with the process over time. It's one that has so many rewards that it's well worth the effort.

Let Tom Peters sum it up for us: "This is your life. You are your clients. It is fair, sensible, and imperative to make these judgments. To dodge doing so shows a lack of integrity."

I'll go one step further and say that doing so is one of the best and smartest business and life decisions you can make. It's crucial to your success and your happiness. Prune regularly and before you know it, you'll be booked solid with clients you love working with.

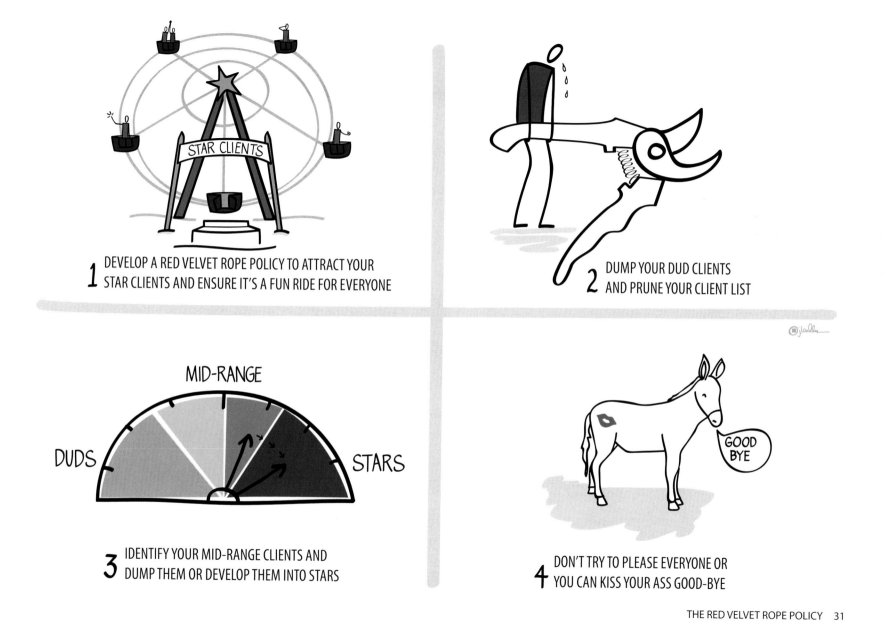

1 DEVELOP A RED VELVET ROPE POLICY TO ATTRACT YOUR STAR CLIENTS AND ENSURE IT'S A FUN RIDE FOR EVERYONE

2 DUMP YOUR DUD CLIENTS AND PRUNE YOUR CLIENT LIST

3 IDENTIFY YOUR MID-RANGE CLIENTS AND DUMP THEM OR DEVELOP THEM INTO STARS

4 DON'T TRY TO PLEASE EVERYONE OR YOU CAN KISS YOUR ASS GOOD-BYE

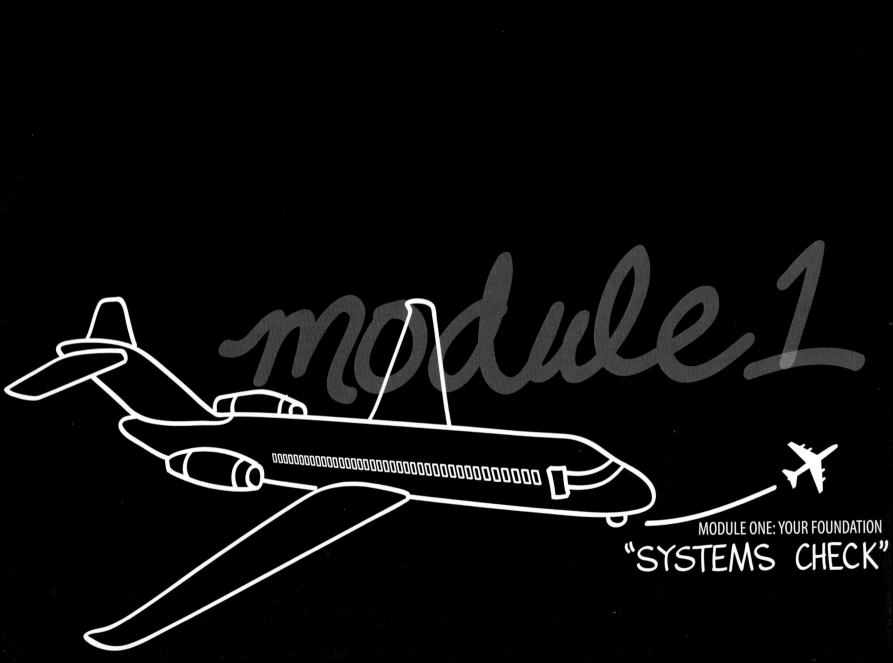

MODULE ONE: YOUR FOUNDATION
"SYSTEMS CHECK"

CHAPTER 2
Why People Buy
What You're Selling

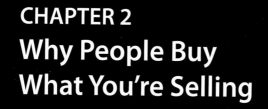

1.2 WHY PEOPLE BUY WHAT YOU'RE SELLING

CREATE RELENTLESS DEMAND FOR YOUR SERVICES

EMOTIONAL BENEFITS

FINANCIAL BENEFITS

PHYSICAL BENEFITS

SPIRITUAL BENEFITS

1 IDENTIFY YOUR TARGET MARKET

2 UNDERSTAND YOUR CLIENTS' URGENT NEEDS

3 DETERMINE THE #1 RESULT YOU PROVIDE

4 DEMONSTRATE THE BENEFITS OF WHAT YOU GIVE

1.2 WHY PEOPLE BUY WHAT YOU'RE SELLING

Before everything else, getting ready is the secret of success.

— Henry Ford

The next few steps we take down the Book Yourself Solid path will either feel like you're skipping over stepping-stones or like you're taking giant leaps of faith. Either way, these few steps will be well worth the time spent. The most important thing is to submit to the process. Stay by my side as we walk and work together on getting you booked solid.

Taking the following four steps will help you keenly understand why people buy what you're selling, an essential component in creating relentless demand for your services.

STEP 1: Identify your target market.

STEP 2: Understand the urgent needs and compelling desires of your target market.

STEP 3: Determine the number one biggest result your clients get.

STEP 4: Uncover and demonstrate the benefits of your investable opportunities.

Identify Your Target Market

Now that you've looked at the qualities of the people you want to work with, it's time to identify your target market, that is—the specific group of people or businesses you serve. For example, your target market might be seniors in Vancouver, BC, or mothers who have their own home-based networking marketing business or orthopedic surgeons. Your ideal clients are a small subset of the target market you choose to serve. Remember, your ideal clients are those individuals who energize and inspire you; your target market is the demographics of the group you're most passionate about serving. It is just as important to identify the right target market, as it is to identify the ideal clients.

It's also important to understand the difference between your target market and your niche. If you've done other research or reading on the subject of building your business, you may have heard both of these terms before, and you may have heard them used interchangeably. However, in the Book Yourself Solid system, they are not synonymous. There's an important distinction between the two: Your target market is the group of people you serve, and your niche is the service you specialize in offering to your target market. For example, you and I may both serve the same target market, say, service professionals, but offer them different services. I might specialize in getting clients and you might help them create systems for their business.

Even if you believe you have identified and chosen a target market, please don't skip this section. I often see service professionals who are struggling because either they've chosen a target market that isn't as specific as it needs to be, or they've chosen a target market based on what they think is the most logical and most lucrative choice, rather than one they feel passionate about serving. For the sake of your own success, read through this section, even if you don't think you need to. Trust me. If your target market isn't specific enough or the right one for you, the rest of the book won't be as effective. And besides, you just might be surprised at what you discover.

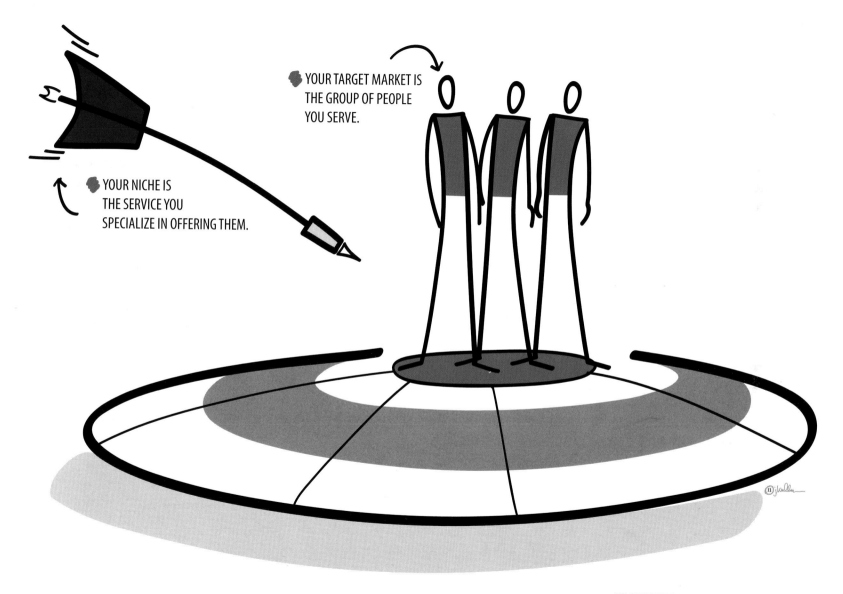

Three Reasons to Choose a Target Market

If you're just starting out in your business, or if you've been working in your business for a while but are not yet booked solid, you may be tempted to market to anyone and everyone with the assumption that the more people you market to, the more clients you'll get. While narrowing your market to gain more clients may seem counterintuitive, that's exactly what you need to do to successfully book yourself solid. That said, there are three primary reasons to choose a target market:

1. YOU'LL KNOW WHERE TO FIND THEM. It helps you determine where to find potential clients who are looking for what you have to offer. If you have a target market, you know where to concentrate your marketing efforts and what to offer that is compelling and well received. You know what associations to speak to, magazines and journals to write for, and influential people with whom to network—you know where your potential clients gather. Voila! You now know where to show up.

2. YOU'LL DISCOVER THEIR NETWORKS. Virtually every target market already has some kind of network of communication established. For your marketing to work, your clients need to spread your messages for you. If they already have a network of communication set up, they can talk to each other about you and your marketing messages can travel that much faster. What are networks of communication? Environments that are set up to help a group communicate—as I mentioned earlier: associations, social networking sites, clubs, various publications, events, and more.

3. THEY WILL KNOW YOU ARE COMMITTED TO SERVING THEM. And, finally, choosing a target market lets the people in that target market know that you've dedicated your life's work to them.

Marketing and sales isn't about trying to persuade, coerce, or manipulate people into buying your services. It's about putting yourself out in front of, and offering your services to, those whom you are meant to serve—people who already need and are looking for your services.

No matter how much you might like to be everything to everyone, it's just not possible. Even if you could be, you would be doing a disservice to yourself and your clients in the attempt. You can serve your clients much better, and offer them much more of your time, energy, and expertise, if you narrow your market so that you're serving only those who most need your services and who can derive the greatest benefits from what you have to offer.

WHEN THE FISH GET FED,
WOULDN'T YOU RATHER BE
A BIG FISH IN A SMALL POND?

Think of narrowing your market this way: which would you rather be—a small fish in a big pond or a big fish in a small pond? It's much easier to carve out a very lucrative domain for yourself once you've identified a specific target market. And once you're a big fish in a small pond, you'll get more invitations than you can handle to swim in other ponds.

Two Primary Ways to Grow Your Business

There are two primary ways to grow a service business.

1. HORIZONTAL EXPANSION: SELL MORE SERVICES TO ONE MARKET. You can choose a target market and, over time, continue to add new products and services to this same target market. For example, if your target market is fitness professionals, and you're currently offering them web design services, as you grow, you might start offering them search engine optimization services and then pay-per-click advertising services.

2. VERTICAL EXPANSION: SELL YOUR SERVICES TO MORE MARKETS. Once you get booked solid in one target market, you can begin to market and sell the same services in additional vertical target markets. So, if you currently serve wood flooring manufacturers, you might offer the same services to manufacturers of tile flooring. Once you get a foothold in that market, you might then begin to focus on carpet manufacturers.

You might be thinking: "If I specialize and only work with a specific group of people, or specific types of companies within a specific industry, won't that limit my opportunities? And what if I get bored?" Let me answer the second question first. If you're someone who gets bored easily, you may have that problem no matter what you do. You may want to spend some time reflecting on why you're not able to stay focused on what you've chosen to do. Or it may be that you've chosen a target market that doesn't excite you, that you aren't passionate about or interested in.

Over time, you can move into other areas. When I started my business, I helped fitness and wellness professionals get booked solid. Once I was fortunate enough to create demand for my services, I leveraged the reputation I built servicing the fitness industry as a springboard into other vertical target markets, like financial services, and others. As you establish your expertise and reputation, if you choose, you can broaden your target market. (I now serve virtually every type of service professional.) So if you want to increase your speed to getting booked solid, choose a very specific target market and stay with that target market until you are booked solid. Then you can move into other markets if you like or stay with your original focus and grow your product and service line.

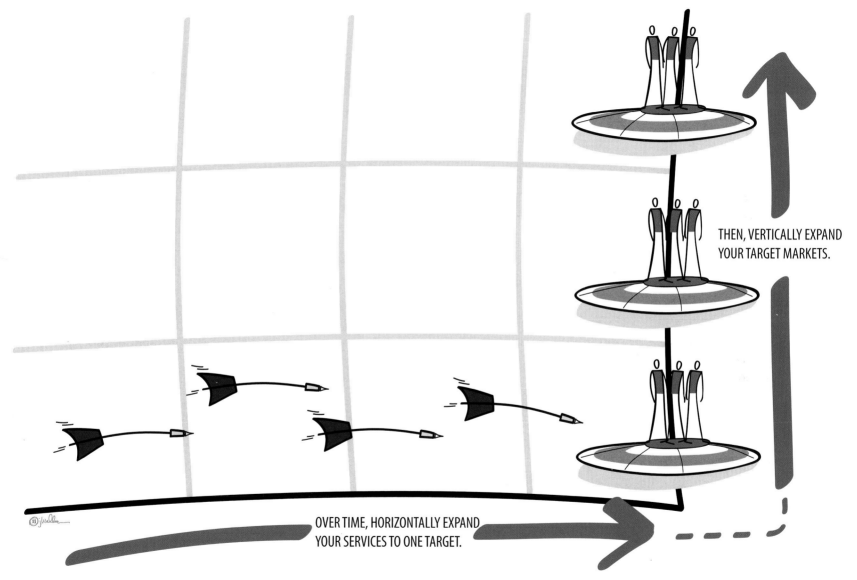

THEN, VERTICALLY EXPAND YOUR TARGET MARKETS.

OVER TIME, HORIZONTALLY EXPAND YOUR SERVICES TO ONE TARGET.

Your Passions, Natural Talents, and Knowledge Are Key

If you haven't yet chosen a target market, or if you know it's time to refresh it, then this is your chance, and I am going to help you. I'm going to ask you to consider what you're most passionate about, what excites you, and what you enjoy doing so much that it feels more like play than work and that will allow you to make the most of your natural talents and your knowledge.

Why start by thinking of your own needs, desires, and passions rather than those of your clients? For one very simple reason: If you are not passionate about what you're doing, if your heart isn't in it, if it doesn't have meaning to you, then you are not going to devote the time and energy required to be successful. You'll never, in a million years, be able to convince people in your target market that you're the best person to help them.

I often discover when I'm working with clients that they've chosen a target market based on what they think makes sense or will earn them the most money. The end result is that they're bored, frustrated, and struggling to book themselves solid. Don't make that mistake. It is imperative that you work with a target market that excites you, that you can feel passionate about serving. If you don't, growing your business will quickly feel like

drudgery, and you'll be miserable. When you choose a target market you're passionate about, growing your business will feel like play and will bring you joy.

Identifying a target market you feel passionate about may sound like a daunting task. But just like John Travolta in *Saturday Night Fever*, if you know what moves you, you'll be king of the dance floor.

That's not to say that you shouldn't also consider your clients. If you've been in business for a while, even if you may not have as many clients as you'd like, the clients you do have can help with this process. Look at the clients you're currently serving. Look for common elements among them— for example, a particular industry, geographic location, age, gender, or profession. If you find that most of your clients share one or more common elements, it may be that you are naturally drawn to those elements or they are drawn to you. Perhaps your target market has already chosen you and you just haven't stopped to think about it long enough to realize it and then focus your marketing there.

FIND YOUR FEVER.

Written Exercise 2A

Take a few moments to think about the following questions and jot down whatever comes to you. Doing so will provide you with clues to the target market you're best suited to serve. Your passion, your natural talents, and what you already know and want to learn more about are key.

CLUES TO THE TARGET MARKET YOU WERE MEANT TO SERVE

Use the visual worksheet on the next page for the following exercise.

STEP 1: Think about all the different groups of people who use the kind of services you provide. List them *in the written exercise sheet*, across the top of the table that has been drawn for you.

STEP 2: Which of these groups do you most relate to or feel the most interest or excitement about working with? To make this quick and easy, mark an "X" in the table in the visual worksheet corresponding to the group(s) you most relate to.

You get the idea, so keep going on this track with steps 3-5, putting an "X" in the table where it fits your sentiments about these groups.

STEP 3: Which group(s) do you know people in or already have clients in?

STEP 4: Which group(s) do you have the most knowledge about?

STEP 5: On the flip side, what group(s) would you find fascinating to learn more about?

Great work! Did you find some clues about the target market you are best suited to serve? My hunch is yes. Let's keep going.

WRITTEN EXERCISE 2A

CLUES
TO THE TARGET MARKET YOU
ARE BEST SUITED TO SERVE

(1) THE DIFFERENT GROUPS OF PEOPLE WHO USE THE KIND OF SERVICES I PROVIDE

	GROUP A:	GROUP B:	GROUP C:	GROUP D:	GROUP E:	GROUP F:
(2) GROUPS I MOST RELATE TO, OR FEEL MOST EXCITED TO WORK WITH						
(3) GROUPS I KNOW PEOPLE IN OR ALREADY HAVE CLIENTS IN						
(4) GROUPS I HAVE THE MOST KNOWLEDGE ABOUT						
(5) GROUPS I WOULD FIND FASCINATING TO LEARN MORE ABOUT						

WHY PEOPLE BUY WHAT YOU'RE SELLING   45

Written Exercise 2B

YOUR PASSION, YOUR TALENTS, YOUR KNOW-HOW

Your passion, your natural talents, and what you already know and want to learn more about are key.

Use the visual worksheet on the next page for the following exercise. For each question, write your answer in the spaces provided.

First let's look at some questions related to your work.

STEP 1: What are you most passionate about as it relates to your work?

STEP 2: What natural talents and strengths do you bring to your work?

STEP 3: What aspects of your field do you know the most about?

Now consider your life experience and interests. You'll be able to more sincerely identify and empathize with your target market if you share common life situations or interests.

STEP 4: What interests or hobbies do you have that might connect you with your target market?

STEP 5: What life situations or roles do you identify with that might connect you to a particular target market?

STEP 6: Now I want you to take a closer look at the visual worksheet you just filled out. What patterns do you see? Is there some cross-over between what you wrote in the different categories?

PASSION, TALENT, KNOW-HOW

DISCOVER WHETHER YOUR TARGET MARKET MAY
HAVE ALREADY CHOSEN YOU

 MY NATURAL TALENTS
I BRING TO MY WORK

④ **MY INTERESTS & HOBBIES**
THAT CONNECT WITH MY MARKET

③ **THE ASPECTS OF MY FIELD**
I KNOW MOST ABOUT

① **MY GREATEST PASSIONS**
RELATED TO MY WORK

 MY LIFE SITUATIONS OR ROLES
THAT MY MARKET MIGHT IDENTIFY WITH

Takin' It to the Streets

Now that you've given some thought to these questions, are some new possibilities beginning to emerge? Let's take a look at a few examples that might help you to see how you can incorporate some of your answers into serving a target market.

- If you're a graphic designer whose whole family is in the construction industry, maybe you'd choose the construction industry as your target market because you know the sensibilities of the people in that industry, and you know a lot about its inner workings.

- Or perhaps you're a fitness professional and one of your parents suffered from a chronic illness all your life. You know a lot about what it's like to go through that kind of situation and you empathize with and want to help people with chronic illnesses.

- Maybe you're a chiropractor who used to be a semipro athlete and you'd really enjoy working with athletes.

KNOWLEDGE
GRAPHIC DESIGNER

+

LIFE SITUATION
FAMILY IN CONSTRUCTION INDUSTRY

=

TARGET MARKET

- If you're an accountant and you grew up in a family business that went bankrupt when you were a teen, you might like to work with family businesses to help them avoid what happened to your family.

- If you're a hairstylist who used to be a stay-at-home mom, stay-at-home moms might be a target market you'd relate well to and enjoy working with.

- Perhaps you're a web designer who is fascinated by—and would like to learn more about—fashion, so you choose the fashion industry as your target market.

- If you're a yoga teacher who loves and naturally connects with children, and you're very creative, imaginative, and patient, you might want to choose children as your target market.

Let's take this last example and examine it more closely. Say this yoga teacher is booked solid. Chances are her full roster isn't just because she's an expert on the specific techniques of yoga for children, but because she has a natural affinity with children. This differentiator is what helped her to book herself solid much more quickly than she would have if she had focused on serving the general population.

INTEREST & PASSION   NATURAL TALENT   TARGET MARKET

YOGA TEACHER   +   GREAT WITH KIDS, CREATIVE, PATIENT   =

Written Exercise 2C

Are you beginning to see the ways in which your passions, natural talents, knowledge, life experience, and even interests and hobbies might help you to choose a more specific target market? Play, explore, and have fun with this process.

CHOOSE YOUR TARGET MARKET

Use the visual worksheet on the next page for the following exercise. For each question, write your answer in the spaces provided.

STEP 1: For now I just want you to answer this question:

Who is your target market? Write it in the center of the target on the visual worksheet on the next page.

Now, maybe you're not ready to make this choice, or perhaps you're close, but not quite there. If so, move to step two.

STEP 2: Go to the outer rings of the target in the visual worksheet. Start listing the possibilities that appeal to you in those outer rings.

STEP 3: Take a step back and look them over. Sit with them for a while (but not for too long) and then choose one, and move it to the center of the target in the visual worksheet.

Even if you're not sure at this point, it will become clearer to you as you work through the next few chapters.

Remember to tune into your intuition. I can't tell you how many times I've worked with clients who knew on some level the target market they most wanted to serve, and for one reason or another discounted it. Turn off your inner censor when doing this exercise and allow yourself to at least explore every possibility, no matter how wild, silly, or unrealistic it may seem on the surface.

TARGET MARKET

LIST THE POSSIBILITIES AND
CHOOSE YOUR TARGET MARKET

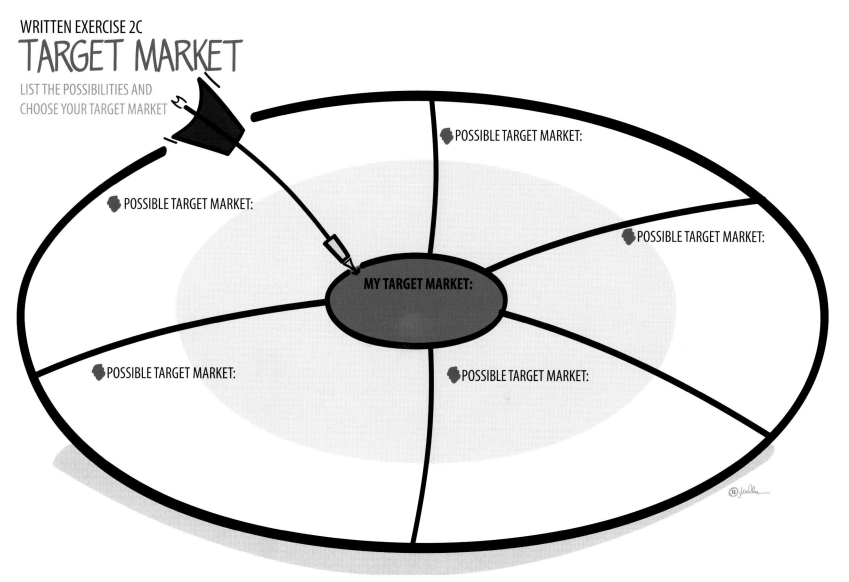

POSSIBLE TARGET MARKET:

POSSIBLE TARGET MARKET:

POSSIBLE TARGET MARKET:

MY TARGET MARKET:

POSSIBLE TARGET MARKET:

POSSIBLE TARGET MARKET:

Identify the Needs & Desires of Your Target Market

Your target market's urgent needs and compelling desires prompt them to go in search of you and your services, so it's critical to be able to identify and address them when they come looking or you'll miss your window of opportunity.

You must offer what your potential clients want to buy, not what you want to sell or think they should want to buy. You must be able to look at your services from your client's perspective—their urgent needs and compelling desires.

Your clients' urgent needs are the things that they must have right away, usually pressing problems, and often the things they would like to move away from. Their compelling desires are the things that they want in the future. Sure, they'd like to have them right now but they may be part of a bigger picture dream, and see themselves moving toward these desires.

IDENTIFY YOUR CLIENTS' URGENT NEEDS.

KNOW THEIR COMPELLING DESIRES.

Written Exercise 2D

URGENT NEEDS & COMPELLING DESIRES

Use the visual worksheet on the next page for the following exercise.

STEP 1: What are five of your clients' urgent needs?
(What problems must they solve right away?)

List them, 1 through 5, on the visual worksheet.

EXAMPLE: *The urgent need that may have prompted you to buy this book might be a feeling of stress because you know you need more clients (and more money) but don't know where or how to begin marketing your business. Maybe the bills are really starting to pile up and you're afraid. Or maybe you know what to do to market your services but just aren't doing it. You're procrastinating and your business is suffering as a result.*

STEP 2: What are five of your clients' compelling desires?
(What would they like to move toward?)

Again list them, 1 through 5, on the visual worksheet.

EXAMPLE: *Let's use you as an example again. Your compelling desire might be to feel confident and in control as you get as many clients as you would like. Maybe you want financial freedom. Maybe you just want to be able to take a real vacation every year. Or maybe it's all about having a thriving business that includes doing what you love and making oodles of money.*

WRITTEN EXERCISE 2D
URGENT & COMPELLING

IDENTIFY YOUR CLIENTS' URGENT NEEDS
& COMPELLING DESIRES

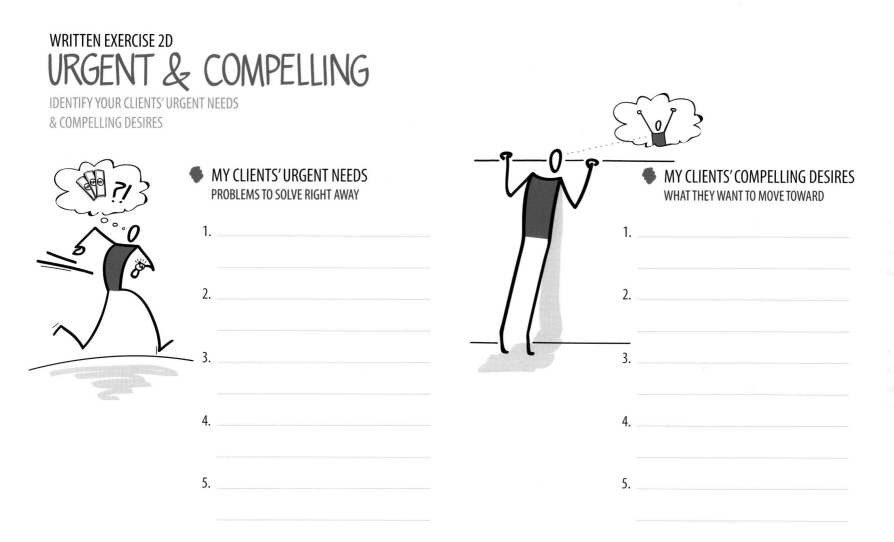

MY CLIENTS' URGENT NEEDS
PROBLEMS TO SOLVE RIGHT AWAY

1. _____

2. _____

3. _____

4. _____

5. _____

MY CLIENTS' COMPELLING DESIRES
WHAT THEY WANT TO MOVE TOWARD

1. _____

2. _____

3. _____

4. _____

5. _____

Determine the Biggest Result Your Clients Get

This simple step might be the most important step in understanding why people buy what you're selling. What is the Number One result you help your clients achieve or get? And, when I say Number One result, I mean one big one. Of course, I know there are lots of things that you help your clients achieve, experience, or get. But, generally, when a client comes looking for you, they're looking to solve one big problem or achieve one big result. I mean, why did you buy this book? To get more clients. Period. End of story. Are there lots of other things you'll get from reading this book? No doubt—from more confidence to more accountability, and even more friends (we'll get to that later). But, bottom line, you want more clients and the Book Yourself Solid system delivers on that promise. In fact, every product or service you offer must have one big promise. Your job is to fulfill that promise in the delivery of your service.

So let's get to it.

WRITTEN EXERCISE 2E:

Use the visual worksheet on the next page for the following exercise.

STEP 1: What is the number one, biggest result you provide for your clients? Describe it in the space provided on the next page. You can either write a short phrase, or a short story example. Make it your own and have fun with it.

Did you wrestle with that one? Good! Remember, if you have trouble picking one thing, you can always list several and then narrow them down.

Great job!

BIGGEST RESULT

DETERMINE THE #1 BIGGEST RESULT YOUR
CLIENTS GET WHEN THEY WORK WITH YOU

THE BIGGEST RESULT I PROVIDE TO MY CLIENTS IS:

Demonstrate the Benefits of Your Investable Opportunities

Do potential clients within your target market see your services and products as opportunities that will give them a significant return on their investment?

They must; if your potential clients are going to purchase your services and products, they must see them as investable opportunities; they must feel that the return they receive will be greater than the investment they made.

My rule of thumb is that your clients should be getting a return of at least 20 times their investment in your services. This return will come in different forms, depending on what you offer, but the return falls into four related categories: financial, emotional, physical, and spiritual, which I'll refer to by the acronym FEPS. Not only should the return on investment be high, this potential reward must be evident before your clients purchase services from you.

Let's look at the financial component as an example. If I sell a product for $49, the buyer can expect a financial return of, at least, $1,000. If one of my coaching programs requires a financial investment of $1,500, the average participant can expect a return of at least $30,000 in new client business (and don't forget about the other FEPS like increased confidence, focus, clarity, and more). If someone hires me to give a speech at $30,000,

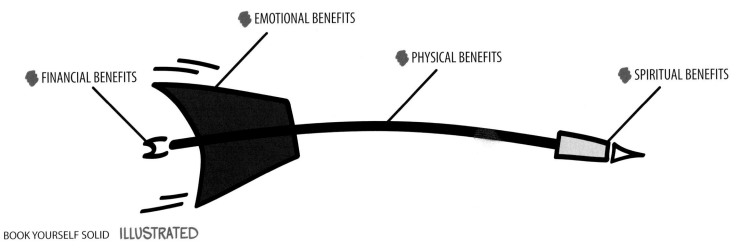

EMOTIONAL BENEFITS

PHYSICAL BENEFITS

FINANCIAL BENEFITS

SPIRITUAL BENEFITS

the financial return for the audience, as a whole, can be, at a minimum, $600,000. I'm afraid that sometimes, as service professionals, we forget how important our clients' return on investment is.

What kind of return on investment will your client get from working with you? Will it be greater than their financial, emotional, physical, or spiritual investment in your services? If so, how much higher? Twenty times?

The secret to having a successful business is to know what your clients want and deliver it. Rather than talking about what you do, focus instead on clear, specific, and detailed solutions that solve your clients' problems. People aren't buying what you do. *The science, technique, or technical name that you use won't get clients to hire you!* Clients who understand the return on investment you offer will jump at the chance to work with you.

To make it obvious that your solutions are investable opportunities for your potential clients, you need to uncover and demonstrate their benefits. The opportunities you offer—acupuncture, financial planning, web site design, career counseling, executive coaching, interior design—are just things that you do. They are the actual services you offer; they are technically what your clients buy but not what they actually buy.

For example, some of my offerings are technically these:

- A book that you can read on how to book yourself solid
- A coaching program that teaches you how to book yourself solid
- Live seminars that teach you how to book yourself solid
- A license to become a Certified Book Yourself Solid Coach®

However, these are still only the features and technical offerings. The core benefits of these offerings are much deeper. Benefits are sometimes tangible results, but more often they're intangible; they're the effects your services have on your clients' quality of life. They are what make your offer an investable opportunity—the FEPS that clients can experience because of your services. They are what people buy. Don't ever forget that.

People buy results and the benefits of those results. So think about the solutions you offer and the subsequent results and benefits they provide.

Written Exercise 2F

DEEP-ROOTED BENEFITS

Use the visual worksheet on the next page for the following exercise.

STEP 1: What are the financial benefits your clients receive when they work with you? Do they receive 20 times their investment? Write your response on the visual worksheet.

EXAMPLES OF FINANCIAL BENEFITS:
- Increase financial security and freedom.
- Save money.
- Maximize profit and return on investment.
- Help make wise financial choices.
- Understand financial alternatives.

STEP 2: What are some emotional benefits your clients experience as a result of working with you?

EXAMPLES OF EMOTIONAL BENEFITS:
- Help clients feel proud of themselves.
- Give them peace that they made the right decision.
- Help be a buffer so the client doesn't have to deal with the stress.

STEP 3: What are the physical benefits your clients experience as a result of working with you?

EXAMPLES OF PHYSICAL BENEFITS:
- Due to reduced stress for the client, their health improves.
- They breathe easier.
- Less indigestion.
- They can sleep better.

STEP 4: What are some spiritual benefits your clients experience as a result of working with you?

EXAMPLES OF SPIRITUAL BENEFITS:
- They are connected to their purpose.
- They are in alignment with what they believe.
- Their work has a positive impact on others.
- Achieving their dreams.
- Life has new meaning.

DEMONSTRATE THE BENEFITS

IDENTIFY THE DEEP-ROOTED BENEFITS YOUR CLIENTS EXPERIENCE
AS A RESULT OF YOUR SERVICES

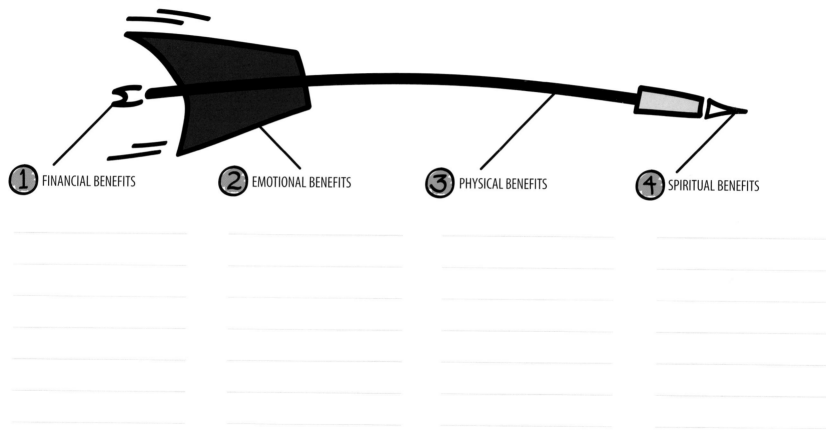

1 FINANCIAL BENEFITS

2 EMOTIONAL BENEFITS

3 PHYSICAL BENEFITS

4 SPIRITUAL BENEFITS

Clients Want You to Help Them

Begin to view your role with your clients as that of a highly important and trusted advisor. You have a moral obligation to offer your services to those who need them. To do anything other than counsel, advise, guide, and coach your clients would be a huge disservice. Start to view yourself as a leader in their life.

We all want someone to believe in. Be that person and you can write your own ticket. If you view yourself as a trusted advisor, clients will never forget you. They will come back to you months or even years later.

Trust is built over time, so a connection you make today may not develop until much later. Continue to share your vision, mission, and obligation to help people. Give clients benefit after benefit and show them exactly how they can fulfill the promise of your offerings.

There is an acronym that is often used in sales—A. B. C.—always be closing. Yuck! Sounds like cheesy sales talk to me. Instead, I say—A. B. C.—always be communicating. Let everybody and anybody know how you help people.

BUT FIRST:

1. Select a target market.

2. Identify your clients' urgent needs and compelling desires.

3. Determine the Number One biggest result you can help them get.

4. Uncover the deep-rooted core benefits of that big result (financial, emotional, physical, and spiritual).

Got it? Good.

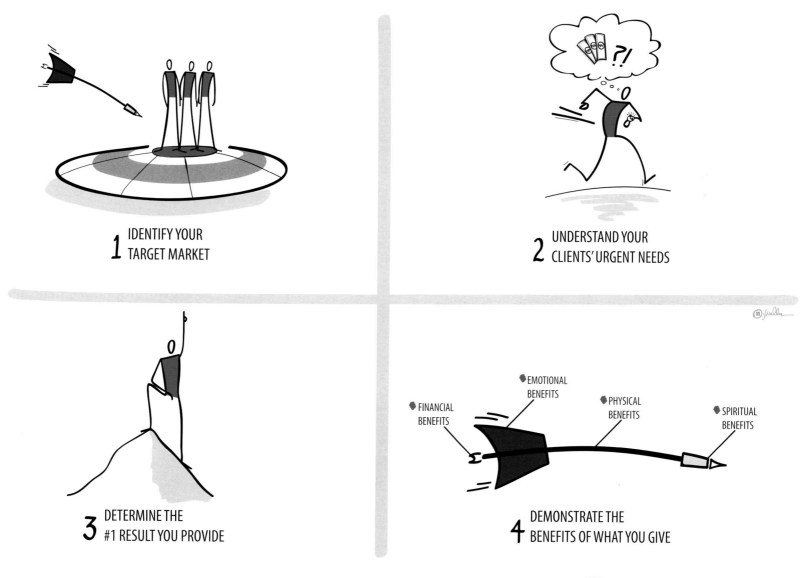

1 IDENTIFY YOUR TARGET MARKET

2 UNDERSTAND YOUR CLIENTS' URGENT NEEDS

3 DETERMINE THE #1 RESULT YOU PROVIDE

4 DEMONSTRATE THE BENEFITS OF WHAT YOU GIVE

EMOTIONAL BENEFITS

FINANCIAL BENEFITS

PHYSICAL BENEFITS

SPIRITUAL BENEFITS

1.3 DEVELOP A PERSONAL BRAND

DEVELOP THE COMPONENTS OF YOUR PERSONAL BRAND
THAT DETERMINE HOW YOU WILL BE KNOWN IN YOUR MARKET

THE GUY YOU CALL WHEN YOU'RE TIRED OF THINKING SMALL®

4 DEVELOP A TAGLINE THAT SAYS
SOMETHING ABOUT WHO YOU ARE

3 DEVELOP YOUR "WHY YOU DO IT"
STATEMENT: YOUR VISION FOR
WHAT YOU HOPE TO ACHIEVE

WHY I DO IT

1 DISTINGUISH YOURSELF
FROM EVERYONE ELSE

WHO I HELP

2 DEVELOP YOUR "WHO AND DO WHAT"
STATEMENT: WHOM YOU HELP
& WHAT YOU HELP THEM DO

WHAT I HELP THEM DO

1.3 DEVELOP A PERSONAL BRAND

Every time you suppress some part of yourself or allow others to play you small, you are in essence ignoring the owner's manual your creator gave you and destroying your design.

—Oprah Winfrey

Having established your target market and identified their urgent needs and compelling desires, the big result you help them get, as well as the benefits of the investable opportunities you offer, you are ready to develop a plan for deciding how you want to be known in your market—in an irresistible and unforgettable way.

You will do this by developing a personal brand. There are three components to your personal brand.

Don't Blend In — Distinguish Yourself

A personal brand will serve as an important key to your success. It will help clearly and consistently define, express, and communicate who you are, who you serve, and why you have chosen to dedicate your life and work to serving your target market so that you can attract your most ideal clients and not those who are less than ideal.

Personal branding is far more than just what you do or what your web site and business cards look like. It is you—uniquely you. It allows you to distinguish yourself from everyone else: what is unique about who you are, what you stand for, and what you do. Blending in and marketing yourself like others in your field can be tempting. It gives the illusion that it's a safer thing to do. But it won't be you, and you won't get booked solid.

Your brand is about making yourself known for your skills and talents. More than that—your brand is about what you stand for. Successful people find their style, build a brand based on it, and boldly express themselves through that brand. To let the world see your true, authentic worth is powerful and it makes you memorable.

The more bold, authentic, and concise your personal brand is, the more easily you'll attract those you're meant to work with.

That's how a personal brand works—it defines you, but first you must define it. Your personal brand will give you the ability to attract fun and exciting clients who understand and get you. And you get them. Develop a personal brand that looks like you, thinks like you, sounds and feels like you—one that is instantly recognizable as your essence.

It should be:

- Clear
- Consistent
- Authentic
- Memorable
- Meaningful
- Soulful
- Personal

DISTINGUISH YOURSELF
FROM EVERYONE ELSE.

Have You Watered Yourself Down?

Before we begin to craft your personal brand, it's important to address any blocks you are inadvertently creating that may hold you back from achieving success. I know it can seem unusual to discuss personal blocks as they relate to personal branding, but this is your life we're talking about. You want to play the biggest game possible, don't you? Of course, you do. The following questions can help you gain clarity about how you want to be known in the world. Consider them seriously.

The greatest strategy for personal and business development on the planet is bold self-expression.

Are you fully self-expressed? Again, I know this may seem like an unusual question. But I ask it because to create a gutsy, passionate, ardent, provocative, courageous, valiant, vibrant, dynamic, luminous, and respected personal brand, you must be fully self-expressed. You can't hide behind the shingle that you've hung over your door and you can't water yourself down in any way, shape, or form. If you do, you won't be of interest to the people you're meant to serve.

As a business owner, you probably already work on your business—creating the framework that supports the business itself, such as setting up an automatic marketing system—and work in your business, serving your clients. How you brand yourself is equally critical and is a reflection of how you work on yourself.

Have you compromised yourself or watered yourself down in any area of your business? For example, have you been in a business situation where you walked away feeling like you settled for less or compromised your integrity? You may be thinking, "I don't sell out. I've never compromised or sold out." If you haven't, you are unique. It's completely normal to compromise yourself or to be out of integrity from time to time. We all are.

It will serve you well to know exactly where you have run into trouble in the past. Since working independently and starting and running your own business is challenging, you can eliminate a lot of pain and surprise right now by acknowledging the issues you may have buried or have had a difficult time confronting in the past.

DON'T WATER YOURSELF DOWN,
OR YOU WON'T BE OF ANY INTEREST.

Written Exercise 3A

LIVING OUT YOUR TRUE COLORS

Use the visual worksheet on the next page for the following exercise.

STEP 1: Tap into instances in your business life where you've felt alive and vibrant—fully self-expressed in your true colors. Everything you did just flowed. Draw on all of your senses. What was happening at that time that made you feel so alive?

STEP 2: What about the flip side? In a business context, list the ways in which you've sold out, settled for less, or compromised your integrity, either now or in the past. When did you "do what everyone else was doing" at the expense of being true to yourself?

STEP 3: Now compare the two areas, the ones where you sold out and the situations in which you felt most fully self-expressed.

- How can you change your behavior to speak boldly and from a place of free expression so that you're working in situations that make you feel fully self-expressed?

- How will you communicate to make sure you stop compromising or watering yourself down in the future?

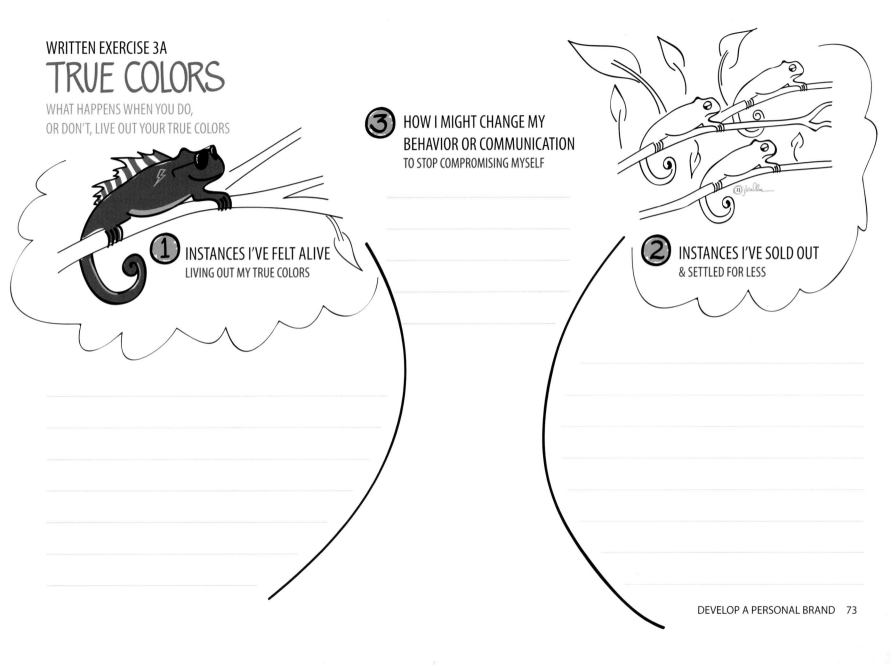

WRITTEN EXERCISE 3A

TRUE COLORS

WHAT HAPPENS WHEN YOU DO,
OR DON'T, LIVE OUT YOUR TRUE COLORS

③ HOW I MIGHT CHANGE MY BEHAVIOR OR COMMUNICATION
TO STOP COMPROMISING MYSELF

① INSTANCES I'VE FELT ALIVE
LIVING OUT MY TRUE COLORS

② INSTANCES I'VE SOLD OUT
& SETTLED FOR LESS

Written Exercise 3B

SITUATIONAL BOLDNESS

Use the visual worksheet on the next page for the following exercise.

STEP 1: Start with a few situations (fairly comfortable ones) in which you could practice speaking from a bolder and more self-expressed place. These ideas go in the far left column.

STEP 2: Write down a few more situations (that seem a little more difficult) that you'd like to work up to speaking more boldly about. Write these thoughts in the middle column.

STEP 3: Really challenge yourself now. What are a few situations that would be stretch goals for you, where you could be more bold? Write these thoughts in the right-hand column.

SITUATIONAL BOLDNESS

LIST THE SITUATIONS WHERE YOU CAN BEGIN TO EXPRESS
YOURSELF MORE FREELY AND BOLDLY

easy

MEDIUM

HARD

SITUATIONS
I COULD BE MORE BOLD

SITUATIONS
I COULD BE MORE BOLD

SITUATIONS
I COULD BE MORE BOLD

Clear Intentions

There are two reasons for the exercises you're doing. The first is so you can help clients understand how you can help them. The second is so you can make sure that your personal and professional intentions are clear.

Clear intentions allow you to gracefully and confidently move toward your goals. Conflicting intentions will undermine your success without your even knowing it. They will hold you back from your dreams. They are the mother of energy drain and confusion. From a perspective of a personal brand identity, conflicting intentions will eventually lead to a bland message and a less successful you.

Here's a story to illustrate this concept. My father is an accomplished psychiatrist. I have always had great respect for him and his work. And, above all, I've always wanted him to be proud of me and my accomplishments. That's natural, right?

When I first launched my service business, I spent lots of time getting clear on my offerings and how I would communicate them to the world.

And then I did just that—or so I thought. I let everybody know what I was up to. However, not too much was happening. I got a few clients, but as I

CLEAR INTENTIONS WILL MOVE YOU
QUICKLY TOWARD YOUR GOALS.

mentioned earlier, I couldn't really pay the bills, and I certainly wasn't happy with the response I was getting. So a few months later, when I was at my wits' end, I did a formal evaluation of my brand. I started with my web site. I locked myself away and read every word on my web site from start to finish. I sat back in my chair, staring at the screen in amazement and shock. The entire feeling of the site was not really me—it was almost as if my father were talking. In fact, I was communicating what I thought he would approve of.

I shied away from being bold and brave and instead played it safe, secretly hoping that he would approve of what I was doing. So I had two very conflicting intentions. One intention was to build a wildly successful business and the second (my conflicting intention) was to make my father proud. The underlying dynamic was not to do anything that he wouldn't approve of. And, here's the rub, if you think about it, many business problems are simply personal problems in disguise.

I had limited myself dramatically. I hadn't given myself the freedom to be truly me. I had been inhibited and unable to offer the full extent of my experiences, point of view, and passion. The result was a rather confusing and bland identity.

In order to set clear intentions for yourself, you must remove the conflicting intentions that you currently have. Your reality is created by your present intentions and action on them. If you want to change your reality, you must change your intentions. My vision for you is that, through this book, the intentions for your business, as well as your life, will become clear to you and to your clients.

Written Exercise 3C

GET CLEAR INTENTIONS

Use the visual worksheet on the next page for the following exercise.

STEP 1: Identify one of your most important intentions as it relates to your business.

EXAMPLE: I intend to book myself solid.

STEP 2: Take a good hard look within to see if you can identify any potentially conflicting intentions for the intention you identified. These are likely to be subconscious and more difficult to identify, and they are nearly always based on fear.

EXAMPLE: If I book myself solid, I won't have time for myself. Or, in order to book myself solid, I'll have to promote myself, and self-promotion will make me feel pathetic and vulnerable. Or maybe you want to book yourself solid but you think self-promotion is unappealing.

STEP 3: Identifying and acknowledging your conflicting intentions is the first big step in releasing them. Awareness is key, but not always enough to prevent conflicting intentions from affecting and blocking your positive intentions. The next step in the process is to identify the underlying fears. Once you've identified them, you can begin to take steps to relieve them.

BOOKED SOLID ACTION STEP: For this step, it's critical that you very carefully choose one or two sincerely and highly supportive friends to share your new insights with. They must be truly supportive and willing to help you change. Often as we begin to make changes in our lives, whether business or personal, some of our most dearly loved friends and family can feel threatened by the process of change. While they may consciously want you to be successful, they may have their own subconscious conflicting intentions and be highly invested in wanting to maintain their own comfort zone by keeping you in yours. These are not the folks you want to ask for help to do this exercise.

WRITTEN EXERCISE 3C

THOUGHTS & FEARS

IDENTIFY THE CONFLICTING THOUGHTS & UNDERLYING FEARS
THAT KEEP YOU FROM YOUR CLEAR INTENTION

1 MY CLEAR INTENTION
RELATED TO MY BUSINESS

2 CONFLICTING THOUGHTS
RELATED TO MY INTENTION

3 UNDERLYING FEARS
RELATED TO MY CONFLICTING THOUGHTS

?

Written Exercise 3D

DISCOVER YOUR HIDDEN TALENTS

Use the visual worksheet on the next page for the following exercise.

To know which secret quirk or natural talent is waiting in the wings to bring you wealth, happiness, and unbridled success in your business, answer the following questions:

QUESTION 1: What are the special talents that you are genetically coded to do? What have you been good at since you were a kid?

QUESTION 2: What do people always compliment you on?

QUESTION 3: What are three things that make you memorable? How are you unique?

QUESTION 4: In your personal life, what do you love or never grow tired of talking about?

QUESTION 5: When you are asked about your work, what would you never grow tired of talking about?

Many times we are too close to see the qualities or quirks that stand out to others. Send a few of these questions to different people in your life to get their responses about you and your personality. Not only will you start to see some of the same truths about who you are, but you'll get back the most touching and warm e-mails—I promise. Try it.

BOOKED SOLID ACTION STEP: Send an e-mail to five or more people (include friends, family, clients, neighbors, and acquaintances from all the different aspects of your life).

- Ask them to provide you with your top five personality traits or quirks.

- Ask for fun or unique experiences they've had with you.

- Tell them to be brave and not to be shy.

WAITING IN THE WINGS

DISCOVER YOUR SECRET QUIRK OR HIDDEN TALENT
THAT IS WAITING TO BRING YOU SUCCESS IN YOUR BUSINESS

① MY SPECIAL TALENTS
THAT I'VE BEEN GOOD AT SINCE I WAS A KID

② 3 COMPLIMENTS
PEOPLE OFTEN GIVE ME

1.

2.

3.

③ 3 THINGS THAT MAKE ME MEMORABLE
AND UNIQUE

1.

2.

3.

④ IN MY PERSONAL LIFE
THINGS I NEVER GROW TIRED OF TALKING ABOUT

⑤ IN MY WORK LIFE
THINGS I NEVER GROW TIRED OF TALKING ABOUT

The Three Components of Your Personal Brand

As I mentioned at the beginning of this chapter, there are three components to your personal brand:

1. Your who and do what statement.
2. Your why you do it statement.
3. Your tagline.

I want you to laser-beam your focus on these three aspects of your personal brand until you feel totally and utterly fully expressed when you put words to your who and do what statement, your why you do it statement, and your tagline. The process may take a week or it may take a few months. It took me six months, but I didn't have this book to help me do it faster. The important thing is to give yourself the time to really give thought to it all.

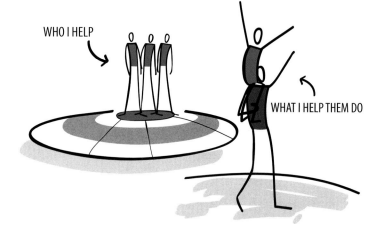

WHO I HELP

WHAT I HELP THEM DO

YOUR WHO AND DO WHAT STATEMENT

Your who and do what statement lets others know exactly who you help and what you can help them do. It is the first filter that people will put you through when considering your services for hire. Your potential clients will look at it to see if you help people like them in their specific situation.

WHY I DO IT

THE GUY YOU CALL WHEN YOU'RE TIRED OF THINKING SMALL®

YOUR WHY YOU DO IT STATEMENT

After potential clients identify with your who and do what statement, they will want to know if they connect with you on an emotional, philosophical, or even spiritual level. They'll want to know if they connect with your why you do it statement—the reason you do what you do, what you stand for. The reason you get up every day to do the work that you do. Those who resonate with your why you do it statement will feel it on a deep level and be strongly, almost magnetically, attracted to you. Many others in your industry will share your who and do what statement. Similarly, your why you do it statement and even your tagline don't necessarily need to be wildly unique. Just deeply meaningful to you—and to the people you're meant to serve.

YOUR TAGLINE

I have become known as "The guy to call when you're tired of thinking small.®" This is no accident; I've been saying this over and over since the day I realized that being "The guy to call when you're tired of thinking small" was a perfect tagline to represent and demonstrate my "why I do it" statement, that I want to help people think bigger about who they are and what they offer the world.

Your tagline, based on your why you do it statement, is something you'll never get tired of hearing. And the first time you hear someone refer to you by it, you'll want to cry tears of joy. You'll formulate one simple sentence that allows people to define you in a manner of your own choosing. You'll never get tired of saying it or hearing it because it's based on what you stand for, what's important to you. And, most importantly, not only will it very deeply and truly mean something to you, it will resonate with the people you're meant to serve. Reading or hearing your tagline will be the defining moment people need to decide whether to purchase your services, products, or programs.

Written Exercise 3E

DEVELOP YOUR WHO AND DO WHAT STATEMENT

Use the visual worksheet on the next page for the following exercise.

STEP 1: Who do you help?

Refer to your target market from Chapter 2. The first time around, just come up with something accurate and clear for now—make sure a five-year-old can understand it. List as many possibilities as come to mind. Finish this statement, "I help …"

STEP 2: What do you help them do? What common problem do you help them solve?

STEP 3: Now blend these together to get your "who and do what" statement.

EXAMPLE: I help … service professionals get booked solid. (Or, for the five-year-old, "I help the store sell more stuff.")

WHO & DO WHAT
WRITE SOME POSSIBLE STATEMENTS TO EXPLAIN
WHO YOU HELP & WHAT YOU HELP THEM DO

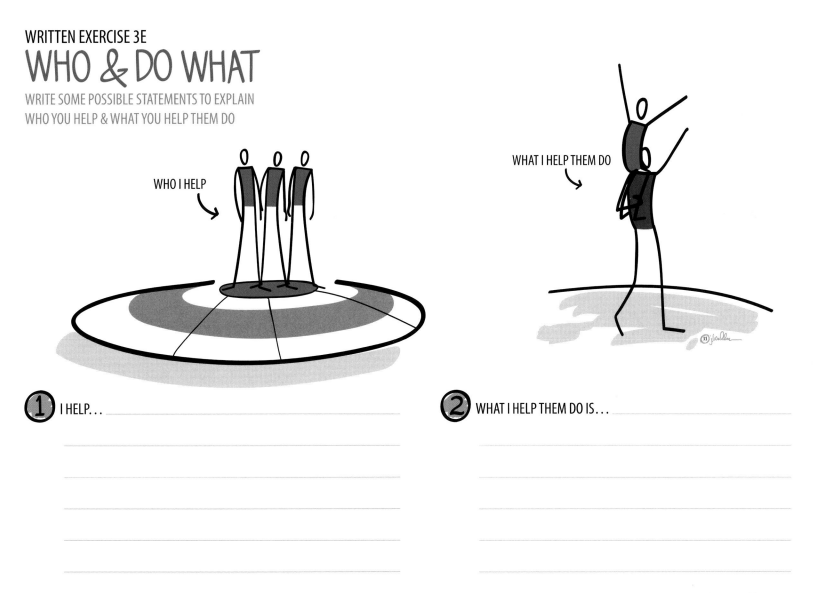

WHO I HELP

WHAT I HELP THEM DO

1 I HELP…

2 WHAT I HELP THEM DO IS…

Written Exercise 3F

DEVELOP YOUR WHY YOU DO IT STATEMENT

It's time to step out of your comfort zone again. Set aside that inner critic and give yourself permission to think big—I mean really big, bigger than you've ever dared to think or dream before. Be your most idealistic, inspired, creative, powerful you.

Use the visual worksheet on the next page for the following exercise.

STEP 1: Why do you do what you do for the people you serve? What drives you to do it?

STEP 2: What is your purpose? What is your vision of what you hope to achieve through your work?

Remember, your work is an expression of who you are. List whatever comes to mind. Keeping the preceding in mind, craft a minimum of two possible "why you do it" statements.

BOOKED SOLID ACTION STEP: If your "why you do it" statement is not immediately and easily identifiable, get together with a group of supportive friends or associates who know you well and ask them to brainstorm it with you. It's often the things about you that are most natural and that you don't even recognize that become key elements of your why you do it statement. Having some outside input and a few more objective perspectives can make all the difference.

WHY YOU DO IT

WRITE ABOUT WHY YOU HELP THE PEOPLE YOU SERVE
& YOUR VISION FOR WHAT YOU HOPE TO ACHIEVE THROUGH YOUR WORK

1 WHY I DO WHAT I DO
FOR THE PEOPLE I SERVE

2 MY VISION FOR WHAT I HOPE TO ACHIEVE
THROUGH MY WORK

Written Exercise 3G

DEVELOP YOUR TAGLINE

Your tagline lets others know what it's like to be around you. It says something about who you are at your core, and it's the essence of what you want to achieve or experience in the world. Think of it as the bigger vision that is the inspiration for what you do in your business. Your why you do it statement and associated tagline is the way in which you want to touch others' lives in a positive and meaningful way.

You may have noticed that my tagline is not necessarily specific to my target market. It may resonate with many people; professional service providers aren't the only ones who want to think bigger about who they are and what they offer the world. But I've chosen to offer my services to this inspired group of people, not to every single soul on the planet. Your tagline is not necessarily about your target market; it's about the emotional connection you make with people in general and with your ideal clients in your target market. Many people serve the same target market you serve,

but your tagline is what will resonate with some people and not with others: It will resonate with those you're meant to serve.

Why have you dedicated your life to serving others? How do you want to make a difference?

If you don't want to make a difference, consider making your living as something other than a service professional. The operative word is service.

Use the visual worksheet on the next page for the following exercise.

STEP 1: Review what you developed in the previous exercise.

STEP 2: Write three to five possible taglines that represent and demonstrate your current favorite "why you do it" statement.

WRITTEN EXERCISE 3G
YOUR TAGLINE
DEVELOP A TAGLINE THAT SAYS SOMETHING
ABOUT WHO YOU ARE AT YOUR CORE

THE GUY YOU CALL WHEN YOU'RE TIRED OF THINKING SMALL®

POSSIBLE TAGLINES

1.

2.

3.

4.

5.

6.

Rome Wasn't Built in a Day

Rome wasn't built in a day, and neither was my personal brand. I went through many, many versions, even one per month, before I got to a "why I do it" statement and tagline that worked for me. I didn't get caught up in trying to find the perfect brand message or positioning statement. I didn't worry about it because I knew I could change it. I knew that creating a tagline that represented what I stood for was a process and that I'd just keep changing it until I got there. If I didn't start with something, though, what would I have had? I'd have had nothing.

First I got clear on my who and do what statement, that "I help professional service providers get more clients."

Then I got clear on my why I do it statement, that "I want to help people think bigger about who they are and what they offer the world."

What took longer was nailing down my tagline. I worked really hard on trying to find it. It took about six months. I thought about it every day, but the amazing thing was that it came to me by accident. I was with a bunch of people and we were masterminding and brainstorming about our businesses and everyone was talking about what they did. I was giving the others a hard time, teasing and questioning, asking, "Why would I hire you for that?" I was playing devil's advocate until finally, one of the women gave it right back to me and said, "Yeah, well why would I hire you?" I blurted out, "Because I'm the guy to call when you're tired of thinking small.®" Suddenly the whole room went silent, as if everyone was holding their breath. After a few moments the same woman shouted out, "Yes! That is so you!" Everyone in the room was cheering and the air was charged with excitement.

As I began using my why I do it statement and tagline to let others know why I do what I do, I found that the people for whom it resonated would immediately comment on how much they connected with it. Those who didn't get it, wouldn't. That's okay. It's all about attracting those people who are meant to work with you.

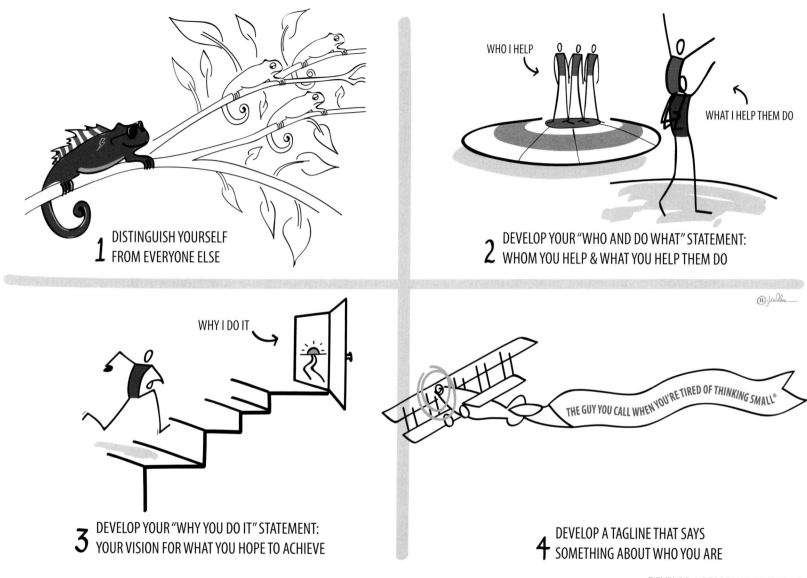

1 DISTINGUISH YOURSELF FROM EVERYONE ELSE

WHO I HELP

WHAT I HELP THEM DO

2 DEVELOP YOUR "WHO AND DO WHAT" STATEMENT: WHOM YOU HELP & WHAT YOU HELP THEM DO

WHY I DO IT

3 DEVELOP YOUR "WHY YOU DO IT" STATEMENT: YOUR VISION FOR WHAT YOU HOPE TO ACHIEVE

THE GUY YOU CALL WHEN YOU'RE TIRED OF THINKING SMALL®

4 DEVELOP A TAGLINE THAT SAYS SOMETHING ABOUT WHO YOU ARE

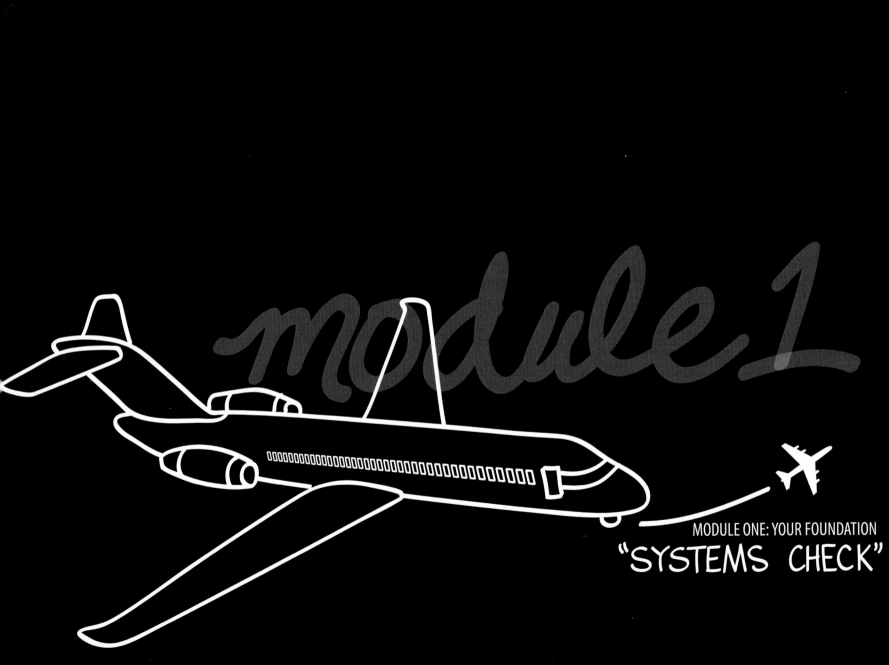

module 1

MODULE ONE: YOUR FOUNDATION

"SYSTEMS CHECK"

CHAPTER 4
How to Talk About What You Do

HOW TO

TALK ABOUT WHAT YOU DO

WITHOUT SOUNDING CONFUSING, BLAND, BORING, OR IRRELEVANT

1 KILL THE ELEVATOR SPEECH

2 AVOID USING ONLY YOUR PROFESSIONAL CATEGORY SO YOU DON'T GET BOXED IN

3 USE THE 5-PART FORMULA TO TALK ABOUT WHAT YOU DO IN A WAY THAT IS ORGANIC & REAL

4 DITCH THE SCRIPTS SO YOU DON'T SOUND LIKE A ROBOT

1.4 HOW TO TALK ABOUT WHAT YOU DO

A conversation is a dialogue, not a monologue. That's why there are so few good conversations: due to scarcity, two intelligent talkers seldom meet.

—Truman Capote

A primary reason that many service professionals fail to build thriving businesses is that they struggle to articulate in a clear and compelling way exactly what solutions and benefits they offer. They don't know how to talk about what they do without sounding confusing or bland or like everyone else—and without using an elevator speech. Yes, you heard me, without using an elevator speech.

Kill the Elevator Speech

The elevator speech (aka: the elevator pitch or 30-second commercial) reflects the idea that it should be possible to wow someone with what you do in the time it takes an elevator to go from the first to the fifth floor.

I've been polling audiences of thousands for years on this issue. During each speech I ask, "How many of you love, love, love listening to someone else's elevator speech?" No hands go up. I then ask, "How many of you love, love, love giving your elevator speech?" Same thing. No hands. So what gives? If we don't like listening to or giving the speech, why is it still being taught? Because, of course, we need to be able to talk about what we do—I get the concept. However, in this case, the elevator speech has been inappropriately appropriated by the service professional. Not only does it not work well, it makes us look foolish, or, worse yet, obnoxious.

The elevator pitch was born so that the entrepreneur could pitch an idea to a venture capitalist or angel investor in the hopes of receiving funding, not for the service professional to try to build a relationship of trust with a potential client. Venture capitalists often judge the quality of an idea on the basis of the quality of its elevator pitch. Makes perfect sense, in that situation. But this is not how a relationship develops between a client and a service professional. You're trying to earn the status of a trusted advisor not trying to raise money to create some new product like metal-detecting sandals. Totally different context. Totally different dynamic.

To support my beautiful community of service professionals, I'm on a mission to kill the elevator speech, to remove it from the business vernacular—for the service professional. I hope you'll join me on this mission and learn how to talk about what you do without ever resorting to an elevator speech.

Have a Meaningful Conversation

So, what do you do instead of the elevator speech?

You use this crazy concept I call a *conversation*. Weird, I know. Over the course of this chapter, I'm going to teach you a Book Yourself Solid Dialogue, a creative—but not scripted!—conversation that will spark curiosity and interest about you and your services, products, and programs.

The Book Yourself Solid Dialogue will allow you to have a meaningful conversation (conversation being the operative word) with a potential client or referral source. The dialogue is a dynamic, lively description of the people you help, what challenges they face, how you help them, and the results and benefits they get from your services. It is intended to replace the static, boring, and usual response to the question, "What do you do?" "I'm a business consultant," "I'm a massage therapist," or "I'm a graphic designer";

answers that often elicit nothing more than a polite nod, comment, or awkward silence and a blank stare. Once you get that response, anything more you say about yourself or your services will sound pushy. Worse yet, you could supplement the rote answer with an overblown, highfalutin, hyperbole-laden elevator speech that's supposed to make you look like a rock star in 30 seconds. Unfortunately, I doubt the one-two punch of boring answer, followed by excessively exuberant elevator pitch is going to compel the listener to whip out his credit card right then and there.

Instead you'll learn the Book Yourself Solid way to create a meaningful, connected dialogue with a potential client or referral source. Think of it as a conversation between two people each of whom actually cares about what the other has to say. The beautiful thing is that the interchange is based

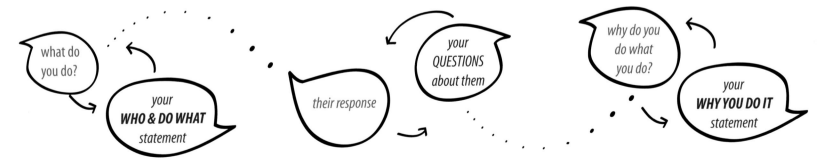

on successfully understanding why people buy what you're selling. And because of the work we did together in Chapter 2, you already know why people buy what you're selling.

You previously created your who and do what statement. That's a fantastic first step and an excellent tool for starting a conversation about what you do. Now you must be sure that you can captivate and actively engage the person you're talking to in a conversation that elicits questions rather than just polite acknowledgment. You must talk with people, not at them, which means listening to them, too, and really hearing what they're interested in, and what their needs are. After all, their needs may be exactly what you serve. Never give anyone a prepared script. Doing so is a train wreck waiting to happen. The long, medium, and short version of your Book Yourself Solid Dialogue will allow you to have conversations with different people in different situations, so you're always prepared. You tell them about the people you work with and then you listen to their response. You build on their response, and before you know it, you are having a conversation that is informative and inspiring—and that's the key to talking about what you do without being bland or confusing or, worse yet, obnoxious, albeit, unintended.

So, What Do You Do for a Living?

We hear the question "What do you do for a living?" all the time. Your professional category alone is the wrong answer. It will put you in a box.

You are so much more than your profession. Let's toss out the generic labels for now. Teacher, doctor, designer, accountant, acupuncturist, personal fitness trainer, yoga teacher, consultant, coach, or other dictionary description defines you as one of the masses.

Think about it for a second. Let's say you're a yoga teacher and you meet someone who really needs your help who would also be an ideal client. The only problem is that she has a preconceived notion of what yoga is all about and what a yoga teacher is like, and it's not a preconceived notion that sets you up for success.

Imagine this scenario: The potential client asks you what you do. You say, "I'm a yoga teacher." Before you know what's happened, you see the potential client's face contort, her left eyebrow lifts along with the left side of her upper lip, and her nostrils begin to flare. The potential client says, "Oh, yeah … I had a yoga teacher as a neighbor once. She was really weird and made my life miserable. In fact, I had to move out of that apartment because of her and I loved that apartment! She had scores of people coming in and out at all hours of the day, blasting strange music and chanting like the world was about to end—I think they must have been members of a cult. Oh, and you wouldn't believe the awful smell that I was subjected to from the perpetual cloud of incense that invaded my home."

Uh-oh.

Would you like to get that kind of response when you tell someone what you do? And this can happen to any service professional, not just to a yoga teacher.

How much more are you than your professional title? Your Book Yourself Solid Dialogue will allow you to set yourself apart from everyone else whose professional title is the same as yours. It provides you with the opportunity to highlight the ways in which you and your services, products, and programs are unique—and do so with passion.

If your Book Yourself Solid Dialogue reads like your resume, you'll bore people to tears, and although they may not say it, they'll be thinking, "Who cares? So what? What has any of that got to do with me?" Your potential client wants to know: "What's in it for me?"

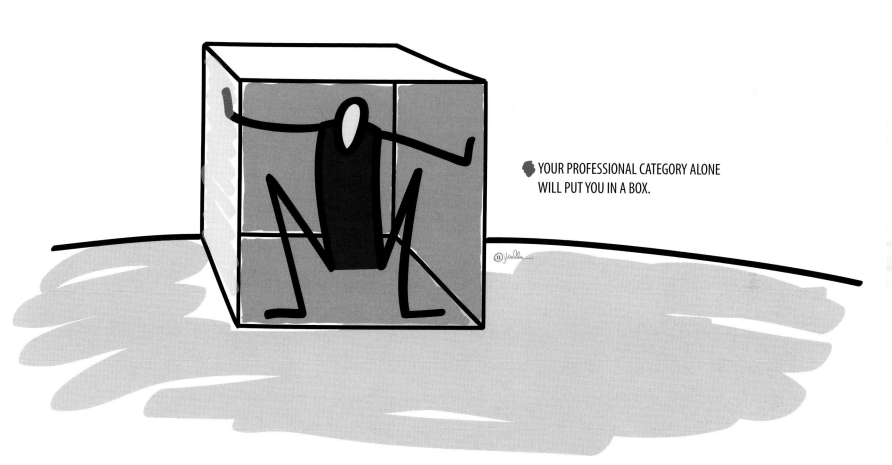

YOUR PROFESSIONAL CATEGORY ALONE
WILL PUT YOU IN A BOX.

Written Exercise 4A

We're going to break this down into its smallest components and gather all the information we've worked hard to compile in the previous pages. You've chosen your target market and you've begun to develop your personal brand by crafting your:

- Who and do what statement
- Why I do it statement
- Tagline

Now we're going to go back through all the exercises you've done and clean up your core message. If you've kept up on the exercises, crafting your Book Yourself Solid Dialogue will be a relatively simple process, and yet this powerful piece will make all the difference in your business and your message.

Let's put it all together and create a few different versions of your Dialogue: short, medium, and long. Please, please, bear in mind, we are not crafting a speech. I am just giving you some structure so that you can begin to imagine the possible content of the Book Yourself Solid Dialogue that is a conversation.

5-PART BOOK YOURSELF SOLID DIALOGUE FORMULA

Each of the following five parts has already been answered in previous exercises. All you need to do is pull the pieces into the formula below.

PART 1: Summarize your target market in one sentence. Who do you help?

PART 2: Identify and summarize the three biggest and most critical problems that your target market faces.

PART 3: List how you solve these problems and present clients with investable opportunities.

PART 4: Demonstrate the Number One most relevant result you help your clients achieve.

PART 5: Reveal the deeper core benefits your client's experience.

WRITTEN EXERCISE 4A

5-PART DIALOGUE FORMULA

PREPARE TO TALK ABOUT WHAT YOU DO
BY PULLING TOGETHER THE POSSIBLE COMPONENTS OF YOUR DIALOGUE

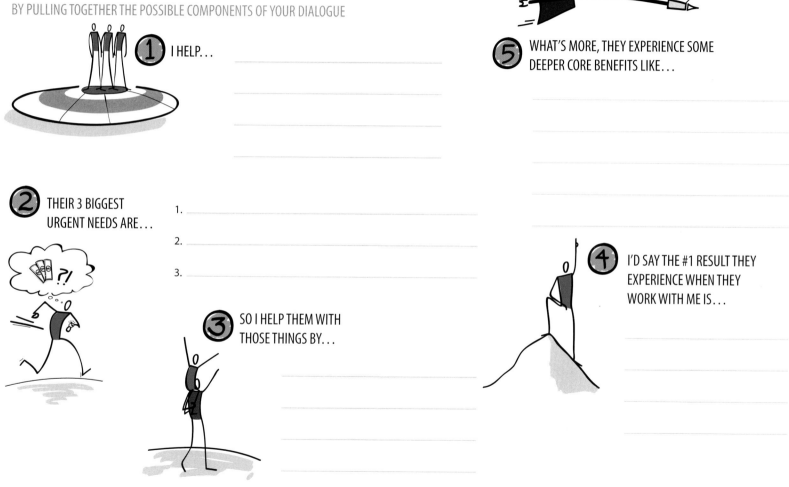

1 I HELP...

2 THEIR 3 BIGGEST URGENT NEEDS ARE...

1.
2.
3.

3 SO I HELP THEM WITH THOSE THINGS BY...

4 I'D SAY THE #1 RESULT THEY EXPERIENCE WHEN THEY WORK WITH ME IS...

FINANCIAL BENEFITS

EMOTIONAL BENEFITS

PHYSICAL BENEFITS

SPIRITUAL BENEFITS

5 WHAT'S MORE, THEY EXPERIENCE SOME DEEPER CORE BENEFITS LIKE...

Apply the 5-Part Formula

You now have an outline that will help you clearly articulate what you do without sounding confusing and bland. In fact, you'll sound like a superstar because you can use this outline or framework to have a meaningful conversation with another human being. I know I'm being redundant here, but it's so important that I'm willing to. *This is not a speech. Don't stay married to the format. Be sure to improvise. Using the structure can be helpful but you may not need to go through every element of this framework in every conversation.* The person you're engaged with might end up doing all the talking and even supply your side of the dialogue accurately. Then you can just sit back and relax.

The point is, if you're prepared with these five elements, you have the required ingredients for talking about what you do so you can cook up a sweet and tasty business, booked solid with high-paying, high-value clients. (Make note of how each part of the exercises you've just done fits into the conversations that follow, and note also how each part flows as the result of a natural conversation.)

I HELP _____ _____ .
               (TARGET AUDIENCE)   (BIG RESULT)

Example: *Checkout line at the supermarket.*

BOBBY: Nice to meet you, Michael. What do you do?

MP: I'm a small business advisor. I help small business owners (TARGET AUDIENCE) get more clients, (BIG RESULT)

BOBBY: Oh, that's very interesting. My wife has a home-based business. Can you help her?

MP: Tell me a bit about what she does and what kind of support you think she needs.

Now, we're talking …

the MEDIUM VERSION

I HELP _____ _____ . YOU KNOW HOW _____ _____ ?
       (TARGET AUDIENCE)   (BIG RESULT)   (TARGET AUDIENCE)   (THEIR COMPELLING NEEDS & DESIRES)

WELL WHAT I DO IS _____ AND AT THE SAME TIME, THEY _____ .
       (HOW I HELP / MY "DO WHAT" STATEMENT)   (THE DEEPER CORE BENEFITS THEY EXPERIENCE)

Example: *Industry conference.*

LISA: Nice to meet you, Michael. What do you do for a living?

MP: I'm a small business advisor. I help small business owners (TARGET AUDIENCE) get more clients. (BIG RESULT)

LISA: That's so important... getting more clients.

MP: Ain't that the truth. Business owners are always looking to find more clients but often (TARGET AUDIENCE) (URGENT NEED) complain that they hate marketing and selling.
(THEIR PROBLEM/CHALLENGE)

LISA: Can I confess something to you, Michael? I'm one of those business owners, and I always need new clients, but I really hate marketing and selling!

MP: I hear that! But it SO doesn't have to be that way. In fact, I teach people just like you (TARGET AUDIENCE) how to love marketing and selling, and at the same time, get as many clients as their heart desires. (HOW I HELP / MY "DO WHAT" STATEMENT) (THE DEEPER CORE BENEFITS THEY EXPERIENCE)

LISA: Tell me more! Please tell me more!

Listen and Be Flexible

The 5-Part Formula is a pretty good way to have a real conversation with someone about what you do. Of course, I wrote that scene so it works perfectly. In real life, it won't always be this smooth or successful. But, if you listen well, are flexible, and can adapt to the dynamic and specifics at hand, more often than not, you'll knock the conversation out of the park.

If I didn't use the 5-Part Formula, I could start by saying I'm a *New York Times* bestselling author of four books, appear regularly on network and cable TV shows, am one of the most sought-after speakers in the business, and run one of the most respected coaching programs in the world. But then I'd sound like an arrogant jerk. These kinds of credentials should come out over time, when appropriate, not three seconds after someone says, "What do you do?"

Of course, you can go back to the way you've always done things and say, "Hi, I'm [your name here]. I'm a [add professional title]." Or, you could try to use an elevator speech, but I think you see that you're not going to have quite the same impact and more likely than not, you'll end the conversation rather than start a relationship.

Once you've clearly identified your target market, understand their needs and desires, and can articulate how you help them by identifying the core benefits associated with the results of your services, you'll never be caught off guard again. I suggest you continue to hone and refine your message and then practice over and over. I do.

Practice Being Human

Start in the comfortable confines of your home; it may take some time for your Book Yourself Solid Dialogue to feel natural. While you don't want your dialogue to sound stiff and rehearsed, you do want to practice it. The more you practice it, the more comfortable you'll get with it, the less rehearsed it will sound, and the more improvisational you will be. You only get one chance to make a first impression. Present yourself and your business in a powerful and compelling way.

Practicing in this way will help you to become comfortable with the multitude of ways in which your Book Yourself Solid Dialogue will unfold when you're speaking with a variety of people. It is truly a dialogue, not a speech or script, so every time you have a dialogue with someone about what you do, it will be unique. Since the people you'll be speaking with won't be reading a script, they may or may not respond in similar ways to what I outlined earlier, but you'll soon discover that when you know your Book Yourself Solid Dialogue well, it won't matter. You'll easily and effortlessly respond in the most appropriate way.

BOOKED SOLID ACTION STEP: Practice with a colleague or two. Call one another spontaneously to ask, "What is it that you do?"

The most important principle of the Book Yourself Solid system is actually using what I teach you. Learning it is only a means to an end. Taking action will get you booked solid.

Use this exercise as the great opportunity it is to get honest, open feedback so that you can fine-tune your Book Yourself Solid Dialogue and make it the best it can be.

DON'T SOUND LIKE A ROBOT WHEN YOU TALK ABOUT WHAT YOU DO.

Speak from the Heart

Be sure to speak with lots of expression. Get excited and show the passion you have for the problems you solve and what you do in the world. If you're not very interested in what you do, no one else will be, either.

When you're passionate and excited about what you do and you let it show, it's incredibly attractive. Real passion can't be faked and there's nothing more appealing and convincing than knowing someone is speaking from the heart.

And don't forget to:

- Smile. I mean really smile—a big, bold, friendly smile.
- Make eye contact. You can't connect with others on a deep level if you aren't making eye contact.
- Be confident. Use confident, open body language. Stand up straight, yet be relaxed.

Listen! Stop and listen intently to the needs and desires of the person you're speaking to so that you can address whatever is most important and relevant to her.

A well-crafted Book Yourself Solid Dialogue that is delivered with ease and sincerity and infused with your own unique brilliance and passion is incredibly powerful. Claim your passion, claim your voice, and share it with the world one person at a time.

1 KILL THE ELEVATOR SPEECH

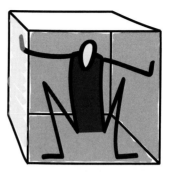

2 AVOID USING ONLY YOUR PROFESSIONAL CATEGORY SO YOU DON'T GET BOXED IN

3 USE THE 5-PART FORMULA TO TALK ABOUT WHAT YOU DO IN A WAY THAT IS ORGANIC & REAL

4 DITCH THE SCRIPTS SO YOU DON'T SOUND LIKE A ROBOT

THE RUNWAY TAKEOFF

In order for a plane to lift into the air it needs maximum thrust; the bigger the plane, the longer the runway required. The amount of energy necessary just to lift the wheels off the ground is massive, as is the effort required by the new service business owner to become known as a credible expert in her field.

Few business owners hit the speed needed in order to take off because they only give 80 percent effort. Imagine if a pilot did the same when attempting liftoff? What would happen? The plane wouldn't take off. The passengers would find themselves driving to their destination.

The choice is yours. Make a full "non-reversible" commitment to give 100 percent effort (for a relatively short period of time) so as to maximize and concentrate your marketing, and your business will surely get off the ground.

module 2

MODULE TWO: BUILDING TRUST & CREDIBILITY

"RUNWAY TAKEOFF"

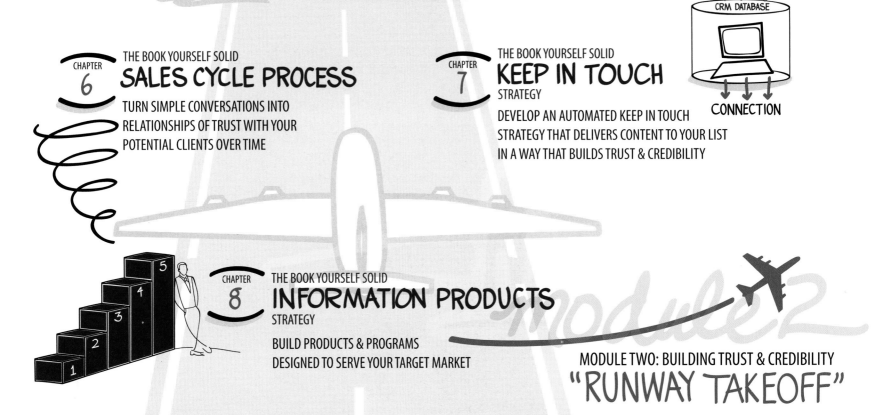

CHAPTER 5 — CREDIBILITY & LIKABILITY

ESTABLISH YOURSELF AS A CATEGORY AUTHORITY
& UNDERSTAND HOW YOUR LIKABILITY
WILL HELP YOU GET BOOKED SOLID

COLLECTION

CRM DATABASE

CONNECTION

CHAPTER 6 — THE BOOK YOURSELF SOLID SALES CYCLE PROCESS

TURN SIMPLE CONVERSATIONS INTO
RELATIONSHIPS OF TRUST WITH YOUR
POTENTIAL CLIENTS OVER TIME

CHAPTER 7 — THE BOOK YOURSELF SOLID KEEP IN TOUCH STRATEGY

DEVELOP AN AUTOMATED KEEP IN TOUCH
STRATEGY THAT DELIVERS CONTENT TO YOUR LIST
IN A WAY THAT BUILDS TRUST & CREDIBILITY

CHAPTER 8 — THE BOOK YOURSELF SOLID INFORMATION PRODUCTS STRATEGY

BUILD PRODUCTS & PROGRAMS
DESIGNED TO SERVE YOUR TARGET MARKET

module 2

MODULE TWO: BUILDING TRUST & CREDIBILITY
"RUNWAY TAKEOFF"

Building Trust & Credibility

MODULE TWO

To be booked solid requires that you are considered credible within your marketplace, that you be perceived as likable, and that you earn the trust of the people you'd like to serve. Now that you've got a solid foundation, it's time to look at how to develop a strategy for creating trust and credibility so that you stand out from the crowd and begin to build relationships with your potential clients.

YOUR STRATEGY WILL BE BASED ON:

- Becoming and establishing yourself as a likable expert in your field.
- Building relationships of trust over time through your sales cycle.
- Implementing an automated Keep in Touch Strategy.
- Developing brand-building information products and programs.

As before, I walk you step-by-step through the process and you'll begin to see that marketing and selling don't have to be so hard after all. In fact, I think you'll find that they can even be exciting and fun.

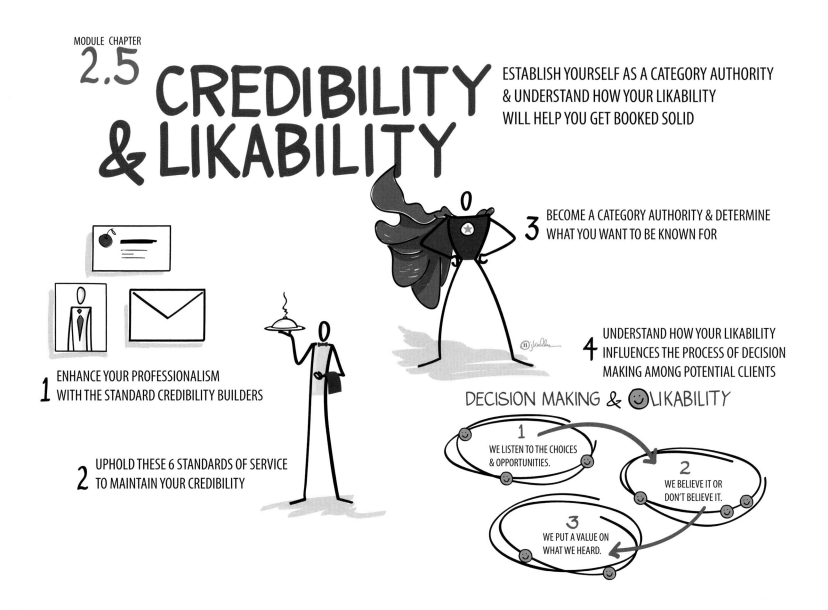

MODULE CHAPTER
2.5 CREDIBILITY & LIKABILITY

ESTABLISH YOURSELF AS A CATEGORY AUTHORITY & UNDERSTAND HOW YOUR LIKABILITY WILL HELP YOU GET BOOKED SOLID

3 BECOME A CATEGORY AUTHORITY & DETERMINE WHAT YOU WANT TO BE KNOWN FOR

1 ENHANCE YOUR PROFESSIONALISM WITH THE STANDARD CREDIBILITY BUILDERS

2 UPHOLD THESE 6 STANDARDS OF SERVICE TO MAINTAIN YOUR CREDIBILITY

4 UNDERSTAND HOW YOUR LIKABILITY INFLUENCES THE PROCESS OF DECISION MAKING AMONG POTENTIAL CLIENTS

DECISION MAKING & ☺LIKABILITY

1 WE LISTEN TO THE CHOICES & OPPORTUNITIES.

2 WE BELIEVE IT OR DON'T BELIEVE IT.

3 WE PUT A VALUE ON WHAT WE HEARD.

2.5 CREDIBILITY AND LIKABILITY

All credibility, all good conscience, all evidence of truth come only from the senses.

—Friedrich Nietzsche

Even before we discuss how to position yourself as an expert within your field, let's get down to the nitty-gritty—the standard credibility builders. The standard credibility builders are the things that you need to do and have in place to appear credible and professional. Once you have all your basics covered, then and only then can we discuss how to establish your reputation as an authority in your field and look at how your likability influences your ability to get booked solid.

The Standard Credibility Builders

The standard credibility builders may seem obvious, but without them you won't be taken seriously, so they're worth reviewing:

- You must have a professional e-mail address, preferably one that includes your domain name. juicytushy@aol.com doesn't qualify. Neither does 175bb3c@yahoo.com. If you don't yet have a web site, then at least use your name: johndoe@gmail.com.

- Invest in quality business cards. Business cards with perforated edges that you've printed at home, or the free cards with the printing company's name on the back, will undermine your credibility. On the flip side, overproduced cards with hyped-up text or a highly stylized head shot may undermine your authority. Only do something unusual with things like business cards if you're an expert at that kind of differentiation. If you're a designer and brand specialist, it might make sense to have a very unusual business card because it's likely so well done that it'll come off as remarkable. Otherwise, keep it simple.

- If you don't have a web site, have one built now! Actually, wait until you read Chapter 16, *The Book Yourself Solid Web Strategy*. If you do have a web site and it's out of date or created using a lower-end, old-school free template, build a new one. Please don't design your site yourself unless you're a professional.

- Have professionally produced photographs taken. Display them on your web site and in promotional materials. A photo of you in your pajamas with your cat is not going to inspire a lot of confidence (unless, of course, you own a pet store that also sells pajamas).

- Obtain and showcase specific testimonials rather than general testimonials. A comment from a client named H. G. that says, "Pam was great. She really helped" is not going to hold a lot of weight and it's certainly not going to get you booked solid. However, a very specific testimonial from a person with a name, a company, and maybe even a web site address, if applicable, that says, "In two months, Pam helped me lose 15 pounds. I could not have done it without her!" will carry weight (no pun intended).

- Bonus: Establish an advisory board. If well-known individuals will lend you their names, it will help you establish credibility within your target market. Just your association with other recognized experts will do wonders for establishing your credibility.

YOUR PHOTO

TESTIMONIALS

ADVISORY GROUP

Standards of Service

These are the basic standards of service that are essential for any decent service professional to adhere to and that your clients will expect. They help establish your credibility. The mistake that many service professionals make is thinking that these standards of service are all that are necessary to help them stand out from the crowd.

- **QUALITY OF SERVICE.** Of course you should have a high quality of service. A potential client expects that you offer a high quality of service.

- **METHODS AND TOOLS.** It's expected that you have the best methods and tools.

- **RESPONSIVENESS.** Your clients and customers expect you to be responsive. If you own an ambulance service, maybe responsiveness is paramount, but if you're a photographer, I expect you to respond to my calls and e-mails, but I don't expect you to come to my house on a whim at 3 a.m. on a Sunday to take a family portrait.

- **CREDENTIALS.** For most service professionals, clients don't care as much about credentials as you might think, unless, of course, you're in the medical, legal, or financial field; then credentials are expected and assumed. But you don't get a lot of brownie points for having a degree in acupuncture. If I'm going to come to you for acupuncture, I'll expect that you're credentialed, and if there is a plaque on the wall that displays your credentials, I'm satisfied. However, if you won the Nobel Prize for your work as an acupuncturist, that might be impressive.

- **CLIENT IMPORTANCE.** Your clients and customers expect to be considered important. It's essential to always make your clients feel important—more than important, in fact. You want to make your clients feel like the sun rises and shines just for them, because it does, if you want to book yourself solid. Making clients feel as important as they truly are builds your credibility, and it should be a given.

- **APPROPRIATE PRICE.** People don't generally buy on price (even though they say they do) and certainly not when it comes to their personal satisfaction, family, or their business, which I guess, is almost everything. Offering the lowest price is not necessarily going to help you establish credibility. In fact, many potential clients may be leery if your prices are significantly below market value. More on pricing later.

Please do not assume that these standards of service will set you apart. They won't. They're what every savvy consumer will expect. However, there is something very special that will make you stand out from the crowd every day of the week.

STANDARDS OF SERVICE AREN'T EXCEPTIONAL; THEY'RE EXPECTED.

Don't Just Fake It 'til You Make It

Although being a category authority and establishing yourself as one may, at first glance, appear to be the same thing; they're not. This isn't about faking it until you make it. Before you can establish yourself as a category authority you must be one. How do you do that? You truly become a category authority by learning everything you possibly can about the one thing you've decided you want to become known for.

For many of us, the leap into learning all we can about our field can be immediately overwhelming, as the first thing we often learn is just how much we don't know. But this is a good thing. You can't seek knowledge that you don't know you need, so it is much better to first study what you didn't realize earlier that you didn't know, even if it deflates your ego.

If the thought of becoming and establishing yourself as a category authority immediately induces a sense of panic at the thought of all you'd have to learn and do, you're not alone. Or maybe you feel you already know enough to be an expert, but the thought of having to put yourself so boldly—and publicly—front and center of your target market makes you want to run home for Mom's homemade chicken soup.

For some, the idea of putting yourself out in front of the people you'd like to serve in a big, bold, public way, where you'll be subject to public scrutiny, can trigger a multitude of insecurities. You'll know your dark side has taken over when thoughts start racing round and round inside your head like, "Who am I to call myself an expert? What do I know? I'm such a fraud. I don't know enough yet. Maybe I'll never learn enough to be an expert. I don't even know where to begin." Or worse yet, "What if I put myself out there and fall flat on my face? What if I look silly and embarrass myself? What if everyone hates me? What if I get made fun of or criticized?"

Does this sound familiar? I'll bet it does. Again, you're not alone! It doesn't have to be that way. If your dark side is running rampant, lock it in a soundproof closet and give control back to the bold and brilliant you that you know you really are, and keep reading.

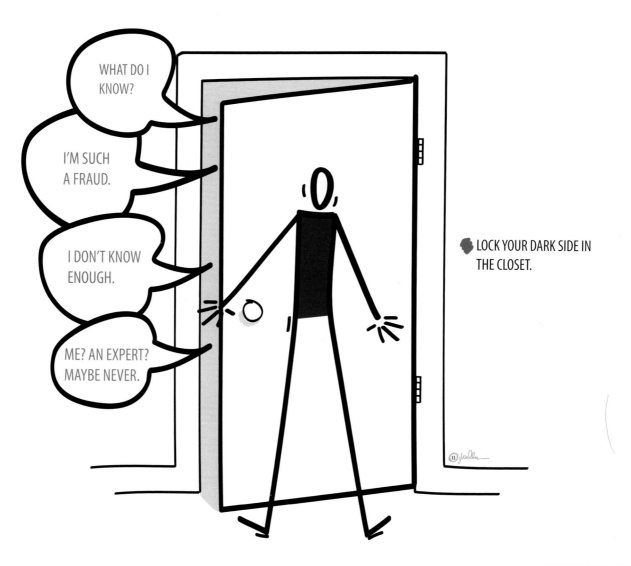

There Is a Hero in You

If, now that you've thwarted the dark side, some other side of you has taken over and is whining, "Do I have to?" the answer is a firm and resounding, "Yes, you do!" Like it or not, becoming a category authority, an expert in your field, isn't optional if you want your business to be as successful as it can be. It's a must. There is a hero in you, and the Book Yourself Solid system will help you become and establish yourself as a category authority. It will have such a powerful effect on the success of your business, and it will be so incredibly rewarding, that it's well worth the effort and perceived risk (which means no real risk at all).

BECOMING A CATEGORY AUTHORITY WILL:

- Establish the credibility and trust necessary for potential clients to feel comfortable and confident about purchasing your services, products, and programs.

- Get your message out to the world in a big way as it raises awareness of yourself and your business within your target market. The idea is to be the first to come to mind when someone needs the kind of services, products, and programs that you offer.

- Help you gain clients and increase sales more easily and effortlessly while also allowing you to earn higher fees. It will give you the edge you need to stand out from the crowd of others who offer similar services, products, and programs. Suddenly, you'll no longer be just one of the masses.

- Create the visibility you'll need to reach all of your target market.

- Make it much easier to move and expand into new markets of your choosing.

- Increase your own confidence in your ability to provide the best possible services, products, and programs to those who most need and want them.

Written Exercise 5A

IDENTIFY WHAT YOU WANT TO BE KNOWN FOR

You first have to identify what you'd like to become known for within your target market. If what you want to be known for is too broad or you try to become a category authority on too many topics, you'll overwhelm yourself and confuse your target market.

Use the visual worksheet on the next page for the following exercise.

STEP 1: ASSESS YOUR EXPERTISE.

- In what areas are you currently an expert?
- In what areas do you need to develop your expertise?
- How will you develop the expertise you need?

STEP 2: ASSESS THE PROMISES YOU CAN MAKE AND DELIVER.

- What promises can you make and deliver today, to your target market, that will position you as an expert?
- What promises would you like to make and deliver to your target market but don't yet feel comfortable with?
- In order to get comfortable making those promises in the future, what will you do?

STEP 3: ASSESS WHAT YOU ARE KNOWN FOR AND/OR WANT TO BE KNOW FOR.

- What are you currently known for?
- What is the ONE THING you would like to be known for?
- In order to become a category authority for that one thing, what will you do? List the ways in which you could learn the things you identified.

BECOME A CATEGORY AUTHORITY

DETERMINE THE ONE THING YOU WOULD LIKE TO BE KNOWN FOR
& HOW YOU WILL ESTABLISH YOURSELF AS A CATEGORY AUTHORITY

WHERE I AM TODAY	WHERE I WOULD LIKE TO BE	HOW I'M GOING TO GET THERE
① I'M CURRENTLY AN EXPERT IN THE FOLLOWING AREAS:	I NEED TO DEVELOP MYSELF IN THE FOLLOWING AREAS:	TO DEVELOP MYSELF, I WILL:
② I CAN CURRENTLY MAKE THE FOLLOWING PROMISES THAT POSITION ME AS AN EXPERT:	I WOULD LIKE TO MAKE THE FOLLOWING PROMISES IN THE FUTURE, BUT DON'T YET FEEL COMFORTABLE:	IN ORDER TO FEEL COMFORTABLE MAKING THOSE PROMISES, I WILL:
③ I AM CURRENTLY KNOWN FOR:	THE ONE THING I WOULD LIKE TO BE KNOWN FOR IS:	IN ORDER TO BECOME A CATEGORY AUTHORITY FOR THAT ONE THING, I WILL:

Making the Mental Shift

We've discussed what you need to have and do to be credible, and by now you understand the importance of becoming and establishing yourself as a category authority. I hope it's clear that you must actually be an expert. You might think the logical next step would be to implement a plan to establish yourself as a category authority within your target market, but it's not. There's a critical mental shift that must take place first.

All of the Book Yourself Solid marketing strategies that you're going to learn in Module Four will put you out in front of your target market in such a big way that you will establish yourself as a category authority. First consider what you need to learn and what you need to do to establish your expertise so that when the time comes to implement the Book Yourself Solid 6 Core Self-Promotion Strategies, you will be an expert. You will make the crucial mental shift of thinking of yourself as an expert. If you don't believe it, you'll have a hard time persuading anyone else to believe it.

Begin to think of and refer to yourself as a category authority—an expert in your field.

When the time comes to establish yourself as a category authority within your target market, you'll be comfortable with, and confident of, your expertise. If you already consider yourself an expert, then by all means begin including that in your current marketing materials.

Just remember—when communicating with your potential clients, be clear about what you know and clear about what you don't. People who are credible don't actually know everything, and they are just as comfortable saying that they don't know something as they are saying that they do.

There is one other very powerful mental and emotional factor that has a profound impact on your efforts to establish yourself as a category authority, one that may surprise you. I urge you not to discount or underestimate it. It's the power of likability.

SOON YOU'LL BE A CATEGORY AUTHORITY & READY TO PROMOTE YOURSELF AS SUCH.

The Power of Likability

Now that you know what you need to do to become and establish yourself as a category authority, we're going to look at an even more important factor to consider: Do your potential clients like you? Do they perceive you as likable? And I mean really likable.

The fact is that if they don't, none of the rest of your efforts to establish yourself as a category authority will matter. That's a pretty bold statement, and it may come as a surprise to you, but bear with me as I shine some light on the subject, with the help of Tim Sanders and a few concepts from his book, *The Likability Factor: How to Boost Your L-Factor and Achieve Your Life's Dreams*.

When you get right down to it, Sanders points out, "Life is a series of popularity contests." We don't want to admit it, we don't want to believe it, we've been told it ain't necessarily so, but ultimately, if you're well liked, if your likability factor is high, you're more likely to be chosen and to get booked solid.

Mark McCormack, the founder of International Management Group (IMG), the most powerful sports management and marketing company, agrees: "All things being equal, people will do business with a friend; all things being unequal, people will still do business with a friend."

To make choices, we go through a three-step process. First, we listen to something out of a field of opportunities. Then we either do or do not believe what we've heard. Finally, we put a value on what we've heard. Then, we make our choice.

With so many demands on our attention these days, we have to filter and carefully select what we give our attention to. This is why becoming and establishing yourself as a category authority is so important. Your target market and your potential clients need a reason to deem your message important enough to sit up and pay attention, to listen to it. If you're likable, they're much more likely to do so and to remember what they've heard.

Once you have their attention, they're listening, but will they believe what they're hearing? This is where your credibility comes into play. With so many advertising messages coming at us from every direction each day—through spam e-mail, radio and TV commercials, and infomercials, to name a few—we've become highly skeptical of much of what we hear. If you're credible, you're much more likely to be believed.

But wait, that's not the only factor that comes into play when someone is determining whether to believe you. Again, your likability is a critical factor in establishing trust. Think about it for a moment. You're much more likely to trust, and to believe, someone you like. Sanders says, "When people like the source of a message, they tend to trust the message or, at least, try to find a way to believe it."

Your likability factor has an enormous impact on your perceived value. Develop your credibility, establish yourself as an expert, strive to be your best, most likable self, and you'll quickly become the best and most obvious choice for your potential clients.

DECISION MAKING & LIKABILITY

1 WE LISTEN TO THE CHOICES & OPPORTUNITIES.

2 WE BELIEVE IT OR DON'T BELIEVE IT.

3 WE PUT A VALUE ON WHAT WE HEARD.

Be Credible and Likable

Now that you've got the standard credibility builders and you've established your standards of service, you can focus on being a category authority. By identifying and focusing on the one thing you most want to become known for, you simplify and speed up the process, leaving no question in the minds of those in your target market about your area of expertise. This will allow you to create a synergy, not only among your services, products, and programs but among all the techniques you'll use to establish yourself as a category authority.

To powerfully establish yourself as a category authority, you need to demonstrate your expertise on a single subject. To do that, you must focus, focus, focus! Pour yourself into books, Internet research, training programs, and consider apprenticing with a mentor who is already a category authority.

Even if you're already very knowledgable about whatever it is you want to become known for, continuing to learn, and staying up-to-date with the latest information in your field is not only a good idea but is required to remain booked solid. I recommend that you read at least one book a month, if not more, on your chosen subject, which will increase your knowledge, challenge you to see a different perspective, or spark new ideas and thoughts, all of which will enhance the value you provide to your clients.

Finally, don't forget about likability and its role in the level of trust you can gain. If a potential client perceives you as the most credible and likable, you're probably the one she'll hire. And even if all things are not equal, even if you aren't the candidate with the most experience or expertise, if your potential client likes you, it's your likability that will win the day —and the client.

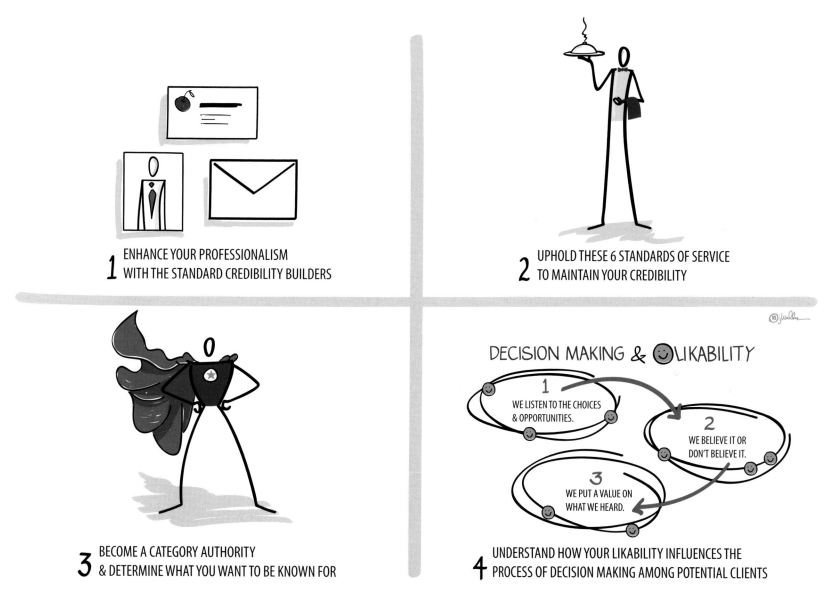

1 ENHANCE YOUR PROFESSIONALISM WITH THE STANDARD CREDIBILITY BUILDERS

2 UPHOLD THESE 6 STANDARDS OF SERVICE TO MAINTAIN YOUR CREDIBILITY

3 BECOME A CATEGORY AUTHORITY & DETERMINE WHAT YOU WANT TO BE KNOWN FOR

DECISION MAKING & LIKABILITY

1 WE LISTEN TO THE CHOICES & OPPORTUNITIES.

2 WE BELIEVE IT OR DON'T BELIEVE IT.

3 WE PUT A VALUE ON WHAT WE HEARD.

4 UNDERSTAND HOW YOUR LIKABILITY INFLUENCES THE PROCESS OF DECISION MAKING AMONG POTENTIAL CLIENTS

module 2

MODULE TWO: BUILDING TRUST & CREDIBILITY
"RUNWAY TAKEOFF"

CHAPTER 6

The Book Yourself Solid Sales Cycle Process

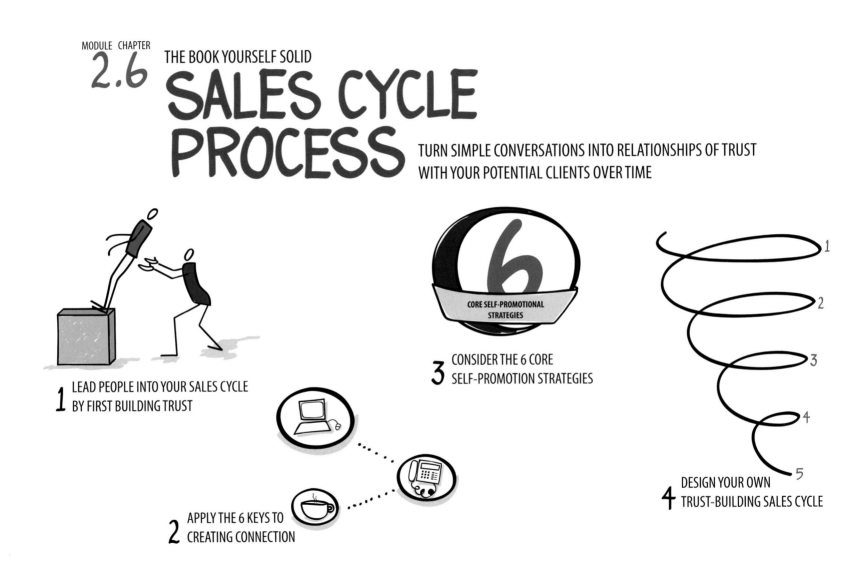

THE BOOK YOURSELF SOLID

SALES CYCLE PROCESS

TURN SIMPLE CONVERSATIONS INTO RELATIONSHIPS OF TRUST
WITH YOUR POTENTIAL CLIENTS OVER TIME

1 LEAD PEOPLE INTO YOUR SALES CYCLE
BY FIRST BUILDING TRUST

2 APPLY THE 6 KEYS TO
CREATING CONNECTION

CORE SELF-PROMOTIONAL
STRATEGIES

3 CONSIDER THE 6 CORE
SELF-PROMOTION STRATEGIES

4 DESIGN YOUR OWN
TRUST-BUILDING SALES CYCLE

1
2
3
4
5

2.6 THE SALES CYCLE PROCESS

It is a mistake to look too far ahead. Only one link in the chain of destiny can be handled at a time.

—Sir Winston Churchill

BUILDING RELATIONSHIPS OF TRUST

All sales start with a simple conversation. It may be a conversation between you and a potential client or customer, between one of your clients and a potential referral, between one of your colleagues and a potential referral, or between your web site and a potential client. An effective sales cycle is based on turning these simple conversations into relationships of trust with your potential clients over time. We know that people buy from those they like and trust. This is never truer than for the professional service provider.

Turn Strangers into Friends and Friends into Clients

If you don't have trust, then it doesn't matter how well you've planned, what you're offering, or whether you've created a wide variety of buying options to meet varying budgets. If a potential client doesn't trust you, nothing else matters. They aren't going to buy from you—period. If you think about it, this may be one of the main reasons you say you hate marketing and selling. You may be trying to sell to people with whom you have not yet built enough trust. All sales offers must be proportionate to the amount of trust that you've earned.

- What are your potential clients thinking?
- Do they really believe you can deliver what you say you can?
- Do they trust you to hold their personal information confidential?
- Do they like the people who work for you?
- Do they feel safe with you?
- Do they believe hiring you will give them a significant return on their investment?

If you want a perpetual stream of inspiring and life-fulfilling ideal clients clamoring for your services and products, then just remember—all sales start with a simple conversation and are executed when a need is met and the appropriate amount of trust is assured.

Seth Godin, author of *Permission Marketing*, implores us to stop interrupting people with our marketing messages and instead:

- Turn strangers into friends by adding value.
- Turn friends into customers by getting permission from them to offer our products and services.

In its most effective form, the Book Yourself Solid Sales Cycle not only turns strangers into friends and friends into potential clients but potential clients into current clients and past clients into current clients.

In order to design a sales cycle for your business, you must first understand how you're going to lead people into your sales cycle through building trust. Then we can actually create a sales cycle process that will attract more clients than you can handle and do so with the utmost integrity.

BUILD TRUST, ADD VALUE, & YOU'LL BUILD FRIENDS WHO TURN INTO CLIENTS.

Key Number 1: Who Is Your Target Client?

We've covered in depth how to choose a target market, but I'm going to reiterate it here because of its importance. You need to choose whom you'd like to bring into your cycle. The more specific you are the better; choose one person (or organization) within your target market to focus on.

Identifying and gearing your marketing to a specific individual (or organization) allows you to make the important emotional connection that is the first step in developing a relationship with your potential client. When you have made the effort to speak and write directly to your ideal client, he'll feel it. He will feel as though you truly know and understand his needs and desires—because you will. That task alone will go a long way toward building the trust you desire with the clients you seek.

If you're not super clear on whom specifically you're targeting, whom you want to reach out to and attract, it's going to be hard to develop a sales cycle that works because you'll be chasing after every potential opportunity and you won't be making a strong connection with anyone.

Describe your customer in specific terms. For example, notice how I describe my target client in the visual at right.

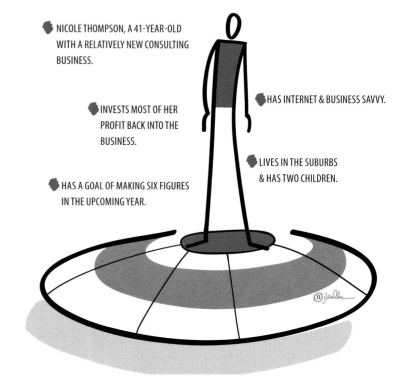

NICOLE THOMPSON, A 41-YEAR-OLD WITH A RELATIVELY NEW CONSULTING BUSINESS.

HAS INTERNET & BUSINESS SAVVY.

INVESTS MOST OF HER PROFIT BACK INTO THE BUSINESS.

LIVES IN THE SUBURBS & HAS TWO CHILDREN.

HAS A GOAL OF MAKING SIX FIGURES IN THE UPCOMING YEAR.

Key Number 2: What Are They Looking For?

You've got to understand what your ideal clients or customers are looking for—the kinds of products or services they think will solve their problems or help them reach their goals. It's very important to be clear on your answers because if you don't know what your potential clients are looking for, you won't know what kind of product and service offers to make in your sales cycle. We usually make offers that we think are relevant. It's time to put your target market first and work to truly understand what they know is relevant. Then you can decide on what you're going to offer them that will meet their needs, according to the amount of trust that you've earned, at various stages in your sales cycle.

A BOOK THAT CAN HELP THEM GET CLIENTS

PRIVATE MENTORING

BUSINESS COACH TRAINING

Key Number 3: Where Do They Look For You?

Do you know where your target market looks for you? Do they search online? Do they read magazines? Do they call their friends for referrals for the kind of service that you're providing? What other types of business professionals do they trust to get their referrals from? If you don't know, survey your current clients. This should always be one of the first questions you ask a new client: "How did you come to find me?" If you don't have any clients of your own yet, ask a colleague how her clients find her.

ONLINE SEARCH

ASK A FRIEND
FOR A REFERRAL

PHONE DIRECTORY

Key Number 4: When Do They Look For You?

When do the people (or organizations) in your target market look for the services you offer? What needs to happen in their personal life or work life for them to purchase the kind of service you have to offer? How high do the stakes need to be before they decide to purchase the service you're offering? They may be interested in what you do, and your offerings may resonate with them, but they might not need you at the moment they find you.

This is why the Book Yourself Solid Sales Cycle is so important. You'll want to make it easy for them to step into your environment and move closer to your core offerings over time. When their stakes rise, they'll reach out to you and ask for you. But you've got to keep the conversation going.

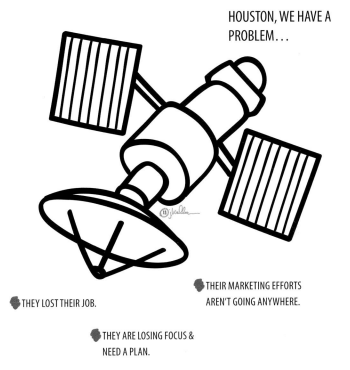

HOUSTON, WE HAVE A PROBLEM...

THEIR MARKETING EFFORTS AREN'T GOING ANYWHERE.

THEY LOST THEIR JOB.

THEY ARE LOSING FOCUS & NEED A PLAN.

Key Number 5: Why Should They Choose You?

That's a big question. Why are they going to choose you? Are you a credible authority in your field? What makes you the best choice for them? What is unique about you or the solutions you offer?

It's crucial that you set your modesty aside and express yourself clearly and with confidence—no wishy-washy answers to these questions. Think back to the last time you went in search of expert help. When you first spoke to the service provider to inquire about his services, his expertise, and whether he could help you, the last thing you wanted to hear was, "Well, I kinda know what I'm doing. I might be able to help you. I'll give it a shot."

You've got to be able to say, "You've come to the right person. Yes, absolutely, I can help you. I'm an expert at what I do and this is how I can help."

Declaring your strengths, your skills, your expertise, and your ability to help is not bragging but expressing confidence in what your potential clients expect, want, and need to hear from you

MY STRENGTHS ARE...

EXPERTISE IN...

EXPERIENCE IN...

TRAINING IN...

Key Number 6: How Do You Want Them to Engage With You?

Once potential clients have learned about your services, how would you like them to interact or engage with you? Do you want them to call your office? Do you want them to sign up for your newsletter on your web site? What is it that you want potential clients to do?

Naturally, we'd love for them to immediately purchase our highest-priced product, program, or service, but this is rare. Most of your potential clients need to get to know you and trust you over time. They need to be eased gradually toward what they may perceive to be your high-risk offerings.

It's often said that, on average, you will need to connect with a potential client seven times before they'll purchase from you. Not always, but if you understand this principle, you will be on the road to booking yourself solid a lot faster than if you try to engage in one-step selling. "Hi, I'm a consultant. Wanna hire me today?" isn't going to be effective. That's definitely not the Book Yourself Solid way. Maybe we should call one-step selling one-stop selling because that's what it'll do—stop your sales process dead in its tracks.

Clearly defining these six keys will help you to determine what you want to offer your potential clients in each stage of your sales cycle and will help you craft the most effective sales cycle possible.

FIND ME ONLINE.

CALL ME.

MEET FOR COFFEE.

Written Exercise 6A

THE SIX KEYS TO CREATING CONNECTION

The Book Yourself Solid Sales Cycle works when you know your responses to these six keys. This exercise was created to ensure that the offers you are making in your sales cycle process are right on target.

Use the visual worksheet on the next page for the following exercise.

STEP 1: Who is your target client or customer? Describe what she is like. Get really creative with this one. List as many specific details as you can.

STEP 2: What are your potential clients looking for?

STEP 3: Where do your ideal clients look for you?

STEP 4: Describe the situations that are likely to drive potential clients to seek your services, products, and programs. When do they look for you?

STEP 5: Why should your potential clients choose you? (Don't you dare skip this one! Be bold! Express yourself fully. Remember, this is not the time for modesty.)

STEP 6: How do you want your potential clients to interact or engage with you? (Note: Establishing a line of communication is the first step in developing a relationship of trust.)

THE 6 KEYS TO CONNECTION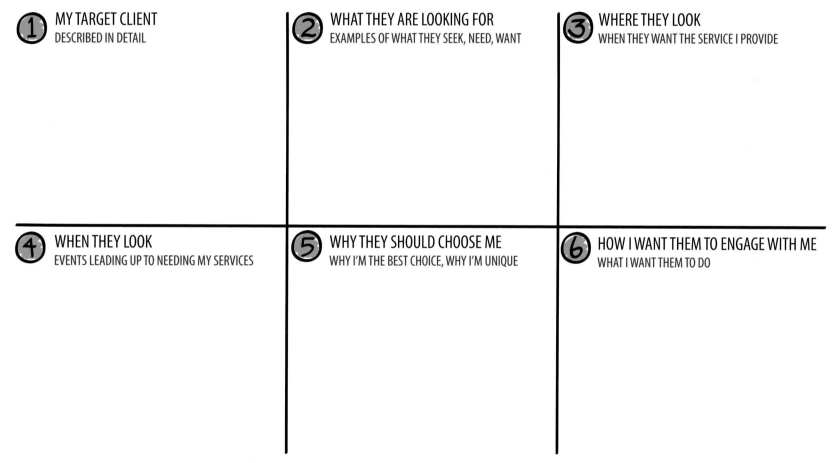

KNOW YOUR RESPONSES TO THESE SIX KEYS TO MAKE SURE THE
OFFERS IN YOUR SALES CYCLE ARE ON TARGET

① MY TARGET CLIENT
DESCRIBED IN DETAIL

② WHAT THEY ARE LOOKING FOR
EXAMPLES OF WHAT THEY SEEK, NEED, WANT

③ WHERE THEY LOOK
WHEN THEY WANT THE SERVICE I PROVIDE

④ WHEN THEY LOOK
EVENTS LEADING UP TO NEEDING MY SERVICES

⑤ WHY THEY SHOULD CHOOSE ME
WHY I'M THE BEST CHOICE, WHY I'M UNIQUE

⑥ HOW I WANT THEM TO ENGAGE WITH ME
WHAT I WANT THEM TO DO

A Preview to the 6 Core Self-Promotion Strategies

In Module Four, you'll learn how to use the Book Yourself Solid 6 Core Self-Promotion Strategies, including networking, direct outreach, referral, speaking, writing, and using the web to create awareness for the solutions you offer. However, rather than attempting to sell to a client, you will simply offer her an invitation that has no barrier to entry.

To best do this, you need to create awareness for the services, products, and programs you offer using one or all of the Book Yourself Solid 6 Core Self-Promotion Strategies.

You will have your choice of the Book Yourself Solid:

1. Networking Strategy
2. Direct Outreach Strategy
3. Referral Strategy
4. Speaking Strategy
5. Writing Strategy
6. Web Strategy

CHAPTER 11

THE BOOK YOURSELF SOLID

NETWORKING
STRATEGY

ADD VALUE & EXPAND YOUR NETWORK WITHOUT SCHMOOZING OR MANIPULATING

CHAPTER 12

THE BOOK YOURSELF SOLID

DIRECT OUTREACH
STRATEGY

REACH OUT DIRECTLY TO PROSPECTIVE CLIENTS & REFERRAL PARTNERS WITHOUT BEING PUSHY OR SPAMMY

THE BOOK YOURSELF SOLID

6

CORE SELF-PROMOTIONAL STRATEGIES

CHAPTER 13

THE BOOK YOURSELF SOLID

REFERRAL
STRATEGY

LEARN HOW TO APPROACH THE REFERRAL PROCESS IN PHASES SO THAT EACH REFERRAL BUILDS UPON ITSELF

CHAPTER 14

THE BOOK YOURSELF SOLID

SPEAKING
STRATEGY

GET IN FRONT OF POTENTIAL CLIENTS & SHARE THE FRUITS OF YOUR KNOWLEDGE

CHAPTER 15

THE BOOK YOURSELF SOLID

WRITING
STRATEGY

WRITE TO EDUCATE THE PEOPLE YOU SERVE & PROMOTE THE SERVICES YOU SELL

CHAPTER 16

THE BOOK YOURSELF SOLID

WEB
STRATEGY

DESIGN YOUR SITE GET MORE VISITORS & BUILD YOUR SOCIAL NETWORK

The Book Yourself Solid Sales Cycle Process

Your services have a high barrier to entry. To potential new clients, your services are intangible and expensive—whether you think they are or not—especially to those who have not used the kind of services that you offer or who have not had good results with their previous service providers.

The Book Yourself Solid Sales Cycle is a sequence of phases that a client moves through when deciding whether to buy your services or products.

As opposed to the typical sales cycle, which has the same start and end points for all prospective clients, the Book Yourself Solid Sales Cycle works in a way that allows buyers to enter at any point in the process, depending on their situation. A client hires you when the circumstances in his life or work match the offers that you make. If you're a mortgage specialist, I may not need your services right now. But perhaps, six months from now, I stumble upon a "FOR SALE" sign in the front yard of my dream home. You can bet that I'll not only want your services, I'll need them immediately. Do you see how the stakes have changed? Chances are that if you haven't built trust with me over the last six months by offering great value along the way (without expecting anything in return, mind you), it's unlikely you'll cross my mind when I look to secure a mortgage for my dream house.

The following example will give you a framework for the process. Your sales cycle may include 3, 10, or even 15 stages, depending on your particular business and the different services and products you offer. I'm going to teach you the principles that govern an effective sales cycle so that you can craft one that serves your particular business and meets the individual needs and tastes of your clients and customers.

I will explain each stage and give you a real example from my business to help you visualize exactly how each stage works. I'm going to also ask you to write out your objective for each stage and how you're going to achieve your objective. This way, by the end of the chapter, you'll have completed your very own Book Yourself Solid Sales Cycle. I'll do my best to make it as easy as possible to absorb and implement the information. If you do get a bit overwhelmed, please stay with it. This is an important part of the Book Yourself Solid system, and understanding the principles behind these techniques will ensure that you're well on your way to being booked solid.

As you work through this process, remember all that you are doing is having a simple conversation with someone. You are making a connection that will build trust so that you will then be able to share your services with another person. How cool is that?

THE BOOK YOURSELF SOLID

SALES CYCLE PROCESS

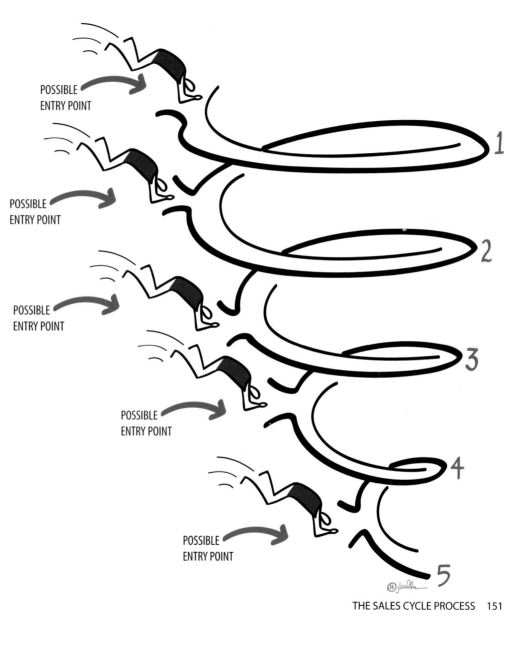

POSSIBLE
ENTRY POINT

POSSIBLE
ENTRY POINT

POSSIBLE
ENTRY POINT

POSSIBLE
ENTRY POINT

POSSIBLE
ENTRY POINT

1

2

3

4

5

Book Yourself Solid Sales Cycle—Stage One

You begin your sales cycle by making no-barrier-to-entry offers to potential clients. A no-barrier-to-entry offer is one that has no risk whatsoever for a potential client so that she can sample your services. I'm not talking just about offering free services, which is a common practice for many professional service providers. I take this concept much further with much more success.

To book yourself solid, perform daily tasks that will keep your name in front of potential clients. In Stage One, your objective is to get a potential client to do something—go to your web site, call a number, fill out a form, or another action that begins to affiliate them to you.

Your objective for Stage One of the Book Yourself Solid Sales Cycle should be simple and measurable, like driving prospective clients to your web site. Or maybe you want them to call your office directly. It's up to you. But once you've chosen an objective, you'll choose the strategies you would like to use to achieve it.

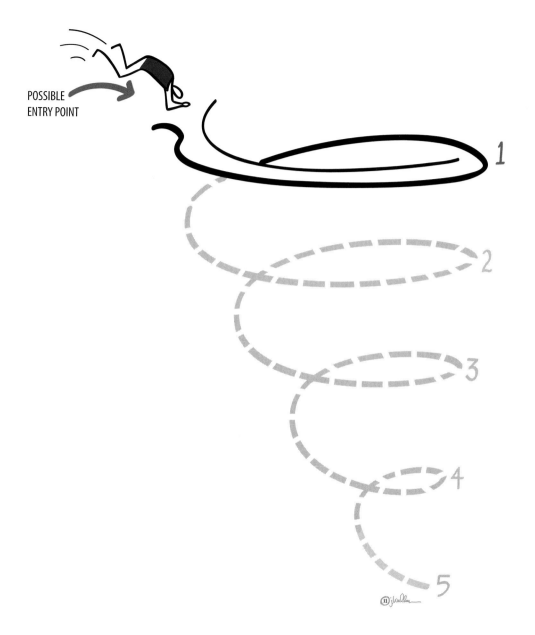

POSSIBLE
ENTRY POINT

1

2

3

4

5

MICHAEL'S STAGE ONE EXAMPLE:

My Stage One objective is to drive potential

clients to my web site. (This is the answer to the

sixth key to creating connection, "How do you

want your potential clients to engage with you?")

To do so, I use the Book Yourself Solid Speaking,

Writing, and Web Strategies.

Book Yourself Solid Sales Cycle—Stage Two

In this stage you will demonstrate your knowledge, solutions, and sincere desire to provide value to your target market free of charge, with no barrier to entry and at no risk to them. The benefits include increased trust—they will feel as though they know you somewhat better.

To familiarize your prospective clients with your services, you need to offer them solutions, opportunities, and relevant information in exchange for their contact information and permission to continue communicating with them over time. What does that communication look like? You may provide a tip sheet, special report, or white paper that addresses their urgent needs and compelling desires. You might give a discount coupon for an initial session. It could be your always-have-something-to-invite-people-to offer, which I discuss in detail at the end of this chapter. No matter what you select, it should be something that speaks not only to their needs but also what you want them to know about how you can serve them.

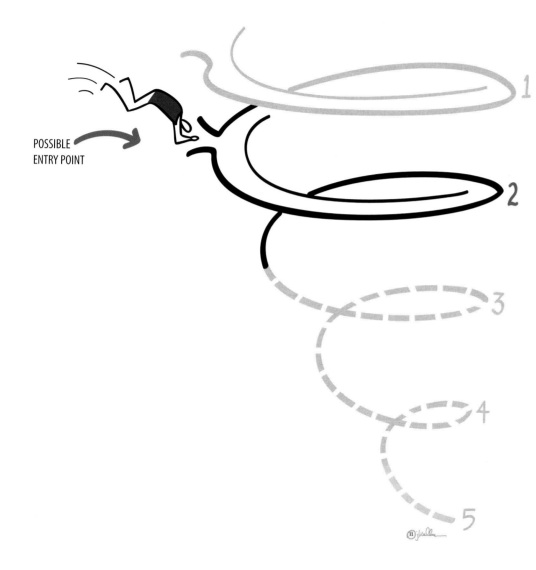

POSSIBLE
ENTRY POINT

MICHAEL'S STAGE TWO EXAMPLE:

My Stage Two objective is to encourage my web site visitors to subscribe to my newsletter by entering their name, e-mail address, and location. If they do, they will also get a free chapter from each of my books, *Book Yourself Solid*, *Beyond Booked Solid*, *The Contrarian Effect*, and *The Think Big Manifesto*, along with a high-quality 60-minute audio recording in which I expand on certain concepts, principles, and strategies.

Book Yourself Solid Sales Cycle—Stage Three

Now that you've started building trust between you and your potential clients, you're going to work on developing and enhancing that trust and cultivating the relationship.

In Stage Three of the sales cycle your objective is twofold: to continue to add value by helping your potential clients incorporate the information that you gave them in Stage Two of the cycle and to make a sale. If you gave them a free report, you should follow up with automated e-mails that help them use the content in the report to create value.

You should also offer them something that will surprise them. It could be a complimentary pass to a workshop you're doing or a personal note on your stationery or branded postcard with a list of books on your area of expertise that you know will speak to their urgent needs. Remember, the value you add doesn't have to be all about you. If you recommend a resource to your potential clients, they will very likely associate the value they received from that resource with you.

As I mentioned, this is the first time in the sales cycle where you might also offer your potential clients a service or product that will cost them money:

an in-person seminar or intake session. It might be one of your information products: e-book, published book, CD, DVD, workbook, manual, guidebook, or teleseminar, all of which we'll get to in the book. When you send your follow-up e-mails, you will let your potential clients know of the opportunities you have for them that speak directly to their urgent needs and compelling desires, and you'll continue to add value without expecting anything in return.

What's important to understand is that the monetized offer you are making does not have a very high barrier to entry. You're not going to rush out of the gate and surprise potential clients with your highest-priced offer, just as you wouldn't propose marriage on a first date, no matter how smitten you are. You want to offer them something they are ready for, and if they're ready for more at that moment, they'll ask for it. Of course, you'll always let potential clients know how to view the page on your web site that lists your various services, just in case they are ready to walk down the aisle.

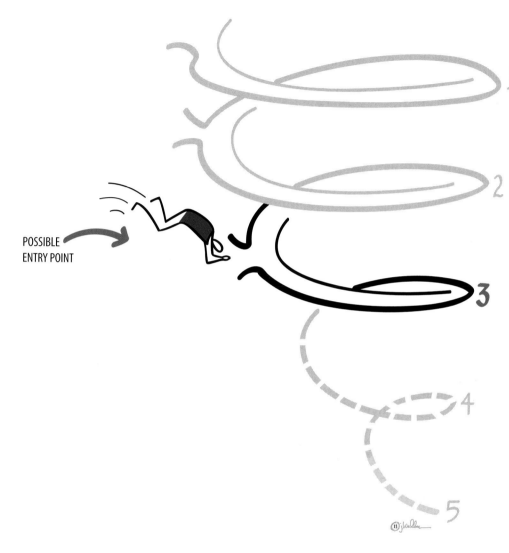

POSSIBLE
ENTRY POINT

MICHAEL'S STAGE THREE EXAMPLE:

My Stage Three objective is to give those who previously opted in for my newsletter, four free chapters, and 60-minute audio the incentive to purchase one of my books from Amazon.com.

(You don't have to have a published book to do this. You can offer an intake session, needs assessment, e-book, CD, class, or any other low-barrier-to-entry offer.)

Book Yourself Solid Sales Cycle—Stage Four

Your focus now is to help your potential clients move to the next level of your sales cycle. Let's say a potential client bought your low-barrier-to-entry product or service or has even become a client, thanks to your efforts in Stage Three of the sales cycle. Now is the time to over-deliver on the product or service he purchased. What does that mean? Here's an example: Your client has recently purchased your e-book, and you notice that you have a workshop or presentation scheduled on the very same topic. To over-deliver, you could call the customer, send the customer an e-mail or card inviting him to the workshop, or, if he can't attend, send him a copy of the notes after the event. What a great way to give more than the potential client expected to receive.

When he has received great value from that service or product, you then offer your next level of product or service, something that requires more of an investment than the previous product or service he purchased. Notice how this client is moving closer and closer to your core offerings and your higher-priced offerings. This is usually the case but only after you've increased the client's trust factor and proven that your solutions work and that you deliver on the promises that you make.

I believe that when people have read one of my books, thoughtfully done the exercises, and taken the action steps necessary, they will be well on their way to achieving their goals. They will also be confident that what I have to offer them is valid and valuable and that I can serve their most relevant, personal, and immediate needs and desires. However, they may also want the opportunity to work through the concepts, principles, and strategies in the book with me, my team, and other inspired service professionals for a number of reasons: opportunity for more personal coaching and attention, higher levels of accountability, networking opportunities, or maybe they want to bathe in the Book Yourself Solid fountain of inspiration.

The point is, I don't want to try to sell them these online and phone-based coaching courses until they've had the opportunity to read one of my books. I want them to be excited about meeting me and my team and know that we can serve them before they sign up for a coaching course. That one factor, knowing that we can serve them, will give our participants better results, and that's our goal—to help our clients get the results they want.

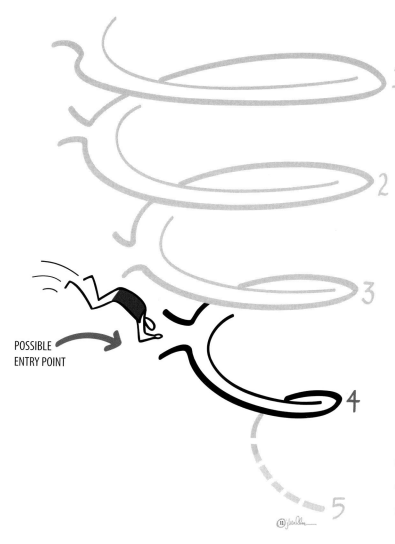

POSSIBLE
ENTRY POINT

MICHAEL'S STAGE FOUR EXAMPLE:

My Stage Four objective is to enroll ideal clients in my online and on-the-telephone courses on marketing, business growth, and even information product creation, the same people who have already visited my web site, opted in for free chapters and the audio recording, and purchased my book.

Book Yourself Solid Sales Cycle—Stage Five

Your objective in Stage Five is similar to the previous one: to help potential clients move to the next level of your sales cycle by offering them a higher-level product or service. What's important to understand about this process is that not every person or organization who enters into your sales cycle will move all the way through it, and the time that each potential client takes to do so will be different as well.

Notice that my Stage Five objective is to enroll ideal clients into my in-person small group coaching and mentoring programs and/or larger live events. Again, there are many people who join one of these programs, or attend an event, without participating in an online coaching course, or right after they have read my book, or even before they do, simply because they were referred to me by a person they trust. But you can't count on that. You'll have better success if you lay out a plan for how you introduce people to your offerings.

The in-person small-group coaching programs require more of a financial investment than do the online and over-the-phone coaching courses. That's why it's very important to me that those who join these programs know

that it is the right place for them to continue their business development and trust that my team and I will over-deliver on our promises. I imagine you would want the same thing. After clients participate in an online and over-the-phone coaching program, which is my Stage Four offering, they will believe this deeply. This is why the Book Yourself Solid Sales Cycle is so effective. You're building trust with people over time, trust that is proportionate to the size of the offer you're making to them.

All of your sales offers should be proportionate to the amount of trust that you've earned.

As a professional service provider you don't want to try to convince people that what you're offering is right for them. You want to provide value upon value until they believe that your services are right for them. They will get better results that way and be more satisfied with your services, a factor that is way too important to forget about.

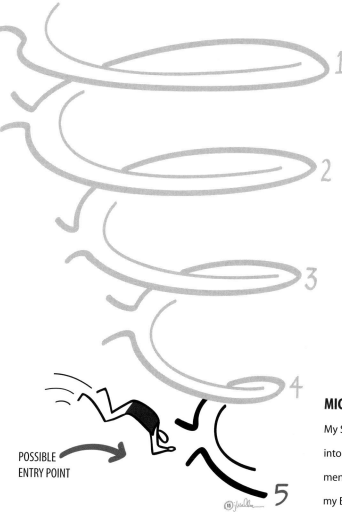

POSSIBLE
ENTRY POINT

MICHAEL'S STAGE FIVE EXAMPLE:

My Stage Five objective is to enroll ideal clients into my in-person small group coaching and mentoring programs and/or larger live events, or my Book Yourself Solid School of Coach Training.

Written Exercise 6B

As you work on the following exercise, keep this in mind: You don't want to try to sell your products and services until your potential client has the opportunity to take advantage of one of your free offers. You want them to be excited about meeting you.

To do the following exercise, you are going to simply replace my example offerings with the appropriate offerings for you and your clients. Remember, your sales cycle will have as many stages as is appropriate for you and your business right now. You might only have three stages in your sales cycle at present, which is A-okay. It will evolve and grow as your business evolves and grows.

DESIGN YOUR OWN BOOK YOURSELF SOLID SALES CYCLE

Use the visual worksheet on the next page for the following exercise and create your own customized plan.

STEP 1: What is your objective for each stage within the sales cycle? In other words, what do you want the client to do or what action would you like them to take? Write it in the first column in the visual worksheet.

STEP 2: What is your strategy for encouraging them to take that action? For ideas, you can choose from the Book Yourself Solid 6 Core Self-Promotional Strategies.

THE SALES CYCLE

DESIGN A SEQUENCE OF TRUST-BUILDING PHASES
THROUGH WHICH YOU WANT YOUR POTENTIAL CLIENTS TO MOVE

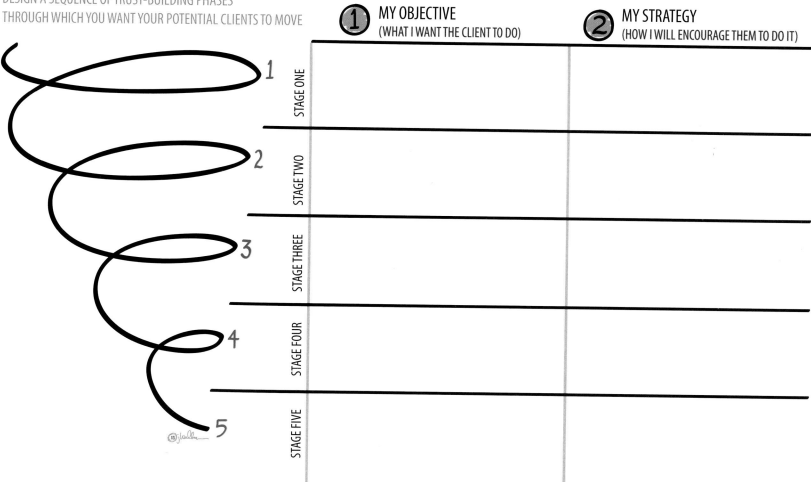

① MY OBJECTIVE (WHAT I WANT THE CLIENT TO DO)

② MY STRATEGY (HOW I WILL ENCOURAGE THEM TO DO IT)

STAGE ONE

STAGE TWO

STAGE THREE

STAGE FOUR

STAGE FIVE

Keeping in Touch Is Key for Your Sales Cycle

The Book Yourself Solid Sales Cycle is most effective when used in conjunction with a Keep in Touch Strategy, which you will learn about in Chapter 7. The size of your network, and especially the number of potential clients in your network, is directly proportional to how booked solid you are. I strongly suggest working diligently on growing your network, which includes potential clients and marketing and referral partners alike.

Sometimes this network is referred to as your database or followers or subscribers or, simply, your list. Your list is made up of people who have given you permission to communicate with them on an ongoing basis. Building a large list and having permission to communicate with them will make it easy to secure new clients whenever you need to. All you have to do is send out a newsletter or e-newsletter, publish a blog post, or tweet a compelling offer, and voilà!—you'll have new ideal clients. I am not being glib; you'll see for yourself just how easy it is once you build trust with a large group of raving fans who have given you permission to add value to their lives and make offers to them at the same time.

Please note, you can never, ever, no way, no how, just add people to your list because you think they'll like what you have to offer. That, my dear friend, is spam, any way you slice it—even if you know them personally. All your marketing, follow-up, keeping in touch, and publishing must be permission-based, which means, the recipient of your message has consented to receive a broadcast from you, regardless of whether it contains marketing messages. You can send a personal e-mail to connect and build your relationship, but you cannot add just anyone to any sort of broadcast list.

Keep in mind, the Book Yourself Solid system is interconnected, with several strategies that build upon, and sometimes rely upon, one another.

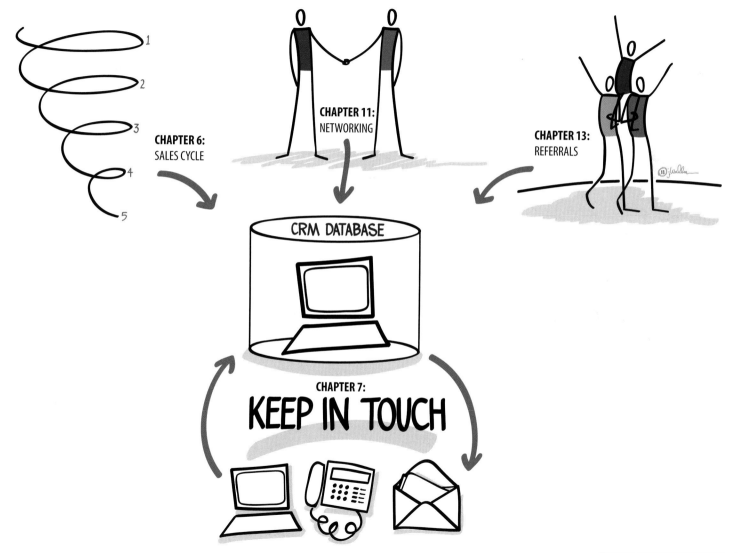

CHAPTER 6:
SALES CYCLE

CHAPTER 11:
NETWORKING

CHAPTER 13:
REFERRALS

CRM DATABASE

CHAPTER 7:
KEEP IN TOUCH

The Always-Have-Something-to-Invite-People-to Offer

This strategy might just be the most effective marketing and trust building strategy on the planet for the professional service provider. You'll want to consider your own always-have-something-to-invite-people-to offer as you design the first few stages of your Book Yourself Solid Sales Cycle. It might be what you choose to direct potential clients to when you use the Book Yourself Solid 6 Core Self-Promotion Strategies.

People generally hate to be sold, but they love to be invited—as long as the invitations are relevant and anticipated. Meaning, they've given you permission to make an invitation. What if I could help you eliminate your need to sell with this one solution? Would that be exciting to you? I bet it would. By my second year in business, this one strategy actually doubled my income.

I offer a weekly complimentary teleseminar (very large conference call) called the "Think Big Revolution." It is designed to help people think bigger about who they are and what they offer the world. Sometimes we discuss a topic related to getting more clients, and other times we cover strategies to help them be more successful in business and in life.

Note that the membership was free. If I met someone I thought would benefit from membership, I'd invite her to join. With the release of my fourth book, *The Think Big Manifesto*, I turned the weekly call into a 24/7 online social networking community, a place where big thinkers can connect with other big thinkers to actually make their dreams come true. Membership is free and it will always be because no one owns big thinking. I'd like to invite you to join. I bet you'll love it. You get an opportunity to participate in something that should add great value to your life and test me out at the same time. And for me it's fantastic because I don't have to sell anything. I can offer really great value to the lives of potential clients and customers at no risk to them. And then they have the opportunity to ask me for more business help if they are so inclined.

To accept my invitation to join the Think Big Revolution, go to ThinkBigRevolution.com and sign up there. See how easy that was? No selling; just an invitation.

Give Too Much, and Then Give More

This strategy works! Of the 93 percent of my clients who successfully book themselves solid, all of them use it in one form or another.

There is another added benefit of this kind of always-have-something-to-invite-people-to offer. It can serve as one of the most effective ways of establishing your personal brand. Your always-have-something-to-invite-people-to offer is the perfect way to integrate and align your who and do what statement (whom you help and what you help them do) and your why you do it statement (the philosophical explanation for why you do what you do).

The value you add in your offer meets the needs and desires of the people you serve. This no-barrier-to-entry offer is an essential component of the Book Yourself Solid Sales Cycle. Then as you continue to build trust over time by offering additional value and creating awareness for the services you provide, you'll attract potential clients deeper into the sales cycle, moving them closer to your core offerings.

Your always-have-something-to-invite-people-to offers should be done in a group format. There are three important reasons for this:

1. You'll leverage your time so you're connecting with as many potential clients as possible in the shortest amount of time.

2. You'll leverage the power of communities. When you bring people together, they create far more energy and excitement than you can on your own. Your guests will also see other people interested in what you have to offer, and that's the best way to build credibility.

3. You'll be viewed as a really cool person. Seriously, if you're known in your marketplace as someone who brings people together, that will help you build your reputation and increase your likability.

Please give away so much value that you think you've given too much, and then give more. Remember, your potential clients must know what you know. They must really like you and believe that you have the solutions to their very personal, specific, and urgent problems. The single best way to do that is to invite them to experience what it's like to be around you and the people you serve.

Use the Sales Cycle to Unconditionally Serve Your Clients

You can have as many stages in your sales cycle as you need to build trust with potential clients for the kinds of offers you make. Just thinking about your sales cycle will help you clarify and expand your offerings. Gone are the days when you can simply have one offering and be guaranteed to book yourself solid. The marketplace is too competitive and diverse. Every day another inspired professional stakes a claim and joins the ranks of free agents around the world. More and more people are feeling the call to stand in the service of others.

Expanding your offerings to create a Book Yourself Solid Sales Cycle may just enhance your business model—the mechanism by which you generate revenue—from only one offering with one stream of revenue to multiple offerings with multiple streams of revenue.

The Book Yourself Solid Sales Cycle is not just about getting new clients to hire you. It is designed to unconditionally serve your current clients as well. It is much harder to sell your services, products, and programs to a new client than to those who have already received value from you as a client or customer. The most successful businesses, both large and small, know this. It's one of the reasons Amazon.com is so successful. Once you've become a customer, they know you, they know what you need, what you read, and they work to continue to serve you. The typical client-snagging mentality suggests that you make a sale and move on. The Book Yourself Solid way requires that you make a sale and ask, "How can I over-deliver and continue to serve this person or organization?" This is not a small thing.

Now it's your turn to develop your own unique sales cycle. Don't limit yourself to just the few examples I've already touched on. There are a multitude of ways to build trust with your potential clients and to ease them toward purchasing your higher price point offerings. Use your imagination and creativity to tailor your sales cycle to what works best, feels most natural, and resonates most with you.

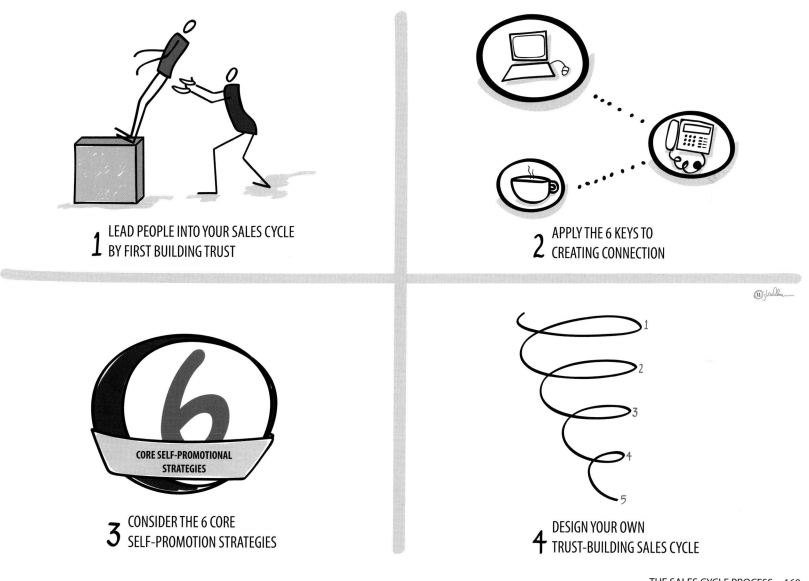

1 LEAD PEOPLE INTO YOUR SALES CYCLE BY FIRST BUILDING TRUST

2 APPLY THE 6 KEYS TO CREATING CONNECTION

3 CONSIDER THE 6 CORE SELF-PROMOTION STRATEGIES

CORE SELF-PROMOTIONAL STRATEGIES

4 DESIGN YOUR OWN TRUST-BUILDING SALES CYCLE

2.7

THE BOOK YOURSELF SOLID

KEEP IN TOUCH STRATEGY

DEVELOP AN AUTOMATED KEEP IN TOUCH STRATEGY
THAT DELIVERS CONTENT TO YOUR LIST
IN A WAY THAT BUILDS TRUST & CREDIBILITY

1 SEE HOW THE BYS STRATEGIES
WORK TOGETHER & RELY UPON
YOUR CRM DATABASE TO HELP YOU
COLLECT & CONNECT

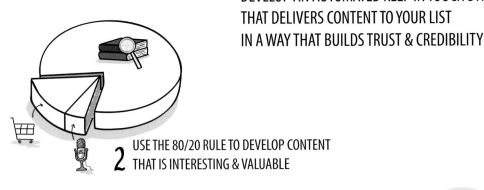

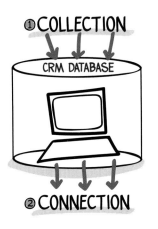

①**COLLECTION**

CRM DATABASE

②**CONNECTION**

2 USE THE 80/20 RULE TO DEVELOP CONTENT
THAT IS INTERESTING & VALUABLE

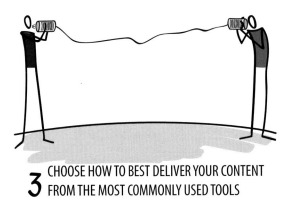

4 USE E-ZINES TO BUILD YOUR LIST,
SELL YOUR PRODUCTS, AND POSITION
YOURSELF AS AN EXPERT IN YOUR FIELD

3 CHOOSE HOW TO BEST DELIVER YOUR CONTENT
FROM THE MOST COMMONLY USED TOOLS

2.7 THE KEEP IN TOUCH STRATEGY

Be well, do good work, and Keep in Touch.

—Garrison Keillor

This Keep in Touch Strategy may be the most important marketing strategy you'll ever use. You already know that you need to connect with potential clients many times before they feel comfortable hiring you or purchasing your products. If you don't have a systematized and automated Keep in Touch Strategy in place, you may, as the saying goes, leave a lot of business on the table. Most important, you'll miss out on the opportunity to serve the people you're meant to serve.

Many businesses fail for lack of a solid Keep in Touch marketing strategy. Either they bombard you with too much information and too many offers that turn you off, or you never hear from them at all, which leaves you feeling unimportant and irrelevant.

Strategies That Help You Collect People

I'm sure you've met hundreds, if not thousands of people over your professional life you've not kept in touch with. Now that you're a service professional wanting to attract more clients than you can handle, I'll bet you wish you had kept in touch with all those folks. Well, no matter! You will Keep in Touch with everyone you meet from this point forward. It is encouraging, however, to reflect on all of the people you have met with whom you did not Keep in Touch because it shows you how easy it can be to build a database of potential clients and networking contacts. Now that you'll put your focus on building your database, you'll be booked solid in no time.

But let's take a step back for a moment because I want you to see the bigger picture. There are two primary reasons you need a CRM (Customer Relationship Management) database system:

1. **TO COLLECT** names of the people you want to reach and valuable information about them.

2. **TO CONNECT** with them and keep track of your interactions, using tools that help automate your efforts.

There are a few strategies shared in this book that help you to collect more names for your database. They are:

- The Book Yourself Solid Sales Cycle Process (Chapter 6) .
- The Book Yourself Solid Networking Strategy (Chapter 11).
- The Book Yourself Solid Referral Strategy (Chapter 13).

Now, I don't just want you to collect names and contact information. Your database should include relevant information so that you can Keep in Touch in a way that is personal and meaningful. So be sure you:

- Segment your people into groups.

- Add tags or keywords to each person, indicating their professional industry, interests, and likes/dislikes.

- Include notes about each person, such as where or how you met and when.

I will go into more depth about databases a little later. For now, I want you see the significance of multiple strategies working in sync, and how they rely on a database to help you get booked solid.

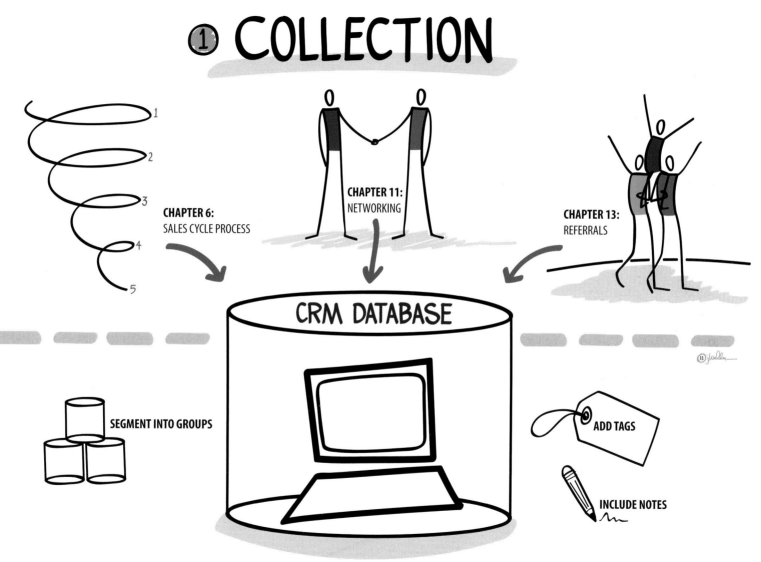

Strategies That Help You Connect with People

Let's switch our focus from collecting to connecting. After all, what is the point of collecting names in a database if we don't create a meaningful, ongoing connection with them? Just like the collecting process, this book includes strategies to help you with connecting. They are:

- Building Trust (an aspect of every chapter in this book)
- The Keep in Touch Strategy (this chapter)
- The Book Yourself Solid Direct Outreach Strategy (Chapter 12)

Building trust is a prerequisite for every strategy, and it is a primary purpose of keeping in touch and deepening our connections. Remember, we only receive what is in direct proportion to the amount of trust we have gained.

The Keep in Touch Strategy gives some insight on a few primary methods for ensuring that your name stays at the forefront of their minds. We break this down into the types of content you can share, and the tools you can use to share it.

But you can't stop there. The activities must be recorded into your database. You must track who, what, when, and where you have connected, so that you can follow up.

Following up with prospects and professional opportunities is a major key to your success. It's an investment that will deliver huge returns. Your Book Yourself Solid Sales Cycle is based on the success of your Keep in Touch Strategy and requires you to deliver great value. Please, I implore you to make this a top priority.

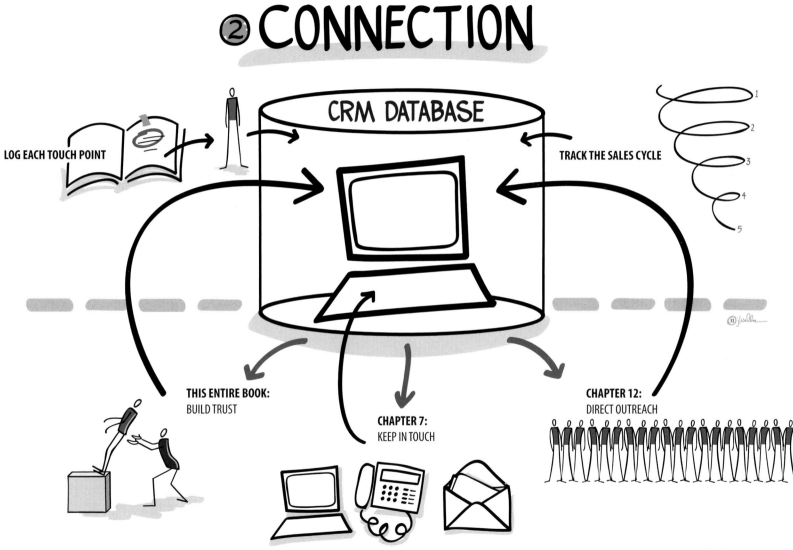

② CONNECTION

CRM DATABASE

LOG EACH TOUCH POINT

TRACK THE SALES CYCLE

1
2
3
4
5

THIS ENTIRE BOOK:
BUILD TRUST

CHAPTER 7:
KEEP IN TOUCH

CHAPTER 12:
DIRECT OUTREACH

Building and Managing Your Database

CHOOSING A DATABASE PROGRAM

To have an effective Keep in Touch Strategy, you'll need a reliable and comprehensive database program. There are many database programs from which you can choose, and more than I can list here, but I'll give you a few examples and important criteria to consider as you make your choice.

There are two important differentiators that I want you to consider: sales management versus contact management. CRM (customer relationship management) systems like the InfusionSoft®, SalesForce®, Goldmine®, or Act® are all designed to manage not only contacts but also the sales process, to turn leads into opportunities and opportunities into clients.

Whereas, contact management systems, like Microsoft Outlook® or Apple® Contacts (Address Book), typically provide a way to organize your company and personal contacts, some of which may be sales opportunities. Others may be networking or referral opportunities but have a very limited functionality related to the tracking and managing of sales leads and sales opportunities. Contact management systems may provide a way to take notes on a record, but they don't provide a good way to track the sales process, or pull reports, which might be the most critical process in your business.

WHY DO YOU NEED MORE THAN JUST AN ADDRESS BOOK?

You see where I come down on this issue: you need to start using a CRM system to manage, not only your contacts but also your sales process, from lead generation to opportunity management to sales conversion. Using a CRM system you'll be able to:

- **TRACK PERFORMANCE OF LEAD SOURCES**—it's likely that a small amount of lead generation efforts will drive the bulk of your sales.

- **CREATE A CONSISTENT SALES PROCESS**—if you have even one person working with you—it will help you see what is driving results.

- **INCREASE THE SPEED OF YOUR SALES CONVERSION**—respond to new leads quickly, follow up frequently with e-mails and calls, and nurture leads that don't convert immediately.

- **KEEP TRACK OF ACTIVITIES**—get things done when you need to and when you say you will.

- **REPORT ON PAST PERFORMANCE**—if you don't know what you've done, how are you going to know what you need to do?

- **FORECAST FUTURE SALES**—if you don't know where you're going, how are you going to get there?

ENTERING DATA

You certainly have to get a new lead's contact information, but that's not where most people fall short. It's that they don't actually do anything with it. You must enter and store it in the system and then continue to connect with the lead, building trust over time. The size of your database, but most importantly the quality of the relationships you have with the people in your database, is directly proportional to the financial health of your business.

BACK UP YOUR DATA

Back it up, baby. You've got to do this daily. Your database is the foundation of your business. If you lose that integral support structure, you can't replace it; you're essentially starting over, which could cost you many hours, if not months, of time and money.

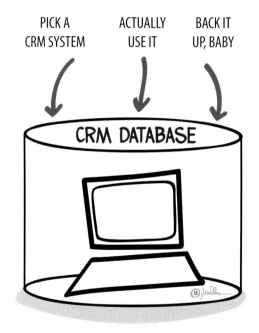

Prerequisites for Communicating to Your List

TWO KINDS OF KEEPING IN TOUCH

I want to make an important distinction between two types of keeping in touch:

1. **TO INDIVIDUALS:** Following up with potential clients, colleagues, and others on a personal, one-to-one level. See Chapter 11 on networking, "Take It Up a Notch" and Chapter 12 on direct outreach, "The List of 20."

2. **TO YOUR LIST:** Developing an automated Keep in Touch Strategy through which you broadcast electronic newsletters, send direct mail campaigns, write blog posts, or use other publishing platforms like social media.

For the rest of this chapter we will focus on the second type, keeping in touch with your list. Just know that before you can communicate to your list, there are two prerequisites:

1. You must have made meaningful connections with each of them.
2. They have given you permission to be on the list.

HAVING A LIST AIN'T ENOUGH

Let's consider the experience of my client Barbara. Within a few short years she had compiled more than 5,000 opt-in names for her database. The names were captured, but Barbara never really followed up with any of them until one day when she created a promotional offer to send to her list, and she eagerly clicked Send. What came back were mostly e-mails from recipients inquiring as to who she was and how they knew each other. Barbara learned a valuable lesson that day: Determine the best approach for using this strategy and build it into your Keep in Touch plans! If your list includes a bunch of people you don't know that well, consider the "Take It Up a Notch" ideas from Chapter 11 and "The List of 20" method from Chapter 12. This will help ensure that your list includes meaningful connections.

Each time I send out my electronic newsletter, which has historically been my primary Keep in Touch Strategy, I get new orders for my products and calls about my services. Every time! Without my solid Keep in Touch marketing strategy in place, I would not be able to build trust with people over time.

A WORD ABOUT PERMISSION MARKETING

When you've met someone and exchanged contact information, you have permission to communicate with him, and to start or continue a dialogue that is valuable to both of you. However, this does not equate to having permission to add that person to your mailing list so you can send him your newsletter or other automated or broadcast messages. All of the broadcast follow-up that you do to groups must be based on the principles of permission marketing, offering a potential client the opportunity to volunteer to be marketed to. According to Seth Godin, in his book *Permission Marketing*, "By only talking to volunteers, permission marketing guarantees that consumers pay more attention to the marketing message. It allows marketers to calmly and succinctly tell their story. It serves both consumers and marketers in a symbiotic exchange."

Permission marketing is:

- **ANTICIPATED**—people look forward to hearing from you.
- **PERSONAL**—the messages are directly related to the individual.
- **RELEVANT**—the marketing is about something the prospect is interested in.

This is essential because you want to communicate only with someone who is looking forward to hearing from you. When potential customers anticipate your marketing messages, they're more open to them. And, of course, when they have not explicitly asked you to send them things like a newsletter, and you do, it's not just possible spam, it is 100 percent pure spam—no matter how much you think they'll enjoy it.

With that said, once you get to know people, you should ask them if they'd like you to subscribe them to your newsletter. Tell them about it, what's valuable about it, when it's delivered, and any other relevant information. Then, if they accept your invitation to be on your mailing list, you have permission to send it to them along with special offers and other promotions.

Use the 80/20 Rule to Create Valuable Content

It's up to you to ensure that the content you share with your potential clients through your Keep in Touch Strategy is relevant, interesting, current, and valuable. There are six basic categories of content that meet those criteria, but I'm going to chunk them into three groups to make it easier to learn and remember:

1. **SHARE HELPFUL INFORMATION**
   - Industry information
   - Strategies, tips, and techniques
   - Content from other sources (experts)

2. **SHARE WHAT YOU OFFER**
   - Product and service offerings

3. **SHOW AND TELL**
   - Cool Keep in Touch
   - Special announcements

As you develop these types of content, apply the 80/20 rule. 80 percent of your content should be free, helpful information for the people you serve. The remaining 20 percent is a vehicle for sharing who you are and how you help them. Remember this is just a rule of thumb, but it will go a long way toward building trust and credibility. The idea is that 80 percent or more of your focus is on them, and 20 percent or less is about you. Some service professionals go too far in the other direction, and they end up disappointed with the results.

1. HELPFUL INFORMATION

80% OF YOUR KEEP IN TOUCH CONTENT SHOULD BE FREE INFORMATION.

2. PRODUCTS & SERVICES OFFERINGS

3. SHOW & TELL

your
KEEP IN TOUCH CONTENT

Share Helpful Information

INDUSTRY INFORMATION

Industry information that is relevant to your target market and that may or may not be widely known is excellent content to deliver to your list. You'll position yourself as an expert within your industry while providing constant value to your current and potential clients. What's more, they will appreciate the information and your generosity for sharing it.

Let's say that you certify yoga teachers. Information regarding industry standards, regulations, and laws would be helpful to your target market. Perhaps if you were a project manager, the latest findings and announcements from OSHA would be meaningful, as would information about safety issues.

Including important information in your Keep in Touch Strategy also makes it more likely that your potential clients will keep the information and refer back to it, keeping you at the top of their minds for future support.

STRATEGIES, TIPS, & TECHNIQUES

Strategies, tips, and techniques is probably the most common type of content, especially for service professionals. It's the primary type of information that I deliver to my e-zine subscribers.

Despite the appeal of this content-rich approach, many service professionals fear they will give away too much of their material. "If I provide all these great tips and strategies for free, then why would anyone ever hire me?" they wonder. Of course there are some who will take everything you offer and never hire you or purchase a product, but they wouldn't be hiring you anyway, and you never know—they may be out in the world talking about what you do and how you help. I've received tons of referrals from people who are not clients just because I've helped them for free. Most people who eventually do hire you or buy your products will need to receive free advice and support to build the trust they need for them to believe that you can really help them. Furthermore, most people will assume that you know a lot more than what you are giving away. They'll think, "Wow! If she gives away this much great stuff, can you imagine what I'll get if I actually pay her?"

CONTENT FROM OTHER SOURCES

I often provide my current and potential clients with relevant content from other people so that I can over-deliver as much as possible. This gives me a break from continuously creating content, it allows me to offer my contacts more than I can offer by myself, and it allows me to position other professionals who appreciate the promotion. There is a bonus as well: The experts I feature often return the favor by promoting me to the people they serve. Isn't that a win for everybody? It's also the easiest way to create great value for the people who have given you permission to serve them when you're first starting out.

Again, if you're concerned that you'll lose customers or clients because you highlight other experts, please recall this Book Yourself Solid principle:

There are certain people you're meant to serve and others you're not. If you can help other professionals attract business through you, you're creating more abundance for everyone involved.

Share What You Offer

If you don't make offers to your potential clients, how will they know you can help them? If you aren't doing everything you can to serve the people who need your help, what are you doing? Seriously, I believe you have an obligation to offer your services to those who need them and to those whom you know you can help in a meaningful and connected way. There are certain people you're meant to serve and others you're not. If you can help other professionals attract business through you, you're creating more abundance for everyone involved.

Here's another way of looking at it: Most of us express our values through the things we buy. We are what we purchase. Think about it. If you didn't know me but came across my personal and business financial statements from the past three months, you'd know a heck of a lot about me, like what I value and how I spend my time. If my financial records showed that I was at the bar every night and spent most of my money playing the slot machines in Vegas, you'd get a sense of what I value. If those records showed that I attend meditation class five times a week, purchase four books a month, and spend thousands of dollars a year on private schooling for my son, you'd see a person with different values.

Most of us want the opportunity to express ourselves through the things we purchase, especially when those things are adding value to our life or work. So please give the people you serve the opportunity to express their values by buying what you have to offer.

Remember, the people who have expressed interest in your services want to know how they can work with you, and it's your responsibility to tell them and show them their options.

WE EXPRESS OUR VALUES BY WHAT WE PURCHASE.

Show and Tell

SPECIAL ANNOUNCEMENTS

This is a valuable method of keeping in touch if the special announcement is relevant, important, and presented as a learning tool to your target market.

But be careful—it's often an overused category and can be irrelevant and annoying when it comes in the "all-about-me" form, like news about your company that is irrelevant to your contacts. How many times have you received announcements telling you about a new development in a company or about a change in management that you really cared about?

Instead, consider announcing the upcoming events where you will be speaking or attending, and give some free content along with the announcement.

COOL KEEP IN TOUCH

You know that I love it when you express yourself. And you also know by now that you will more easily and quickly attract your ideal clients when you do. This category is the cool Keep in Touch category because it can include any fun, different, unique, or exotic method of keeping in touch, some of which may expose your quirks! Please remember that quirky does not mean weird or bizarre. It means unusual, unique, and special. So get creative! Be bold! Dare to stand out from the crowd!

For example, Susan is a hairstylist and dog lover. Each month her Keep in Touch includes a photo shoot of her and her dogs with new fun, wild, and outrageous hairstyles and colors. It is fun, memorable, and totally Susan!

What is your special, unique, and entertaining quirk that can be turned into a cool Keep in Touch Strategy? The possibilities are limitless.

BE MEMORABLE.
EXPRESS YOURSELF WHILE YOU
KEEP IN TOUCH.

Written Exercise 7A

KEEP IN TOUCH CONTENT STRATEGY

We just learned about three categories of Keep in Touch content:

1. **SHARE HELPFUL INFORMATION**
   - Industry information
   - Strategies, tips, and techniques
   - Content from other sources (experts)

2. **SHARE WHAT YOU OFFER**
   - Product and service offerings

3. **SHOW AND TELL**
   - Cool Keep in Touch
   - Special announcements

Now it's time to apply it. What is the best kind of content to include in your Keep in Touch Strategy based on your interests and the needs and desires of your target market? What ideas do you have to make that content relevant, interesting, current, and valuable?

Use the visual worksheet on the next page for this written exercise:

1. Think about your target market, the people you were meant to serve, and more specifically, the people on your list. Put yourself in their shoes and think about what kinds of content would be most helpful to them. Write your ideas in the space provided.

2. What products and services would you like to include when you Keep in Touch with your list? As you write these down, imagine someone from your list who values what you offer.

3. What special announcements might you share with your list? How can you help ensure that these announcements are helpful and relevant? And are there creative ways to be self-expressed when you make those announcements?

KEEP IN TOUCH CONTENT STRATEGY

BRAINSTORM CONTENT IDEAS
FOR KEEPING IN TOUCH WITH YOUR LIST

① HELPFUL INFORMATION

INDUSTRY INFO:

TIPS & TRICKS:

FROM EXPERTS:

② MY OFFERINGS

MY SERVICES:

MY PRODUCTS:

SPECIAL DEALS:

③ SHOW & TELL

ANNOUNCEMENTS:

COOL SELF-EXPRESSION IDEAS:

Choosing Your Keep in Touch Tools

Once you've got great content to share with your clients and potential clients, you've got to choose how best to deliver that content to them. Let's review the most common tools used:

PRINTED & MAILED NEWSLETTERS. Paper newsletters can be effective marketing tools, but they can be costly and time-consuming to print and mail.

E-MAIL NEWSLETTERS. E-zines (e-mail newsletters) continue to be the easiest and most cost-effective way to Keep in Touch with large numbers of people. However, marketers should continue to watch trends in consumer behavior. Most of us ignore as much e-mail as we possibly can because of the never-ending, mass proliferation of spam.

SOCIAL MEDIA. The advent and rise of social media is an alternative Keep in Touch tool that may likely replace e-mail altogether, depending on the market you serve. We'll talk about how to use social media (Facebook, Twitter, and LinkedIn) to Keep in Touch with large groups of people, in Chapter 16.

PHONE CALLS. The phone is a wonderful direct outreach tool and it's a great way to create a stronger human connection. But remember, cold calling can be perceived as spam, which isn't the Book Yourself Solid way. So wait to get on the phone until you've had at least one positive interaction with your direct outreach subject.

DIRECT MAIL. Postcards and mailers are great for one-on-one correspondence, but again, they are costly and time-consuming endeavors when you are attempting to Keep in Touch with large groups of contacts. When you grow to a multimillion-dollar small business, we'll talk about including paper direct mail tools in your marketing campaigns to increase your touch points with your subscribers and contacts.

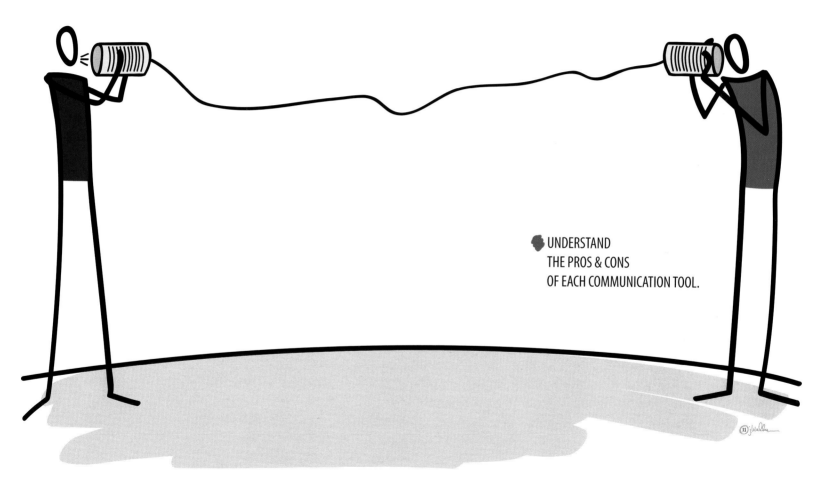

UNDERSTAND
THE PROS & CONS
OF EACH COMMUNICATION TOOL.

Using E-Zines to Keep in Touch

For now, let's focus on e-zines, which are still an effective marketing tool to:

- Build your mailing list, add value, and market to your subscribers over and over again.

- Sell your products and services while delivering great content and adding value.

- Position yourself as an expert within your industry or field.

- Keep in Touch with all the people who have expressed interest in your products or services, and reach them all with the click of a button.

- Create a viral marketing campaign (it grows exponentially as it's passed along to others) because your subscribers will send it to their friends when they think it will help them.

- Create ongoing marketing campaigns that cost virtually nothing and reap great rewards.

Ninety percent of my product and service sales are generated from 20 percent of the space in my monthly e-zine as well as through other direct e-mail promotions. Let me be clear about this because it's so important. I track my sales and know that 90 percent of my online sales are in direct response to my monthly newsletter, not from a new visitor landing on one of my web sites. As you'll learn when we discuss your web strategy, your web site is used most effectively as a vehicle for enticing people to opt in to your subscriber list so that you deliver value and build trust over time. Your follow-up is where you reap the financial and personal rewards of your marketing efforts.

E-ZINE FORMAT

You don't need an HTML newsletter to appear professional. Some of the most successful Internet marketers use text-only e-zines, which generally have a higher rate of delivery success because they are less likely to get caught in spam filters. Spam filters tend to detect more HTML than plain text, and the filters block a higher percentage of HTML e-mails.

E-ZINE LAYOUT

The layout of the text in your e-zine is just as important as what you have to say. Most of your readers will not actually be reading your e-zine. First, they'll scan it. Then, if the issue seems relevant and interesting, they'll read it more carefully.

To make the layout support your content, consider the following criteria when you're writing any kind of Keep in Touch or promotional content:

- Use headlines to get your readers interested, but make sure the headline isn't too ambiguous. If the title doesn't include a keyword that tells them what the article is about, they won't bother reading further.
- Use case studies and testimonials to add credibility to your claims.
- Write from your reader's point of view.
- Write about benefits, not just features.
- Read your text out loud to make sure it sounds conversational.
- Get a colleague or customer to review your e-zine and make suggestions.
- Be specific and concise, using simple concepts.

E-ZINE FREQUENCY

Frequency depends on a lot of factors but should be mostly based on what you're trying to accomplish with your e-zine. Some people send out weekly e-zines, some twice a month, and others monthly or quarterly. I've even seen some daily e-zines. I suggest you begin with a monthly e-zine. Daily, and even weekly may be a bit much for you and your subscribers when you're starting out, and quarterly probably won't get the visibility you're looking for. That said, I do a weekly e-zine, plus special announcements and promotions. The weekly frequency keeps me plenty busy and is just right for my readers.

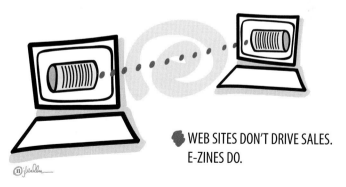

WEB SITES DON'T DRIVE SALES. E-ZINES DO.

Keep in Touch or Bust

The Book Yourself Solid Keep in Touch Strategy is the key to ensuring that your marketing efforts are effective and successful. A variety of Book Yourself Solid strategies will help you collect more names for your database, and your database, along with the Keep in Touch Strategy, will help you connect with the people you are meant to serve.

To better connect with them, you will need to develop content to share that is interesting, relevant, and valuable. Eighty percent or more of that content will be free and helpful information for them, and the remaining 20 percent is a little about you.

There are a variety of tools with which you could use to deliver that content, each with pros and cons to consider. E-Zines are often used as a primary tool for keeping in touch due to their low cost and high potential for return.

Remember, keeping in touch with your potential clients is critical to developing trust and credibility. It will keep you foremost in the minds of your potential clients when they need you, your services, or the products and programs you offer. Your business depends on it.

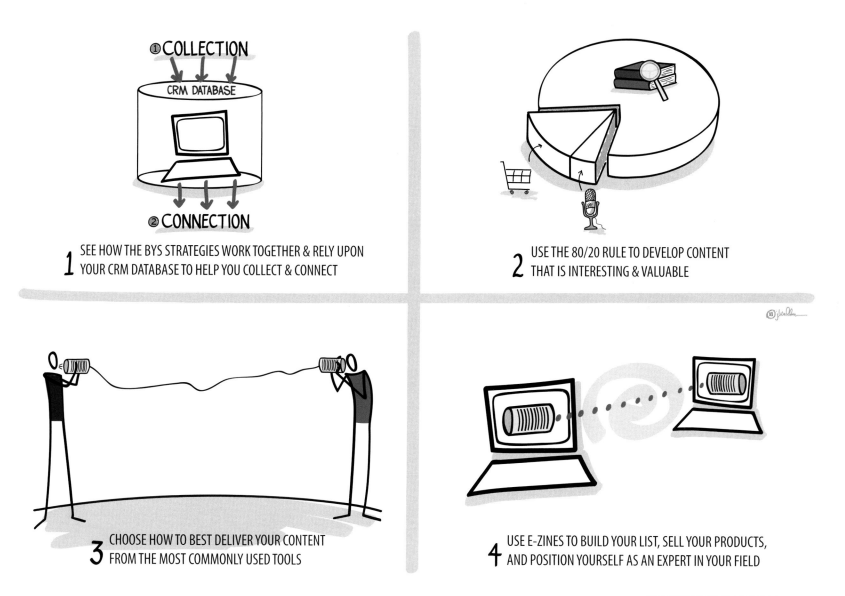

① COLLECTION

CRM DATABASE

② CONNECTION

1 SEE HOW THE BYS STRATEGIES WORK TOGETHER & RELY UPON YOUR CRM DATABASE TO HELP YOU COLLECT & CONNECT

2 USE THE 80/20 RULE TO DEVELOP CONTENT THAT IS INTERESTING & VALUABLE

3 CHOOSE HOW TO BEST DELIVER YOUR CONTENT FROM THE MOST COMMONLY USED TOOLS

4 USE E-ZINES TO BUILD YOUR LIST, SELL YOUR PRODUCTS, AND POSITION YOURSELF AS AN EXPERT IN YOUR FIELD

module 2

MODULE TWO: BUILDING TRUST & CREDIBILITY
"RUNWAY TAKEOFF"

CHAPTER 8

The Book Yourself Solid Information Products Strategy

THE BOOK YOURSELF SOLID

INFORMATION PRODUCTS STRATEGY

**BUILD PRODUCTS & PROGRAMS
DESIGNED TO SERVE YOUR TARGET MARKET**

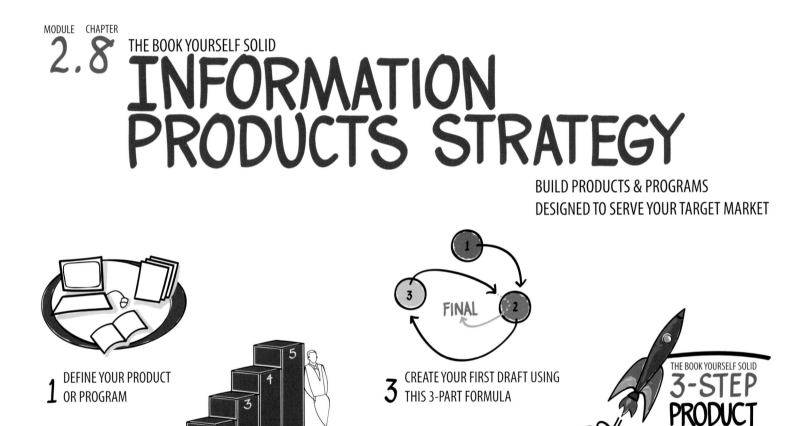

1 DEFINE YOUR PRODUCT OR PROGRAM

2 TAKE THE 5 STEPS TO DEVELOPING YOUR PRODUCT

FINAL

3 CREATE YOUR FIRST DRAFT USING THIS 3-PART FORMULA

THE BOOK YOURSELF SOLID
3-STEP PRODUCT LAUNCH

4 LAUNCH YOUR INFORMATION PRODUCT USING THIS SIMPLE 3-STEP SEQUENCE

2.8 THE INFORMATION PRODUCTS STRATEGY

Know where to find the information and how to use it—that's the secret of success.

—Albert Einstein

Nothing helps to build your credibility like products and programs designed to serve your target market's very specific urgent needs and compelling desires. People love to buy packaged learning and experiences. They're easy to understand, and therefore easy to buy. Perhaps you think that your service may not be as easily defined as a packaged product or program, and necessarily has a high barrier for entry.

I think you underestimate what you have to offer. As you continue to develop and enhance your Book Yourself Solid Sales Cycle, you will want to produce products and programs that will fully round out the many possible stages of your sales cycle, including the early stages, where barriers to entry must be low.

Red-Hot Benefits to Information Products

I just love the opportunity offered through information product creation because you can follow a simple step-by-step system that leads you to so many red-hot benefits. Let's take a quick look:

- Products create opportunities for multiple streams of passive or leveraged income. They can be in retail stores or online, at your web site and the web sites of your affiliates, 24/7/365, with worldwide availability. You can consistently get orders for your products from people all over the world.

- Having a product enhances your credibility with your prospects, your peers, meeting planners, and the media because it establishes you as a category expert and sets you apart from your competitors.

- Products can help you land more clients because they speed up the sales cycle. Since your core services have a high barrier to entry, your potential clients may need to jump a few high hurdles to persuade themselves they need to hire you. Having a product to offer based on your services gives potential clients the opportunity to test you out without having to take a big risk. Then if they connect with you and are well served by your product, they will upgrade from the lower-priced product to the higher-priced service.

- If you use public speaking as one of your marketing strategies, having a product at the back of the room when you speak gives you credibility, and you also have a relatively low-cost way to introduce prospects into your business and generate ancillary revenue at the same time.

- Products leverage your time. One of the biggest problems service professionals face is the paradigm of trading time for money. If all you ever do is trade your time for money, your revenues are limited by how much you charge per hour. For example, if you speak in front of 100 of your prospects and you're able to sell a couple of dozen of your information products at $50 each, then you've just increased your hourly rate from $100 to more than $1,000 an hour. Again, remember, many more people are willing and able to buy an information product than they are willing and able to hire you for your higher-priced service.

MAKE MONEY WHILE YOU SLEEP.

CREATE A LOW BARRIER-TO-ENTRY OPTION.

ENHANCE YOUR CREDIBILITY WITH EVERYONE YOU MEET.

STOP TRADING YOUR TIME FOR MONEY. THIS IS LIMITING YOU.

SPEED UP THE SALES CYCLE.

INCREASE YOUR "HOURLY RATE" FROM $100/HOUR TO $1,000/ HOUR.

red HOT BENEFITS

The Sky's the Limit

You may be in the beginning phase of building your business and just be setting out on the course to book yourself solid, but as Dr. Stephen Covey (*The 7 Habits of Highly Effective People*) says, "Start with the end in mind." If you want to seriously build a long-lasting career as a service professional, you'll want to start thinking just as seriously about creating information products.

Don't let the idea of creating products intimidate you; you can start where you are and then the sky's the limit. For example, you can:

- Publish a free-tips book.
- Write an e-book.
- Produce an audio CD.
- Write an article.
- Write a workbook.
- Compile and publish a glossary of inspirational quotes.

Here are a few thoughts on your first information product:

- Keep it simple.
- Don't overwork it or feel that it needs to be perfect.
- Don't worry about being wildly original.
- Tips, guides, or resource manuals are great formats.
- Continually strive to add value to your clients' lives in any way you can.

When considering how to create an information product, start by examining the different possibilities and ask yourself, "How can I leverage my existing knowledge and experience to create a quality product that I can produce and launch in the shortest amount of time possible?"

Be sure you don't overlook any content you may already have created. If you've written an article, you have content that you can leverage into multiple formats. You can quickly and easily turn your article into an e-course, use it as the foundation for an e-book, print book, or program, or present it as an introductory presentation or teleclass. A single article can be leveraged into any or all of these formats, making it possible to create an entire sales cycle from a single source of content.

Written Exercise 8A

DEFINE YOUR PRODUCT OR PROGRAM

Choose the one product idea that you're most passionate or excited about right now—and most important, one that is in line with your current business needs. If you're starting out and need to build your database, you'll need to create a lead-generating product first, a product that you give away to create connection with a potential client. You will then leverage that free lead-generating information product into other monetized information products over time. If you already have a lead-generating product and you're ready to produce higher-priced information products like an audio program or a book, then go for it!

As you define your product, you will need to consider not only the type of product you will create but to whom you're selling it, the promises it makes, the benefits and solutions it offers, the look and feel you want your product to convey, and the ways in which you can leverage the content.

For now, keep it simple. Use the visual worksheet on the next page to get your ideas out of your head and onto paper.

STEP 1: What type of product or program would you most like to create? What would you be most passionate about creating and offering to your target market?

STEP 2: To whom would you be offering this product? (Refer to target market.)

STEP 3: What benefits will your target market experience as a result of your product?

STEP 4: How do you want your product to look and feel? What image or emotion do you want it to convey?

STEP 5: How might you leverage the same content into a variety of different formats and price points for your sales cycle?

DEFINE YOUR PRODUCT

JOT DOWN YOUR INITIAL THOUGHTS
& CHOOSE THE PRODUCT IDEA THAT MOST EXCITES YOU

THE TYPE OF PRODUCT
I WOULD MOST LIKE TO CREATE

THE TARGET MARKET
WHO WILL RECEIVE MY OFFER

THE RED HOT BENEFITS
MY PRODUCT WILL GIVE THEM

THE LOOK/FEEL
OR EMOTION IT WILL CONVEY

HOW I WILL LEVERAGE
THIS CONTENT INTO DIFF. FORMATS

Written Exercise 8B

ASSESS THE NEED

It's important to be clear about your intentions for your product or program, and it's critical that your product or program meets the needs of your target market. No matter how much you might love to create something, if your target market doesn't need it you'll be defeating your purpose.

Use the visual worksheet on the next page to answer the following questions:

STEP 1: Why does your target market need your particular product now?

STEP 2: What does your product need to deliver for it to meet your customer's need?

STEP 3: What about your product, if anything, will be different from similar products on the market?

BONUS: How can you over-deliver on your promises by adding unexpected value to make your product remarkable? If you're unsure of your target market's need for a particular type of product or program, doing market research will help you ensure you're creating something your target market will find valuable. Survey friends, clients, and groups, such as online discussion groups or local organizations. And certainly search Google, using keywords that your target audience would use. It's the best research tool out there.

ASSESS THE NEED FOR YOUR PRODUCT

ENSURE YOUR PRODUCT OR PROGRAM
MEETS THE NEEDS OF YOUR TARGET MARKET

WHY MY TARGET NEEDS
MY PRODUCT RIGHT NOW

WHAT MY PRODUCT DELIVERS
TO MEET MY TARGET'S NEEDS

HOW MY PRODUCT DIFFERS
FROM OTHER SIMILAR PRODUCTS

5 Steps to Developing Your Product

I'm sure your bookshelves are lined with products and programs that you've purchased from other service professionals over the years. In fact, you're reading one right now.

You have the opportunity to create your own self-expression product or program. I use the phrase self-expression because the kind of programs and products that I'm referring to gives you an opportunity to express yourself to the world and serve your target market at the same time. That's the beauty of being a service professional.

The five simple steps to developing your product are discussed in the following subsections.

STEP 1: Choose the role you are playing.

STEP 2: Choose your product framework.

STEP 3: Choose a title that sells.

STEP 4: Build your table of contents.

STEP 5: Create your content.

Step 1: Choose the Role You Are Playing

Whatever product you choose to create, as the author you will essentially be telling a story. To do so, you'll need to choose the role you wish to play when delivering your content. I'll use books to illustrate my point because books are simply bigger information products:

- **EXPERT.** Here's what I've done, and here's my theory on why it works. This is the role that I chose as the author of this book. Or maybe you're the Mad Professor, the Reluctant Hero, or the Reclusive Genius?

- **INTERVIEWER.** Compile information from other experts. You can compile a product by interviewing others who are experts in their respective fields. A good example of that is Mitch Meyerson's book, *Success Secrets of the Online Marketing Superstars*. He interviewed more than 20 online marketing experts and compiled their interviews into a book.

- **RESEARCHER.** Go out and gather information to serve the needs and desires of your target market. Compile the results to create a product that meets those needs and desires. Research can turn you into an expert at a future date. Jim Collins's book, *Good to Great*, is a perfect example. It's a research study, and it has made him an authority on creating great results in large corporations. You don't need to do a 10-year clinical study as Mr. Collins did, but the concept is the same.

- **REPURPOSER.** Use and modify existing content (with permission) for a different purpose. Many of the guerilla marketing books are excellent examples of this. Jay Conrad Levinson created the "Guerrilla Marketing" brand, and then many other authors co-opted that material and offered it for a different purpose—for example, *Guerrilla Marketing for Job Hunters* by David Perry.

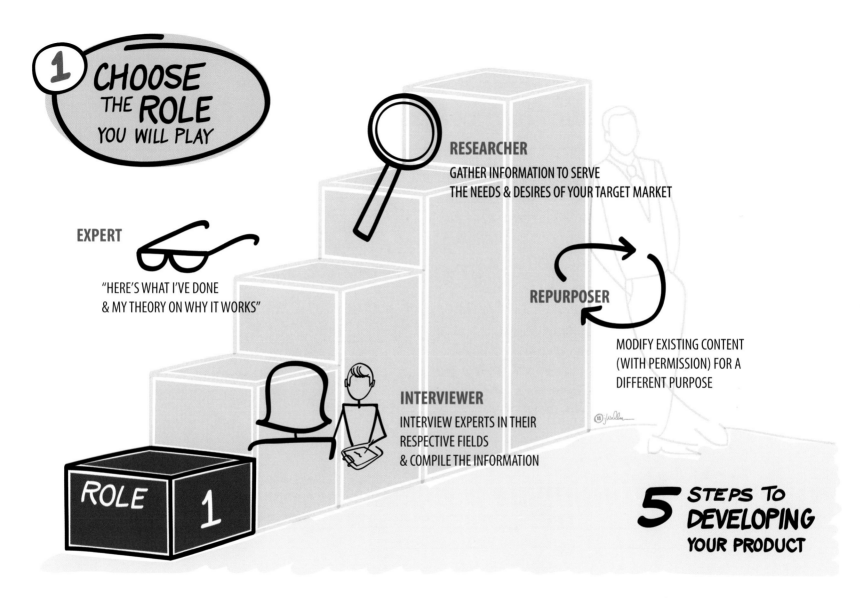

Step 2: Choose Your Product Framework

You'll need a framework in which to organize and present your content. A framework will make it easier not only for you to develop your content but also for your potential client to understand it and get the greatest possible value from it.

Keep in mind, your product may work well in more than one framework. An information product or program often uses a combination of frameworks. Here are six of the most common:

1. **PROBLEM/SOLUTION.** State a problem and then present solutions to the problem. *The Magic of Conflict: Turning Your Life of Work into a Work of Art* by Thomas F. Crum is written in this framework. He presents a number of problems that people face in their lives and at work and presents solutions to those problems using the philosophical principles of the martial art of aikido.

2. **NUMERICAL.** Create your product as a series of keys or lessons. A well-known example of this would be Stephen Covey's *The 7 Habits of Highly Effective People*.

3. **CHRONOLOGICAL.** Some products need to be presented in a particular order because that is the only way it would make sense. Step A must come before Step B, as in *Your Pregnancy Week by Week* by Glade B. Curtis and Judith Schuler.

4. **MODULAR.** This book is a perfect example. The book consists of four modules: Your Foundation, Building Trust & Credibility, Perfect Pricing & Simple Selling, and the Book Yourself Solid 6 Core Self-Promotion Strategies. Within each module are additional tracks presented in a chronological framework. So you see that the book has both a main framework (modular) and a secondary framework (chronological).

5. **COMPARE/CONTRAST.** Showcase your creation in terms of presenting several scenarios or options and then compare and contrast them. Jim Collins, in his book *Good to Great*, compares and contrasts successful and not-so-successful companies.

6. **REFERENCE.** Reference is just as it sounds. You may be creating a product that becomes a valuable resource to members of your target market. A compilation of information is best showcased in a reference format like that in *Words that Sell* by Richard Bayan. It's a reference guide of good words and phrases that help sell.

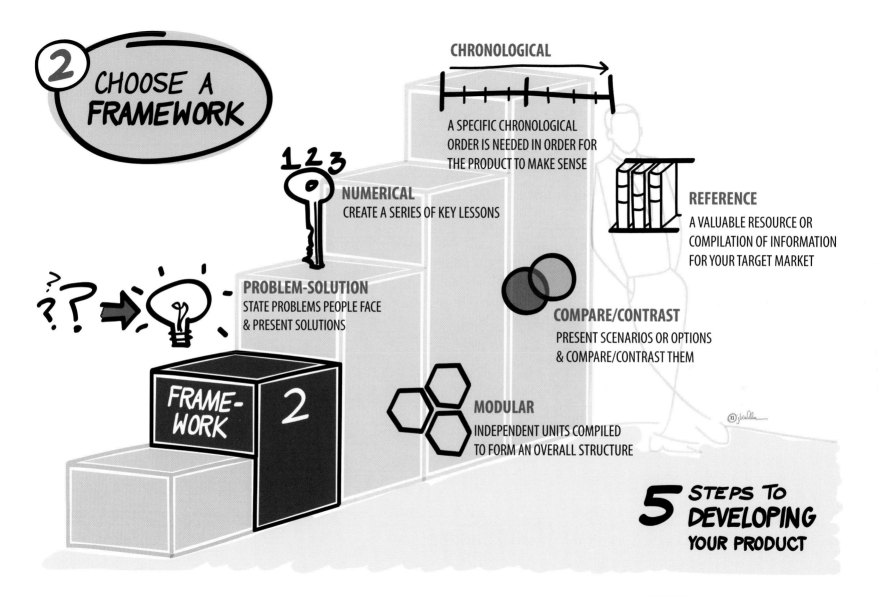

Step 3: Choose a Title That Sells

The title of your product or program can make a big difference in whether your product sells. It's the title that initially catches consumers' attention and determines whether they look any further. Your title must be compelling enough for the prospect to want to know more. The consumer should be able to know exactly what you're offering by reading or hearing your title. Investing time to craft a captivating title can have a significant impact on your bottom line. Here are six types of titles that you can adapt to your needs:

1. **SUSPENSE:** The Secret Life of Stay-at-Home Moms

2. **TELL A STORY:** The Path of the Successful Entrepreneur

3. **ADDRESS A PAIN OR FEAR:** The Top 10 Fears Every Leader Has and How to Overcome Them

4. **GRAB THE READER'S ATTENTION:** Caught! The Six Deadliest Dating Mistakes!

5. **SOLUTIONS TO PROBLEMS:** Focus: The Seven Keys to Getting Things Done Even If You Have ADD

6. **EMOTIONAL CONNECTION:** What My Son's Tragedy Taught Me about Living Life to the Fullest

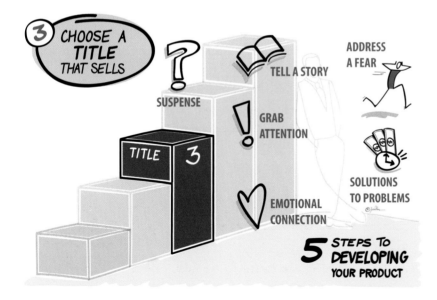

Step 4: Build Your Table of Contents

Your table of contents is another key piece in organizing your content so that it's easy for you to present and easy for your potential clients to understand and follow. Regardless of the role in which you present your content, the creation of a product gives the impression that you are an expert, and this is how your target market will view you.

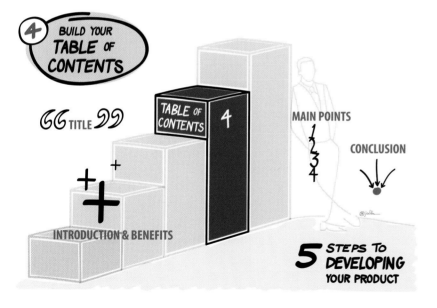

The table of contents should be very well organized and easy to scan through to gain an understanding of the concept and the main points. Creating a table of contents also allows you to break your content into manageable pieces. The thought of writing even a simple article, e-book, special report, or book may at first glance seem overwhelming. Use your table of contents, or outline, to break the process down into smaller steps that will be much easier and less intimidating to work on.

When building your table of contents include the following:

1. **THE TITLE OF YOUR PRODUCT.** You already developed a title that sells in Step 3. Just make sure you include it in your table of contents.

2. **THE INTRODUCTION & BENEFITS.** This covers the benefits of the product, the end result that the consumer will experience, and any FEPS (Financial, Emotional, Physical, Spiritual) benefits.

3. **THE BODY, OR MAIN POINTS.** Break it down into manageable chunks to provide a sense of what the information product will cover. Make sure these main points are solution-oriented, not metaphor-based or mysterious. Use keywords they can scan and know if this product is for them.

4. **THE CONCLUSION.** Tie it up, reaffirm the end result, and tell them what to do next.

Written Exercise 8C

DEVELOP YOUR PRODUCT

Use the visual worksheet on the next page for the following exercise.

STEP 1: Which role most appeals to you or is most appropriate to your product or program, and why?

STEP 2: Which framework will you choose and why?

STEP 3: Choose one of the title types that fits your product or that you find especially appealing, and brainstorm a number of different title ideas. Have fun with this. Just get your creative juices flowing.

STEP 4: Create your table of contents. Keep the following questions in mind:

- What are the steps in understanding your content?
- Is the flow logical and easy to understand?

DEVELOP YOUR PRODUCT

CHOOSE THE ROLE YOU WILL PLAY, THE FRAMEWORK YOU WILL USE,
BRAINSTORM TITLES, & WRITE YOUR TABLE OF CONTENTS

**① THE ROLE
I WILL PLAY:**

☐ EXPERT
☐ INTERVIEWER
☐ RESEARCHER
☐ REPURPOSER
☐ OTHER _____

WHY:

**② THE FRAMEWORK
I WILL CHOOSE:**

☐ PROBLEM/SOLUTION
☐ NUMERICAL
☐ CHRONOLOGICAL
☐ MODULAR
☐ COMPARE/CONTRAST
☐ REFERENCE
☐ OTHER _____

WHY:

**③ THE TYPE OF TITLE
THAT BEST FITS:**

☐ SUSPENSE
☐ TELL A STORY
☐ ADDRESS A PAIN OR FEAR
☐ GRAB THE READER'S ATTENTION
☐ SOLUTIONS TO PROBLEMS
☐ EMOTIONAL CONNECTION
☐ OTHER _____

TITLE IDEAS:

**④ MY TABLE OF CONTENTS
OUTLINE:**

Step 5: Create Your Content

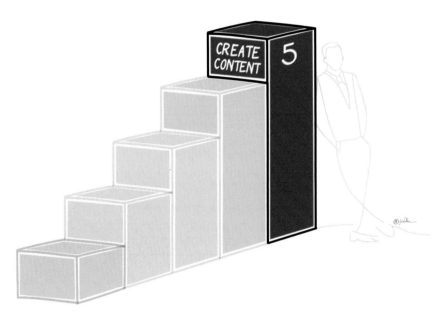

Using your table of contents, create a schedule for completing the first draft of each section. If you write as little as a paragraph or two a day, you could have your content for your product or program completed in as little as a week for an e-course or a month or two for a more in-depth product or program.

STEP 1: Follow the 5-step plan that we just learned for developing the structure of your product. To mitigate the potential overwhelm, just do a data dump to get your thoughts down quickly. Don't edit or judge.

STEP 2: Use the simple 3-part formula on the next page for creating your first draft. Do not expect an end result at this point.

STEP 3: Once you have some initial thoughts down, then you can start to revise. The product is a work in progress. Create your second draft in this step, then a third, until you have the final draft.

3-Part Formula for Creating Your First Draft

PART 1: Based on your table of contents, choose two to five key points that support each section.

PART 2: Flesh out each of the key points per section with supportive content.

PART 3: Repeat Step 2 until you've created the final product.

Yes, it should be that straightforward. I'm even going to get down on my knees right now and beg you not to make it more complicated. Keep it simple and focus on getting it done so you can get down to the business of getting booked solid.

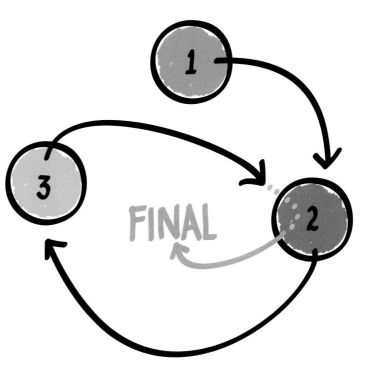

The Simple 3-Step Product Launch Sequence

Listing your product on your web site is a fabulous idea. It's a great start. However, if you don't, at present, have an overwhelming number of visitors browsing through your site, it's unlikely you'll get many orders—even if you're giving it away for free.

On the other hand, if you want to make a big splash with the new product you've created, consider using the following simple 3-step product launch sequence to get your product into the hands of eager and inspired potential clients.

STEP 1: Pre-Launch

STEP 2: Launch

STEP 3: Post-Launch

Step 1: Pre-Launch

Upon completion of your product, you may be tempted to immediately begin promoting it. Hold off for a bit. Instead, consider how you're going to warm up your audience with tidbits of content in the form of video, audio, PDF, and any other format that is easy for them to consume. (I'll show you how to begin to build your audience in a minute.)

During the pre-launch stage, you should focus on giving so much value that you think you've gone too far and then give more. This teaser content should be designed to get your audience thinking about the specific problems that your upcoming product offer addresses and the results it promises—without mentioning the product itself—not yet. This early

stage pre-launch period can last a few days or a few weeks. It gives you the opportunity to evaluate how your audience is responding to your content and adjust your product accordingly.

Perhaps a strength and conditioning coach who created a breakthrough video product on how to increase performance doing three, 30-minute Kettlebell workouts a week might consider writing a series of articles, blog posts, and online press releases that include links to two-minute video clips lifted from the product. This content, sent to her e-mail list, posted on her blog, and in article and press release directories, is designed to stimulate discussion on the topic rather than to explicitly promote the product.

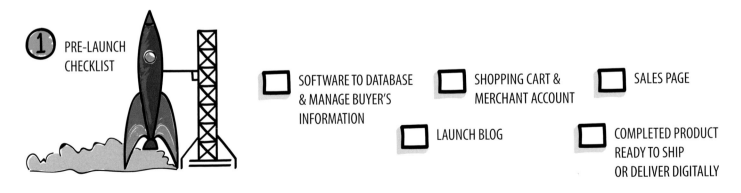

1 PRE-LAUNCH CHECKLIST

☐ SOFTWARE TO DATABASE & MANAGE BUYER'S INFORMATION

☐ SHOPPING CART & MERCHANT ACCOUNT

☐ SALES PAGE

☐ LAUNCH BLOG

☐ COMPLETED PRODUCT READY TO SHIP OR DELIVER DIGITALLY

Instead, she's encouraging her audience to consider particular issues and solutions to those issues before she releases the product itself.

Toward the end of this early stage pre-launch, make mention of an upcoming product in the same places that you seeded with valuable content. Now that momentum and interest in the topic you've been addressing has spiked among your readers, it's time to enter the late stage pre-launch. This is when you announce the details of your upcoming product offer. An offer so packed with value that, again, you and they will think you've gone too far.

But you'll go even further adding more value by piling on additional features, opportunities, and bonuses like:

- Follow-up implementation coaching calls.
- Additional videos, interviews, or e-books.
- Quick-start PDF guides.
- Related software.
- A live event.
- And, certainly, a no-hassle guarantee of some sort.

Your potential buyers should feel like they're getting a significant return on investment; value should overwhelm cost. You'll attempt to focus their attention on the incredible benefits of your product and the problems it solves. Hopefully, by the time you launch, your potential buyers will have very few objections to your product and believe that it is a high-powered vehicle that'll get them where they want to go.

Remember to test every part of the process prior to launch. Guaranteed (well almost), you'll miss something—at least I usually do. Run sample orders to make sure that you clear up any glitches. View all of your pages and videos in all of the most popular browsers, including Internet Explorer, Firefox, Chrome, and Safari. Notify your web host, merchant account provider, and shopping cart solution of your upcoming launch date if you expect a lot more traffic to your site than is usual. Sometimes, hosting companies will freeze an account if they detect activity that is unusual or different from the norm. This happens more often than you might think and can seriously squash your product launch.

Step 2: Launch

② LAUNCH

The success of your launch is, in large part, due to the structure of your offer. How you make it, what comes with it, how long it lasts, and more. A word to the wise: Be careful of what kind of tactics you use to encourage people to buy. I discuss pricing models at length in Chapter 9, so I won't discuss them here. I suggest that you carefully consider how you want to be perceived, however, when promoting your information products. Will you create a hyperkinetic, high-intensity product launch based on the principle of scarcity? Will you try to tap into the buyer's fear that they'll miss out if they don't act right away, or the perception that if they don't buy what you're offering they'll never move forward and will, basically, fail at whatever it is you're offering to help with? Or, will you create a reasoned, sensible, and appropriate product launch based on integrity? Look, I'm comfortable with special time- and space-limited offers as long as they are based on integrity and they're not too hyped up and aggressive. There is a well-known marketing expert who says, "If you're not annoying some of your prospects, then you're not pushing hard enough." I'm not hip to that concept. You are how you market. Consider what you stand for and how you want to be known. And, of course, how the people to whom you are trying to sell want to be treated.

Okay, so, now the big day is here! It's time to press "Send" on your "we're live" e-mail as well as announce the product launch on the social network sites to which you belong, your blog, or any other relevant platform. This is where all of your hard work pays off. Take a deep breath.

Don't stress the process. You know already the launch is unlikely to unfold as planned. Hey, it might go better than planned. The live period of the launch usually lasts from three to seven days, depending on your preference. The first day or two is a great time to introduce the urgency of acting as the time or available units are dwindling (but please see the earlier note). Feel free to share new and exciting testimonials as they come in, or announce added bonuses.

Step 3: Post-Launch

Sales generally die down after the first few days of the launch. There are ways to reignite them, however. For example, you can announce an added bonus. This may encourage people sitting on the fence to go for it and hit the buy button. This bonus will also please all previous buyers, as they'll get extra value that they had not anticipated. Maybe you're holding a special live event to which the buyers of the product get free tickets? Or perhaps, you've added an entire product to the offer that is complementary to the topic covered in the initial product? Sort of like the extended free trial that comes with this book, of the Book Yourself Solid® software that does your marketing for you using all the strategies and tactics you're learning in this book. Go to www.solid.ly to get your free trial.

See?

When you close out the launch, what do you do with the product? Are you planning on continuing to sell it from your site but at a different price point or, maybe, you're taking it off the market for six months and will then do a second launch? If you do take the product off the market, make sure you put up a special web page thanking visitors for their interest in the product and suggest that they opt in to a web form so they can be the first notified when the product becomes available again. This way you'll have the opportunity to earn their trust before your next product launch.

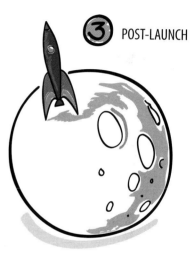

POST-LAUNCH

Joint Venture Partners & Affiliates

When you don't yet have a substantial group of followers or subscribers, or even if you do, for that matter, one of the keys to increasing your reach is to team up with what are usually referred to as joint venture (aka JV) partners or affiliates.

Other professionals, who already have established relationships of trust with your target market, might be willing to partner with you and promote your product in exchange for a commission on each product sold or some other incentive. Note that I said might. As you'll learn when we discuss direct outreach in Chapter 12, before you make any kind of JV request of a successful professional, it's wise to have already established a relationship with them and to understand what incentivizes them. You might be surprised to learn that they are not, in fact, interested in what you think is a financial incentive. When a JV partner promotes your product for you, she expends a considerable amount of her social and professional capital. There is also an opportunity cost associated with every promotion made to a group of subscribers or followers. Be prepared to demonstrate the viability of your offer with sound metrics. You need to have a sound commission structure in place as well as a detailed analysis of your opt-in and conversion rates. When you ask someone to promote a product for you, you're asking a lot—more than you might realize at the moment. You're asking for access to what might be his most prized business asset—the trust he has built with his subscribers. Read the chapter on direct outreach before you attempt any kind of joint venture campaign.

If you want joint venture partners to enjoy working with you, you'll want to make promoting you easy and breezy. Once you have your joint venture partners in place, have the following materials available for them:

• E-mail copy ready to use during the pre-launch and launch periods.

• A contest with prizes to excite and rally the partners with a little friendly competition (just make sure you get their approval before you include them in any competition among JV partners).

- A separate, password protected, JV partner blog for updates on the contest and continued motivation for them to promote your product. It's sort of like doing a launch within a launch.

- Affiliate accounts for your JV partners in your shopping cart system that provide custom affiliate links.

Big, deep, authentic success is truly only realized when we share our gifts with others through mutually valuable, long-term partnerships. Some of your JV partners may even become your best friends and closest allies.

If you are new to the concept of launching a product on the Internet, some of this can seem daunting. It can be a big process with many more moving pieces than I included in this section. Nonetheless, you can do this. Keep your launch simple at first and take it one small step at a time. Look at it this way: Once you create a successful launch, you can do it again and again. Just duplicate your initial success with some small changes for the new product. Most of the hard work is done the first time around.

If you need more help on how to launch your product, David Jehlen, an expert in information product launches and a Certified Book Yourself Solid Coach, can help you. Visit his site at DavidJehlen.com.

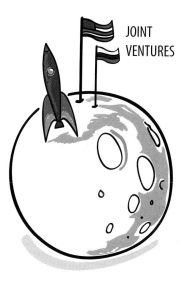

JOINT VENTURES

A Necessary Step in Your Business Development

Creating a product or program is a powerful—and possibly necessary—step in your business development. When you do so, your business has the potential to skyrocket. One product will turn into another and another—the possibilities are endless.

Just imagine this: You open your e-mail first thing in the morning and you see 15 new orders—one from Switzerland, one from Australia, one from India, and a dozen from all over the United States—all for the product you recently made available on the web. It's 7:00 a.m., you're still sipping your first cup of coffee and only half awake, and you've already earned $3,479.27.

While this scenario may seem more like a dream than reality to you right now, it's entirely possible to achieve, and it's much easier to do than you might imagine; just follow the steps I outlined earlier for creating an unlimited number of information products on virtually any topic you can think of! Before you know it you'll be hearing the beautiful, melodic ka-ching, ka-ching sound of your web-site-turned-cash-register as the orders come rolling in.

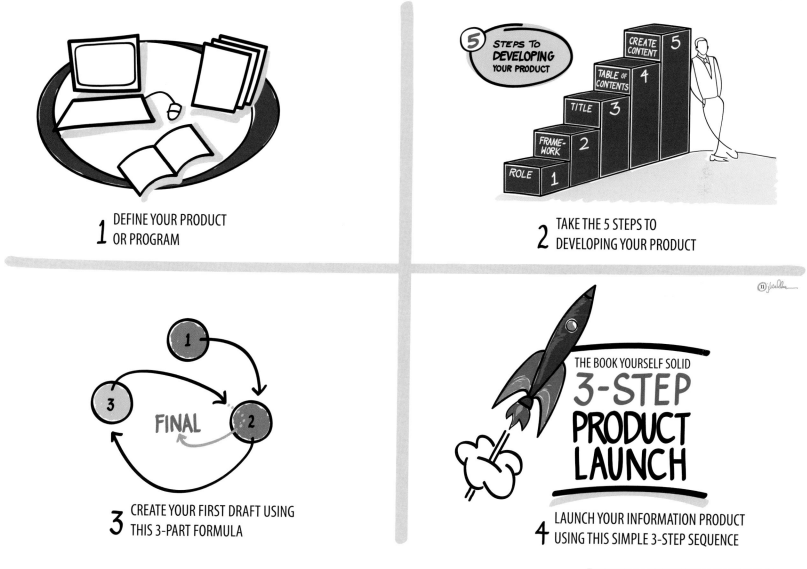

1 DEFINE YOUR PRODUCT OR PROGRAM

2 TAKE THE 5 STEPS TO DEVELOPING YOUR PRODUCT

3 CREATE YOUR FIRST DRAFT USING THIS 3-PART FORMULA

4 LAUNCH YOUR INFORMATION PRODUCT USING THIS SIMPLE 3-STEP SEQUENCE

HITTING FULL THROTTLE

Once a jet has lifted off the ground, it goes to maximum thrust. This is where the pilot (that's you) has to give it all she's got, because the aim is to reach cruising altitude. At the ideal altitude, the thrust-to-weight ratio decreases. The jet will then be flying faster, far faster than it was on the ground, while burning less fuel.

In fact, at the plane's cruising altitude, during a flight that covers, say, 1,000 miles, less fuel is consumed than during the first few miles while ascending due to something called progressive consumption. Think of this part of the Book Yourself Solid system as progressive marketing.

In Module Three you're still ascending, but you need that final push to get to cruising altitude where you level off and then it's smooth sailing from there. So, see if you have the capacity to push the throttle forward just a bit more. You may feel as if you're going pretty fast, but you're not nearly at the redline yet.

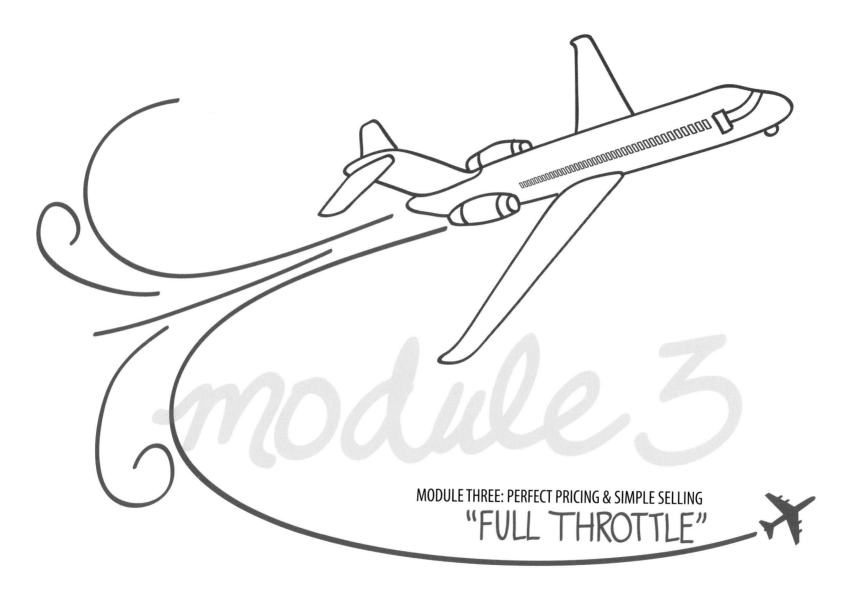

MODULE THREE: PERFECT PRICING & SIMPLE SELLING
"FULL THROTTLE"

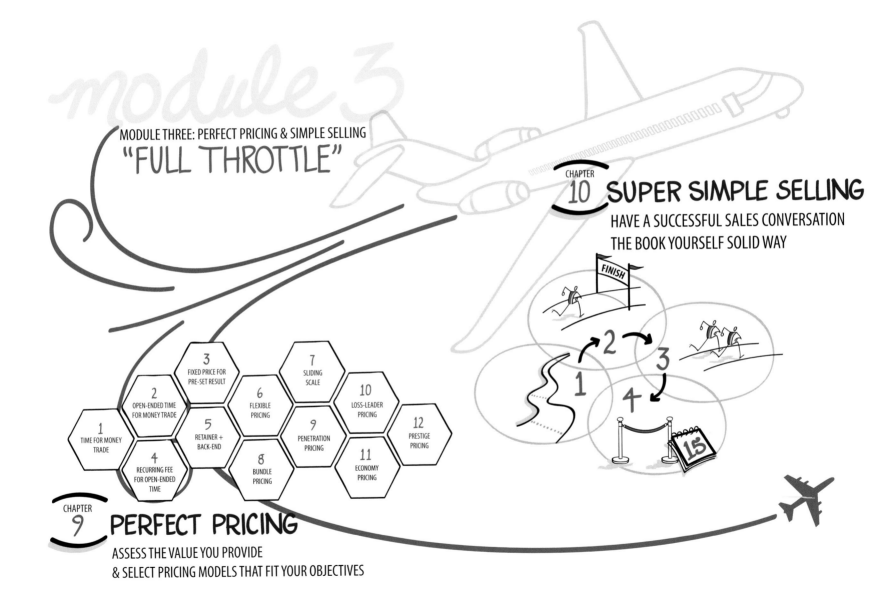

Perfect Pricing & Simple Selling

MODULE THREE

To be booked solid requires that you price your offerings at rates that are compelling to your ideal clients and with whom you're able to have sales conversations that are effortless and effective.

IT MEANS THAT YOU MUST:

- Perfect your pricing strategies using the right models and incentives.
- Master simple selling techniques so you can have sales conversations that feel as easy as a day at the beach.

Module Three consists of two chapters. These two chapters are the culmination of the Book Yourself Solid system because you'll learn how to make offers that are proportional to the amount of trust that you've earned and how to have a sales conversation that books new business. This is the ultimate goal—to get new clients so you can earn new business.

MODULE THREE: PERFECT PRICING & SIMPLE SELLING
"FULL THROTTLE"

CHAPTER 9
Perfect Pricing

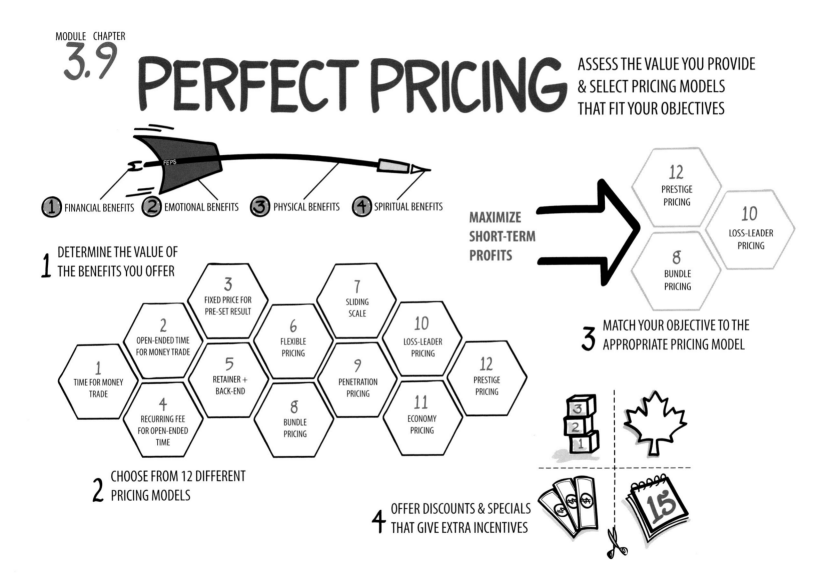

3.9 PERFECT PRICING

Price is what you pay; value is what you get.

—Warren Buffett

What is the value, for example, of having the talent and skills to create a compelling web presence for someone or maybe a training manual for a corporation? Is it the length of time it takes for you to produce it, or the number of pages created, or, how about the number of images used? The answer is . . . D, none of the above. Unfortunately, that's how many service providers price their products and service offerings—as stuff.

The Value of Their ROI & How You Value YOU

I asked Certified Coach Cara Lumen (caralumen.com) for her perspective on the matter because she deals, directly, in ideas and how to make them sell. In fact, as the idea optimizer, she's got it right when she says that "the only way to put a price on ideas is to put a value on what they will produce."

"But it only took me two hours to create it," you might say. How long it takes you to write something, or design something, or think up an idea, or even the amount of time you spend with a client, is irrelevant. What (should) matter to the client is the financial, emotional, physical, and spiritual return on investment your product or service provides—remember, I introduced you to the all-important, life-changing FEPS benefits (financial, emotional, physical, and spiritual).

Think about the value you provide.

- How much income will your service create?
- How long will what you create be a productive, useful resource for the client?
- How much pain will you relieve?
- How much pleasure will you create?
- How are you helping your client connect to their purpose or spirit?
- Will your work create substantial and long-lasting peace of mind?

No less important than the value you create is how you value yourself. And this might just be the difference between simply making ends meet and earning healthy heaps of money. Remember your ideal client. Remember doing your best work. Remember standing in the service of others as you stand in the service of your destiny. You want to work with people who value what you bring to your partnership. But if you don't value it, they won't either.

VALUE IS ABOUT THEIR RETURN ON INVESTMENT & HOW YOU VALUE *YOU.*

Written Exercise 9A

USE THE FEPS MODEL TO PUT A DOLLAR VALUE ON IT

Use the visual worksheet on the next page for the following exercise.

STEP 1: Think of a client who gave you rave reviews.

STEP 2: Make a list of all the FEPS benefits the client received from working with you. Don't be stingy here. Think big.

STEP 3: Now, put specific dollar values on all of those benefits.

Again, think big. No, bigger than that. Because . . . hold on to your hat . . . you may just find that you have been undervaluing yourself and, as a result, underpricing your products and services. You are giving generously of your talents and skills and, it's likely, the value you provide is worth much, much more than what you've been charging.

BENEFITS CONVERTED TO $

THINK OF A PREVIOUS CLIENT, LIST THE BENEFITS THEY
RECEIVED FROM YOU, & ESTIMATE THE DOLLAR VALUE OF EACH BENEFIT

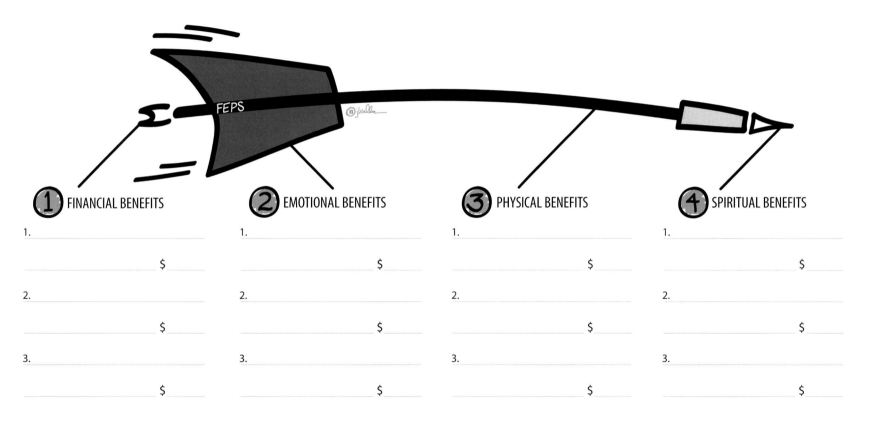

FEPS

① FINANCIAL BENEFITS

1. _____
   _____ $

2. _____
   _____ $

3. _____
   _____ $

② EMOTIONAL BENEFITS

1. _____
   _____ $

2. _____
   _____ $

3. _____
   _____ $

③ PHYSICAL BENEFITS

1. _____
   _____ $

2. _____
   _____ $

3. _____
   _____ $

④ SPIRITUAL BENEFITS

1. _____
   _____ $

2. _____
   _____ $

3. _____
   _____ $

Don't Buy Into a Poverty Mind-Set

Maybe you think . . . I don't want to price my services such that people can't afford them. Or, maybe it was something like . . . I have a new client who says they can't afford much so I'm thinking of lowering my price for them. These thoughts don't necessarily mean you have a "poverty mind-set" but they most definitely play you small. Allow your expectations to be stretched. People rarely buy professional services based solely on price. In fact, people express their values through what they buy—so let them.

Only you can offer you. Whatever it is you offer—it is unique to you. Only you can offer a particular combination of services, skills, talent, and personality. Only you can offer the exact combination of information, style of communication, and value that makes you so uniquely you. Know that. Know and accept, and revel in your value. Come from a place of service. Raise your intention to be well compensated for what you offer. Expect to be paid well. Then ask for it. Put out a price that makes you feel valuable and see others joyously flocking to take advantage of the great value you offer.

BOOKED SOLID ACTION STEP: Right now raise your prices until it makes you slightly uncomfortable. You'll know you've reached the right number when you experience a slight feeling of nausea. That's your new price. Over time you'll grow into it—not the nausea, the price—and, over time, you'll continue to raise your prices, sans nausea.

Ask for what you are worth and you will receive it. But first, truly know and believe you have great value. Then others will know and appreciate all you have to offer. You have to know that what you offer is valuable and you have to charge an amount that shows it is valuable. Only you can choose to think big about who you are and what you offer the world.

Pricing Models

I'm sure you've seen a number of different pricing models employed in various service industries. Some seem to benefit the provider and others are more favorable to the client. However, the picture of perfect pricing has each party thinking that they got the better end of the deal. If the client thinks he snagged a deal, he'll be tickled pink and if the service provider thinks she's scored, she'll feel like the cat who ate the canary. The key is to figure out how to create this win-win dynamic so that both parties feel fortunate. Here are a few of the often-used pricing models for selling professional services:

1. **TIME FOR MONEY TRADE.** A rate is set for a predetermined, agreed-upon amount of time—hourly, daily, weekly, or some other combination thereof (for example, $100 per hour, $1,000 per day, $10,000 per week). This is a very common model and one with which clients are generally comfortable.

2. **OPEN-ENDED TIME FOR MONEY TRADE.** A rate is set that trades your time for money, usually hourly, but no constraint is put on the amount of time required to complete the job. Service providers (especially contractors) like this model for the same reason that it petrifies the client—runaway time piles on additional fees. You know that three-week kitchen remodel that's going on thirty-three weeks? No one likes surprises that cost them money. Imagine, instead of getting gifts on Christmas morning, you woke to find you had to pay for every box that had your name on it.

3. **FIXED PRICE FOR PRE-SET RESULT.** A price is established for the entire project and fees are usually paid in percentages at predetermined dates or upon completion of project milestones (that is, 25 percent up front, another 50 percent halfway through, and the remaining 25 percent upon completion). This model often causes anxiety for the service provider for fear of "project creep" (aka: functionality creep, feature creep, scope creep, and mission creep). This is when the scope of the project gets bigger and bigger but the fee established stays the same. It's different from working on a project with a creep. That sucks, too. Which is worse, however, depends on how much creep or creepiness occurs on the project or with the client, respectively.

Continued on page 246

PRICING MODELS

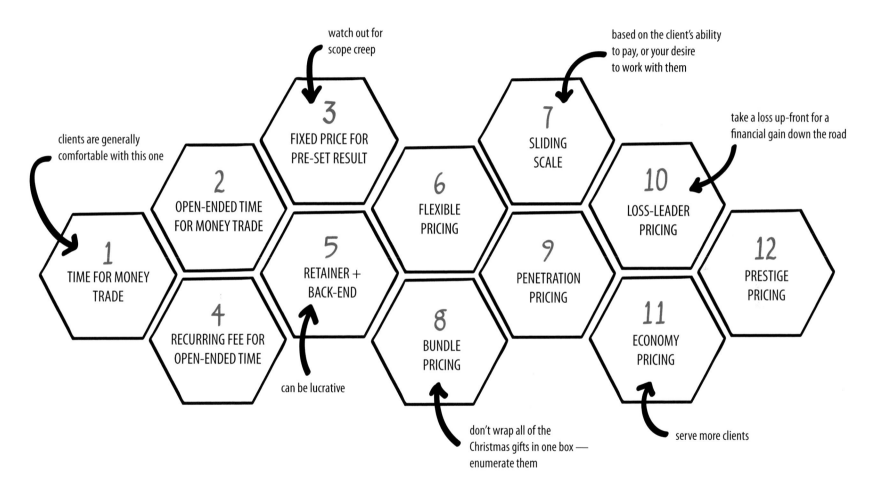

watch out for scope creep

3 FIXED PRICE FOR PRE-SET RESULT

based on the client's ability to pay, or your desire to work with them

7 SLIDING SCALE

take a loss up-front for a financial gain down the road

clients are generally comfortable with this one

2 OPEN-ENDED TIME FOR MONEY TRADE

6 FLEXIBLE PRICING

10 LOSS-LEADER PRICING

1 TIME FOR MONEY TRADE

5 RETAINER + BACK-END

9 PENETRATION PRICING

12 PRESTIGE PRICING

4 RECURRING FEE FOR OPEN-ENDED TIME

can be lucrative

8 BUNDLE PRICING

11 ECONOMY PRICING

don't wrap all of the Christmas gifts in one box — enumerate them

serve more clients

Pricing Models *(continued)*

4. **RECURRING FEE FOR AN OPEN-ENDED AMOUNT OF TIME.** Commonly referred to as a retainer, for which a monthly or quarterly payment is offered for a certain amount of work. Sometimes a time period is associated with the retainer but the arrangement is typically not associated with a period of time and can be canceled at will or with some reasonable amount of notice.

5. **RETAINER PLUS BACK-END.** Includes a retainer that covers expenses and some modest payment might be offered but most of the service provider's revenue is earned on the back end. If the project makes money, the service provider makes money. This pricing model isn't typical but can be very lucrative. Personal injury attorneys use this model. If they win the case, they take a significant percentage of the settlement. Software programmers, especially hungry, entrepreneurial types, also employ this model.

6. **FLEXIBLE PRICING.** Offer the same service to clients at different prices. This is very common in the business-to-business market in which sales are often based on negotiated contracts.

7. **SLIDING SCALE PRICING.** You may also offer flexible pricing based on need. Service providers offer this based on either the client's ability to pay or a provider's desire to work with the client.

8. **BUNDLE PRICING.** Offering a combination of products and services together in a single package to increase the size of the sale can offer savings to both the buyer and to the seller. The buyer gets more value for less money and the seller gets more profit for less marketing effort. However, if you bundle your services, "Don't wrap all the Christmas presents in one box," says economist Richard Thaler. The benefits of the product or service should be enumerated rather than lumped together. So, if you buy "this," we'll also throw in "that." And, if you buy "that," we'll also throw in "this." Or, if you buy "this," you can also have "this" at a reduced price. You want to be sure the client values and appreciates each and every product, program, and service they're getting from you.

9. **PENETRATION PRICING.** Offer very low prices to get into a market. Once you've created a name for yourself, begin to raise your prices.

10. **LOSS-LEADER PRICING.** This is a more common approach to selling products than it is to selling services but can be exploited by service providers, nonetheless. You can offer specific services at a very low price point to get clients in the door who will then, hopefully, buy additional products or other services at a higher price point. You may be willing to take a loss up front for a financial gain down the road.

11. **ECONOMY PRICING.** Offer the lowest prices in the market as a way of differentiating yourself. This is unlike loss-leader pricing in that all your prices are always low when you use economy pricing—it becomes part of your brand, like Walmart. Using the economy pricing model is different from undervaluing yourself. In this case, you're building a model that allows more people to take advantage of your services— which, over time, can actually add value to your brand. Certainly, low prices are often perceived as low value services, but that need not necessarily be the case.

12. **PRESTIGE PRICING.** You may choose to price your services at a price point higher than is typical for your industry in order to create a sense of prestige around you and your company. You may serve fewer clients but end up making more money.

SPECIAL NOTE—REGULATIONS ON PRICING: Before you rush off and start pricing yourself, I should mention that there are various governmental regulations on pricing, for some professions. If you sell outside of your own country, which you might do given that the Internet is a global marketplace, you'll need to familiarize yourself with laws in other countries. In the United States, price discrimination, offering different prices to different buyers, like our flexible-pricing model, has certain limitations. But the Robinson-Patman Act allows for price differentials under certain circumstances, so if you choose to use that pricing model, just check with your attorney to determine what is legal with respect to your services in your particular industry.

How to Choose Your Pricing Model

When considering which of the various preceding pricing models you are going to employ, first consider your objective. You may be thinking, uh, Michael, are you dense? I want to make as much money as I can—that's my objective! Well, yes, but you're reading this book to think more strategically about your business and how you grow it, so humor me for a moment. Consider the following five different pricing objectives:

1. **TO MAXIMIZE LONG-TERM PROFITS.** This should be your default approach. You're building something to last a lifetime, something that will support your dreams, not to mention your family, so you always want to focus on long-term pricing. Any of the pricing models can be applied to achieve this objective.

2. **TO MAXIMIZE SHORT-TERM PROFITS.** Generally chosen when you need to make a bunch of money fast. Prestige pricing may be the way to go but only if you've been in business for a while or are starting up with some sort of unique selling proposition. Or, you might consider bundle pricing to sell more of what you already offer. Or, maybe, aggressive loss-leader pricing will help. Lots of options here.

3. **TO GAIN MARKET SHARE.** That's just a fancy way of saying you're starting up the business or introducing a new product or service line and need to get clients—now. Loss leader or economy pricing or flexible pricing models may be the way to go. They'll help you get in the game and build up a large group of ideal clients that are out in the world talking about your best work. Which, of course, will bring you new ideal clients.

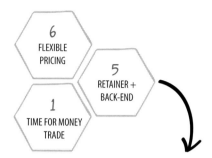

4. **TO SURVIVE.** Hey, look. Sometimes things get rough. You might face, oh . . . what was that little thing that happened in 2008? Oh, yes, a complete global economic recession. Sometimes survival is enough—and that's coming to you from the guy to call when you're tired of thinking small. This is when you employ whatever strategy you think is going to get you through to the next quarter: flexible pricing, time for money trade, retainer plus back-end pricing, and so on. Do what you have to do to make it.

5. **TO DO GOOD.** This is the strategy I use on many of my offerings. My accountant doesn't like this pricing model because he thinks I leave a lot of money on the table. And, he's right. But don't shed any tears for me. I do just fine. I intentionally keep my prices low, compared to my colleagues, for my online and teleseminar courses. This way, newer small business owners (possibly like you) are able to enroll in

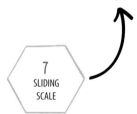

the courses. Sure, it allows more people to participate and you might think that I make bigger profits due to volume but it's not the case because my expenses are also higher. My most profitable offerings are my small-group in-person coaching workshops and big corporate speaking gigs. And yes, they're at prestige prices. Worth every penny, I might add. Even so, you'll often see me using the sliding scale pricing model for these prestige-priced offerings as well. If I think I can help you, and I think you're going to make a positive difference in the world with the help I provide, I'll adjust my prices to fit your current economic situation. The relationship between money and happiness is a complicated one, for sure. The vast majority of research points to this, though: Once you are living above the poverty line, most happiness is a result of meaningful interpersonal relationships and connection to those around you. So, go on, do some good in the world. As my mother says, "C'mon, it won't kill you."

How to Offer Discounts & Incentives

The answer is not always clear but the question remains the same: When should I lower prices or offer discounts and specials? Sometimes you want to offer price discounts or special packages to motivate potential clients to act. Other times, you'll feel the need (or desire) to lower prices because of factors beyond your control like economic conditions, supply and demand issues, competitors' prices, or other market conditions. Or maybe you're in complete control and have found a cheaper, more economical way to produce your services that allows you to lower your prices while increasing your profit margins.

However, use discounting and incentives with care. There's a fine line between over-the-top infomercial-like promotional pricing and authentic, clean, believable, appreciated-by-the-customer, and respectful use of discounting tactics and special offers. You'll know when you step over the line. If you do, take a step back. However, don't be afraid to be fully self-expressed in your sales promotions. There's nothing wrong—in fact, there's something very right about giving your ideal clients an opportunity to take advantage of your services at reduced prices. Remember, what I said before, people buy to express their values. And, you're giving them an opportunity to express their values through the work you do together.

- **QUANTITY DISCOUNTS.** You may be able to encourage clients to buy more of your services if they can get better prices the more they purchase. This model is very common for personal trainers and others like yoga teachers who sell sessions on an ongoing basis. For example, a yoga teacher may sell sessions in 5, 10, 15, and 20 packs. The price per session will decrease for each subsequently larger pack, making the 20-pack the best deal. She may even decide to offer a value-added bonus to the buyer of the 20 pack: a free, three-hour yoga retreat for the client and 20 of her closest friends, for example. Yes, you're right, what a great value-add to the client as well as a remarkable marketing opportunity for the yoga teacher—20 brand new potential clients brought right to her doorstep, or in this case, yoga mat.

- **CASH DISCOUNTS.** A business may offer cash discounts for the costs saved from not having to extend credit and bill the buyer on an open account. This mainly affects business-to-business rather than business-to-consumer sales. However, you'll also find many service professionals offer cash discounts as a way of keeping some, or all, of the work off the books, a practice I can't endorse.

- **SEASONAL DISCOUNTS.** Encourage clients to buy at certain times of the year in anticipation of seasonal needs. Or offer off-season discounts. A landscaper can increase sales in the winter by closing the summer contracts at special off-season prices.

- **MARKDOWNS & TIME-SENSITIVE DISCOUNTS.** Mark down your prices for a particular period of time or until a certain number of sales are made. For example, "25 percent off until the end of March" or "the first three people to respond get 25 percent off." An interior designer who does one-day makeovers can make an offer in her newsletter at a 25 percent discount—but only for the first three people to respond. To avoid sounding like one of those late-night infomercials, she simply explains why she's offering only three spots. She has just a certain amount of time and, as much as she'd love to, she can't do an unlimited number of full-day makeovers.

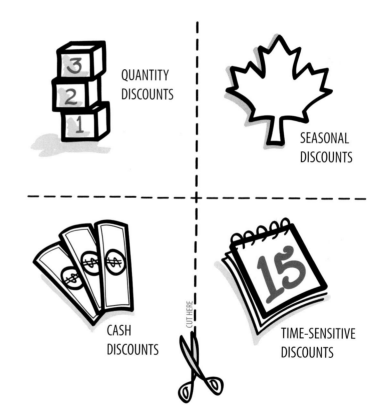

QUANTITY DISCOUNTS

SEASONAL DISCOUNTS

CASH DISCOUNTS

TIME-SENSITIVE DISCOUNTS

CUT HERE

A Strategy for Offering Free Services

Some give away free sessions or services as a sales tactic to get clients. Does it work? Sometimes. Should you do it? Depends on who you ask. Some swear by it. Others have sworn off it. And yet, still others swear every time they do it because it's so frustrating.

Generally, I don't recommend it. Here are some words of caution:

- **CREDIBILITY.** If you're offering free sessions to anybody who happens to stumble across your web site, a potential client may think you are sitting around with lots of time on your hands just trying to give your stuff away for free in the hope that someone will hire you. Credibility is built in large part on perception.

- **MAINTAIN THE RED VELVET ROPE POLICY.** Choose your ideal clients—those with whom you do your best work, not just anyone with a pulse.

- **EXPECTATION MANAGEMENT.** A potential client may perceive that he's supposed to get some big result from that one free session. If he doesn't, he's disappointed and he doesn't hire you, and consequently, he sees you as a low status service provider.

This doesn't mean that there is no way to use this strategy; there is. In my first year in business I used the following "free session" strategy successfully.

Include an offer for a 20-minute laser coaching session into your sales cycle—but only after the potential client demonstrates that she is serious about learning from you. Here's how:

1. When she downloads your seven-part e-mail mini-course, send her the first two lessons during Week One. Each lesson includes two paragraphs of education followed by a detailed written exercise.

2. Send a "congratulations and reward" e-mail, offering praise and appreciation for the work she put in to the first two lessons (all of this can be automated). As a reward, offer a complimentary 20-minute telephone coaching session to address any questions she has about the material from the first two lessons. A number of criteria need to be followed, however, to book the session, which is explained in the "congratulations and reward" e-mail, highlights as follows:

- She must schedule the session using your public calendar. Make only a few spots available on Friday afternoons so that a waiting list develops quickly. This way you don't look like you are sitting around twiddling your thumbs, hoping someone will show up.

- If she misses the session or doesn't reschedule with 24 hours notice, she misses the opportunity and cannot reschedule (again, all of this can be automated).

- If she is more than a few minutes late to the phone session, don't pick up.

- And, finally, one week before the scheduled session, she must send you an e-mail with her responses to the exercises from the first two lessons. This helps because: 1) If she has not already done them, she will now. Getting clients to consume your work is as important as getting them to hire you. 2) By reviewing her written exercises, you know what she needs before she dials your number. It shows you what she is struggling with and how to help her.

So, in just 20 minutes you can solve their problems and create an impressive result.

You might think that all these rules would put potential clients off. You're trying to get clients, not force them to jump through flaming hoops. But, you know what? Over 65 percent of the people who signed up for the free 20-minute session became clients. Figure out a way to use this strategy in your sales cycle and you'll get the opportunity to do something valuable, and free of charge, for your potential clients. You'll enhance your reputation, build credibility, and book more business.

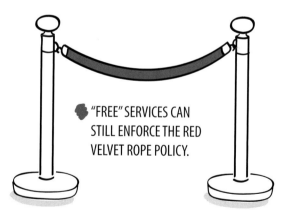

"FREE" SERVICES CAN STILL ENFORCE THE RED VELVET ROPE POLICY.

When to Raise Prices

Whenever you can, but there's no need to race to the top of the pricing ladder to be successful. Here are a few examples of why and how to do it.

- **JUST FOR THE HECK OF IT.** Just for the heck of it. Sometimes, raising prices may simply, and beautifully, lead to a much deserved increase in profit.

- **ECONOMIC CONDITIONS.** You may need to raise prices because of inflation (rising costs unequaled by productivity gains). Inflation usually gets carried over to the consumer—which is why it's such an economic problem.

- **YOU'RE IN DEMAND AND OVERBOOKED.** If demand for your services has increased—I'll be doing the Book Yourself Solid happy dance for you—it may be a good time to raise prices.

- **TRAINING AND SKILL DEVELOPMENT.** If you've recently upgraded your certifications or completed a significant training that is highly relevant to your clients' needs, it may be a great time to raise prices.

- **UPGRADING YOUR PACKAGING.** If you upgrade your web site with a complete redesign and in doing so seriously upgrade the look and feel of your brand, you can raise your prices. If you upgrade your offices, allowing you to become more efficient at what you do, you can up your prices. If you upgrade the packaging of your products, you can also improve your bottom line. Again, credibility is, in large part, based on perception.

Sometimes, when service providers get overbooked, they complain about it. Oh, how easily we forget what it was like when we were struggling our way up the ladder. Worse still, I've witnessed many a service provider resist raising prices, which would have allowed each of them to work with fewer clients, for fear of losing business. Here's a simple story that illustrates my point.

I see an acupuncturist from time to time. He might be the best-known acupuncturist in my town (I live in a small town). He's likely the most experienced, and has an overbooked practice because of it. Every time I see him he complains (in a nice way) that he's overworked and can't keep up with demand. He doesn't want to change the model of his business, in that he still wants to see patients himself and doesn't want to manage other acupuncturists, nor does he want to raise his prices. So, every time I see him, I complain to him (in a nice way) that his prices are too low and, in fact, should be doubled. His answer is always the same, "But, Michael, if I double my rates, I'll lose half my clients." I'll pause here to let that sink in just as I do with him. He never gets it. Maybe you will. First of all, he won't lose half his clients but even if he did, he'd still make the same money and have twice as much free time. More likely he'll lose just a few clients but make much more money overall, because of the price increase.

OVERBOOKED? RAISE YOUR PRICES.

If You Raise Your Rates

If you do raise prices it's a good idea to let clients know why. There's nothing wrong with saying that you're fortunate to be in high demand and are raising your prices so that you can give more attention to your clients. Or, that certain expenses related to serving your clients have increased and you're raising your prices accordingly.

People like the truth. I'd prefer to be open and honest with my clients, running the risk of disappointing a few of them, than be manipulative or obtuse, running the risk of damaging my soul. Just be sure to let them know what the new rates will be and when they go into effect. Give them reasonable notice so they can adjust to the changes. And, most important, remind them of the continuing benefits they'll get from working with you.

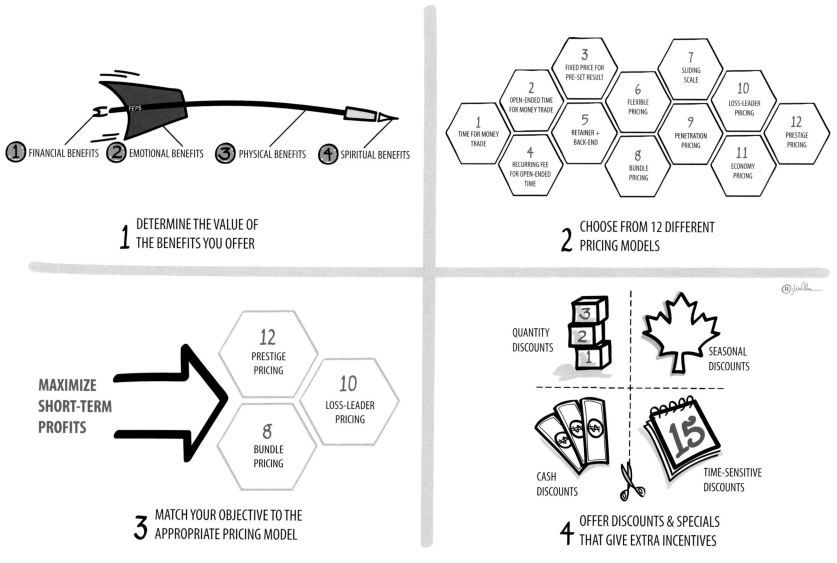

1 DETERMINE THE VALUE OF THE BENEFITS YOU OFFER

① FINANCIAL BENEFITS ② EMOTIONAL BENEFITS ③ PHYSICAL BENEFITS ④ SPIRITUAL BENEFITS

FEPS

2 CHOOSE FROM 12 DIFFERENT PRICING MODELS

1 TIME FOR MONEY TRADE
2 OPEN-ENDED TIME FOR MONEY TRADE
3 FIXED PRICE FOR PRE-SET RESULT
4 RECURRING FEE FOR OPEN-ENDED TIME
5 RETAINER + BACK-END
6 FLEXIBLE PRICING
7 SLIDING SCALE
8 BUNDLE PRICING
9 PENETRATION PRICING
10 LOSS-LEADER PRICING
11 ECONOMY PRICING
12 PRESTIGE PRICING

3 MATCH YOUR OBJECTIVE TO THE APPROPRIATE PRICING MODEL

MAXIMIZE SHORT-TERM PROFITS

12 PRESTIGE PRICING
10 LOSS-LEADER PRICING
8 BUNDLE PRICING

4 OFFER DISCOUNTS & SPECIALS THAT GIVE EXTRA INCENTIVES

QUANTITY DISCOUNTS

SEASONAL DISCOUNTS

CASH DISCOUNTS

TIME-SENSITIVE DISCOUNTS

3.10 SUPER SIMPLE SELLING

HAVE A SUCCESSFUL SALES CONVERSATION
THE BOOK YOURSELF SOLID WAY

HI-YA!

3 USE THE 4-PART FORMULA IN YOUR SALES CONVERSATION

FINISH

2

1

3

4

15

1 LET GO OF LIMITING BELIEFS & SAY IT WITH CONFIDENCE

4 TRASH THE PITCH OF THE DAY & DON'T BE A SLEAZY SALESPERSON

2 FOLLOW THE BOOK YOURSELF SOLID PARADIGM OF SALES

HOT

3.10 SUPER SIMPLE SELLING

Art is making something out of nothing and selling it.

—Frank Zappa

As a service provider you may not want to think of yourself as a salesperson. You're in the business of helping others, and the sales process may feel contradictory to your core purpose. If you're uncomfortable with the sales process, it's likely that you view it as unethical, manipulative, and dishonest. Looking at it that way, who wouldn't be uncomfortable?

Many service professionals also feel uncomfortable charging for services that either come easily to them or that they love doing. There is often a sense that if it comes easily and is enjoyable, there's something wrong with charging others for doing it.

Add the fact that service professionals sell themselves as much as they sell a product, and the whole idea becomes even more uncomfortable. It may feel like you're bragging and being shamelessly immodest.

Letting Go of Limiting Beliefs

Becoming comfortable with the sales process requires that you let go of any limiting beliefs you may have about being worthy of the money you're earning. In fact, developing the right comfort level also requires a shift in your perspective of the sales process itself.

Most people who are successful get paid to do what they do well. You don't usually become successful doing something that you find difficult. You become successful when you exploit your natural talents. Imagine Tom Hanks saying he shouldn't get paid to do movies because he's really good at it and loves it. Or J. K. Rowling saying she should write the Harry Potter books for free because she enjoys it.

Tom Hanks, J. K. Rowling, and anyone else you can think of who is, or was, wildly successful at what they do, work to the bone at becoming even better at what they are naturally gifted at doing. They create extraordinary experiences for the people they serve, whether it's an audience, a fan, or a client. That's why they—and you—deserve to be paid top dollar.

If you don't believe you are worth what you are charging, it is unlikely that a lot of people are going to hire you based on those fees. You need to resonate fully with the prices you are setting so that others will resonate with them as well. To do so, you may need to work on shifting your beliefs so that you feel more comfortable with charging higher fees, rather than lowering your fees to eliminate the discomfort.

There is an old joke about a guy who gets into a cab in New York City and asks the driver how to get to Carnegie Hall, and the driver responds, "Practice, practice, practice." You're going to increase your resonance with practice. It's just like practicing a martial art, or a sport, or singing. Singing is a great example because your voice becomes more resonant the more you practice. At first it's uncomfortable, but over time it becomes easier and more natural. The same thing will happen when you quote your fees. The more you feel comfortable setting your price, the more other people will feel that comfort and the energetic resonance that comes with that comfort, and they'll happily pay you what you're worth.

The Book Yourself Solid Paradigm of Sales

The Book Yourself Solid Paradigm of Sales is all about building relationships with your potential clients on the basis of trust. It is, quite simply, about having a sincere conversation that allows you to let your potential clients know what you can do to help them. You aren't manipulating or coercing people into buying something they have no real need or desire to buy. You're making them aware of something you offer that they already need, want, or desire.

Thinking in terms of solutions and benefits is the ah-ha to the selling process. When you follow the Book Yourself Solid Paradigm of Sales, clients will beg to work with you. You are a consultant, a lifelong advisor. When you have fundamental solutions and a desire to help others, it becomes your moral imperative to show and tell as many people as possible. You are changing lives!

TRUST ESTABLISHED

RED HOT BENEFITS SHARED

PROBLEMS SOLVED

Just the Right Amount of Trust at Just the Right Time

It's no accident that I introduce sales in Chapter 10—after I've taught you how to set your foundation and build trust and credibility. One of the reasons that so many sales conversations are unsuccessful is because they're had at the wrong time—usually too soon—before you've earned the proportionate amount of trust needed for the offer being made. Plus, your clients buy when it's right for them—when something occurs in their life or business that compels them to hire you. If these two factors, trust and timing, come together at just the right moment, you'll have a successful sales conversation and book the business. But this only works if you've built a solid foundation, demonstrating that you:

- Have a Red Velvet Rope Policy so you work only with ideal clients.

- Understand why people buy what you're selling so you know exactly to whom you are selling and what they want to invest in.

- Have developed a personal brand identity so you decide how you're known in the world.

- Are able to talk about what you do without sounding confusing or bland, or like everybody else, and without ever using an elevator speech.

- If you've set this foundation, a potential client will give you the opportunity to earn his trust. But you'll only earn his trust if you:

  1. Use the standard credibility builders and have a high degree of likability.

  2. Have designed a sales cycle that starts with no-barrier-to-entry offers including your always-have-something-to-invite-people-to offer.

  3. Have simple lead-generating information products that enhance your credibility and speed up your sales cycle.

Then, and really only then, are you ready to have sales conversations that work.

Super Simple, 4-Part Sales Formula

Now, let's talk about how to have the sales conversation. I've created the 4-part sales formula for super simple selling—so simple the formula practically works on its own. Why? Because, once trust is assured and a need is met, using this 4-part formula during your sales conversations will book the business. But, please, just like the Book Yourself Solid Dialogue, this is meant to be an open and free-flowing conversation, not a sales script.

When a potential client expresses interest in working with you, open with a simple question . . .

PART 1: What are you working on? Or, what is your goal? Or, what are you trying to achieve? Once you feel certain you know what he wants to accomplish and by when, simply ask . . .

PART 2: How will you know when you have achieved it? What results will you see? What feedback will you hear? What feelings will you have? Once you feel like the potential client has clearly articulated these benefits, make sure he is fully in the hiring frame of mind, and then ask . . .

PART 3: Would you like someone to help you with that (achieve your goal, and so forth)? If he says, no, wish him the best of luck and keep in touch with him. If he says, yes, then offer . . .

PART 4: Would you like that person to be me? Because, you know, you are my ideal client. (To which he'll say, "What do you mean?" because no one has ever said that to him before.) Well, you are someone with whom I do my best work. (He'll ask, "Why?" and you'll tell him . . .) Because you are . . . (Here is where you list the qualities that make him who he is and allow you to do your best work.) As you're listing these qualities you'll see his face brighten as he sits up straight and says, "Wow. That is so me! Thank you for noticing." You'll say, "So shall we look at our calendars to plan a time to get started?" And, the answer will be . . . drum roll, please . . . "Absolutely, yes!"

Don't use the preceding phrases verbatim. Instead, just use the Book Yourself Solid 4-Part Sales Formula as a framework for a super duper simple (successful) sales conversation.

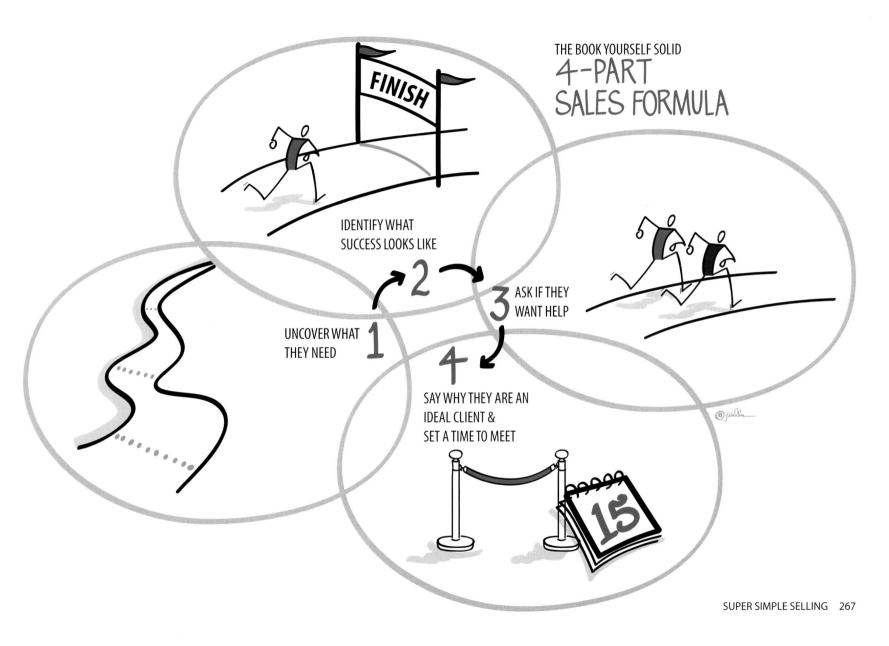

THE BOOK YOURSELF SOLID
4-PART
SALES FORMULA

FINISH

IDENTIFY WHAT
SUCCESS LOOKS LIKE

2

3 ASK IF THEY
WANT HELP

UNCOVER WHAT
THEY NEED

1

4

SAY WHY THEY ARE AN
IDEAL CLIENT &
SET A TIME TO MEET

15

Written Exercise 10A

PRACTICE WITHOUT PRESSURE

Try this 4-part process with a good friend or colleague. Ask her to call you at random a few times in the next week and say, "Hi, I've been getting your newsletter for a while and I think you may be able to help me; can we talk about your services?"

1. **PART 1:** Instead of doing that thing that everyone does—talk about themselves and their business for 20 minutes—use the visual worksheet on the next page while you are on the phone with her. Start with Part 1, Uncover What She Needs. Ask her what she's working on, or what she's trying to achieve. Write her answers in the space provided on the worksheet for each part, which will help you become a better listener.

2. **PART 2:** Once Part 1 is covered, move on to Part 2 and Identify What Success Looks Like. How will she know she has reached success? We have some prompting questions for you in the worksheet, but I encourage you to develop your own great questions too.

3. **PART 3:** If she meets your Red Velvet Rope Policy, then move on to Part 3, and Ask if She Wants Help in getting there. If no, wish her well and be sure to keep in touch. But if she says, "Why, yes, I would like help!" then move on to Part 4.

4. **PART 4:** Tell her why she is your ideal client—the traits that help you do your best work. She will be honored that you noticed. Then, ask if she would like to plan a time to get started. Super simple!

IF THEY'RE UNCERTAIN

What if potential clients are not ready to start working with you? No problem. The good news is that someday the benefits you provide will be a priority. And, something in your potential client's life will change that compels her to hire you. However, if you haven't kept in touch and followed up, she'll look to someone else to help her reach her goals. But, since you're going to become a master at keeping in touch and following up, you'll be waiting in the wings, ready, willing, and able to help her accomplish her goals. (We learned exactly how to keep in touch in Chapter 7.)

THE SALES CONVERSATION

USE THE BOOK YOURSELF SOLID 4-PART FORMULA
TO HAVE A SUPER SIMPLE SALES CONVERSATION

GOAL:	① UNCOVER WHAT THEY NEED	② IDENTIFY WHAT SUCCESS LOOKS LIKE	③ ASK IF THEY WANT HELP	④ SAY WHY THEY ARE AN IDEAL CLIENT & SET A TIME TO MEET
YOUR QUESTIONS:	● WHAT ARE YOU WORKING ON? ● WHAT IS YOUR GOAL? ● BY WHEN?	● HOW WILL YOU KNOW WHEN YOU HAVE ACHIEVED IT? ● WHAT RESULTS OR FEELINGS WILL YOU HAVE?	● WOULD YOU LIKE SOMEONE TO HELP YOU WITH THAT? ● WOULD YOU LIKE THAT PERSON TO BE ME?	● YOU ARE AN IDEAL CLIENT FOR ME BECAUSE... ● SHALL WE PLAN A TIME TO GET STARTED?
YOUR NOTES FOR THEIR RESPONSES:				

The Secret to the Book Yourself Solid System

This simple 4-step process is the secret to the Book Yourself Solid system.

1. You execute a few of the 6 Core Self-Promotion Strategies, which create awareness for what you have to offer.

2. When a potential client becomes aware of your services, she'll take a look at your foundation. If it looks secure, if she feels comfortable stepping onto it, she'll give you the opportunity to earn her trust—but only the opportunity. She's not necessarily going to hire you right then and there. She needs some time to consider the consequences before she will actually trust you.

3. That's when your plan to build trust and credibility comes into play. As a potential client moves through your sales cycle, she will come to like you, trust you, and find you credible.

4. When her circumstances dictate that she needs the kind of help you provide, she'll raise her hand and ask you to have a sales conversation. You have a sales conversation the Book Yourself Solid way and book the business.

The process is simple. The process is sound. It can turn your business life around. And, most important, the process is a complete, repetitive, and self-perpetuating system. While potential clients are going through this process, you're continuing to create awareness for what you have to offer using a few of the 6 Core Self-Promotion Strategies. This gets more new potential clients checking out your foundation for stability and security. They'll like what they see, stand on it, and give you the opportunity to earn their trust. You earn their trust (over time) and when the circumstances are right for them, they'll either raise their hand and ask you to have a sales conversation or they'll accept one of your compelling offers and you'll book the business. The process repeats itself over and over and over again. It's systematic. Once you've set up your own Book Yourself Solid marketing and sales system, it works like a charm. Just rinse and repeat.

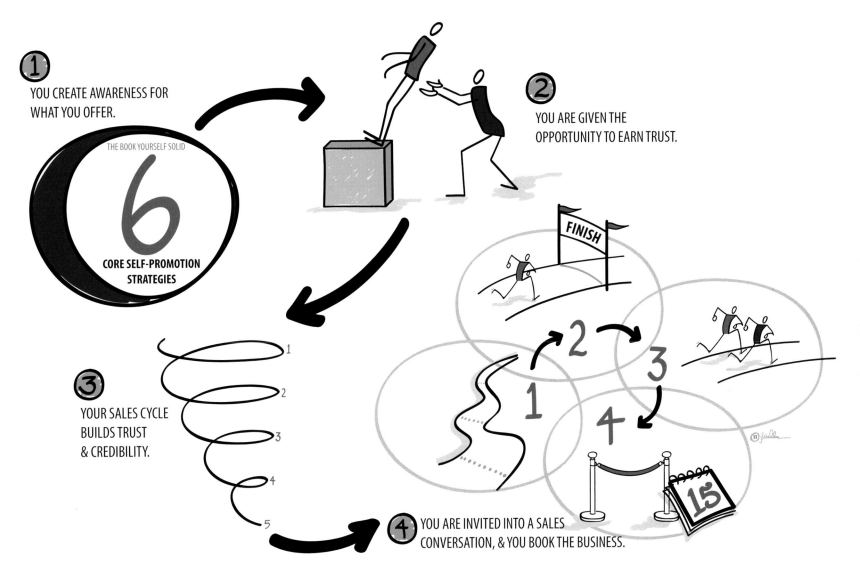

1. YOU CREATE AWARENESS FOR WHAT YOU OFFER.

THE BOOK YOURSELF SOLID

6

CORE SELF-PROMOTION STRATEGIES

2. YOU ARE GIVEN THE OPPORTUNITY TO EARN TRUST.

3. YOUR SALES CYCLE BUILDS TRUST & CREDIBILITY.

4. YOU ARE INVITED INTO A SALES CONVERSATION, & YOU BOOK THE BUSINESS.

FINISH

Cut the Crap Out of Selling

By now you probably can guess that I think traditional sales tactics have about as much validity as a three-dollar bill. I even wrote an entire book about it called *The Contrarian Effect: Why It Pays (BIG) to Take Typical Sales Advice and Do the Opposite.*

In fact, traditional, trite sales tactics, closing techniques, assuming the sale, overcoming objections, and so forth were originally developed in the late 1800s by John H. Patterson of the National Cash Register Company (who ironically enough was found guilty of violating antitrust laws). These contrived sales strategies, created by a convict, are still perpetuated by sales trainers. And for good reason. They give us something to do when we're lost. They provide a standard by which to measure. And the worst part is that they work . . . a little . . . sometimes. But clients detest them.

People don't buy because you want them to. And rarely do they buy because of a sales pitch or something clever you said to persuade them.

If you really want to be successful when selling, you've got to listen to your potential clients.

I've offered you the Book Yourself Solid 4-Part Sales Formula to use as a framework for your sales conversations but there is no perfectly packaged

JUST LISTEN & LET THEM TELL YOU WHAT THEY REALLY WANT.

TRASH THE PITCH OF THE DAY.

SET YOURSELF APART FROM THE SLEAZY SALESPERSON.

process, magic bullet, or foolproof method to crumble every gatekeeper in your path and book every piece of business. It doesn't exist. We must be willing to learn, adapt, and listen to our potential clients.

When you do this, you'll never have to use a canned close again. But you will connect brilliantly with the values your customers want to express. Remember . . .

- Trash the provocative questions, the level-setting statements, and the conversation helpers and just listen while customers tell you what they really want.
- Ditch the pitch of the day and only make relevant sales offers proportionate to the amount of trust you've earned.
- Use the Red Velvet Rope Policy and don't assume you are meant to work with everyone. Maximize your time and energy, and build credibility when you work with people you are meant to serve.

I'm certain you care about what you do: the people you serve, the services you sell, and the reputation you've earned. You wouldn't be reading this book if you didn't. Do not let your guard down for one second. Think bigger about who you are and how you will serve your clients.

When you keep your focus and maintain your integrity, you'll never, ever, be put in the same category as those stereotypical, shady, smooth-talking, handlebar-mustache-twirling, sleazeball "salespeople" ready to screw over the next poor sap just to take home the commission. Your service is important to the world. You are important to the world. Cut the crap out of selling and set yourself apart.

Start Small, End Big

Remember, you've got to let go of those limiting beliefs about selling and getting paid well for what you do. When you exploit your natural talents and work hard to hone them, you can be confident about receiving compensation relative to the value the market places on that talent.

The Book Yourself Solid Paradigm of Sales takes it a step further by shifting the traditional sales tactics of "getting" to a more effective mind-set of "giving." No manipulation, coercion or a free set of knives if they buy in the next 30 minutes. Just a sincere conversation about the benefits of working with you and the solutions you offer.

The paradigm becomes reality through the 4-Part Formula, which is a series of questions you ask your potential client:

1. What are you trying to achieve? Is there a race we are running? Map it out for me.
2. How will you know you have achieved it? What does the finish line look like? Feel like?
3. Would you like help with that? Here are some options that are designed to address the specific challenges you face.
4. Would you like the one to help you to be me? Here's why you are an ideal client for me. When would you like to get started?

I can't emphasize this enough: You must be a good listener. Ask questions that help you understand what they are up against, and at the same time, be listening for clues as to whether they fit your Red Velvet Rope Policy.

There you have it. These are the lovely, easy steps to simple selling and booking yourself solid. Start small, end big, and remember: Successful selling is really nothing more than showing your potential clients how you can help them to live a happier, more successful life.

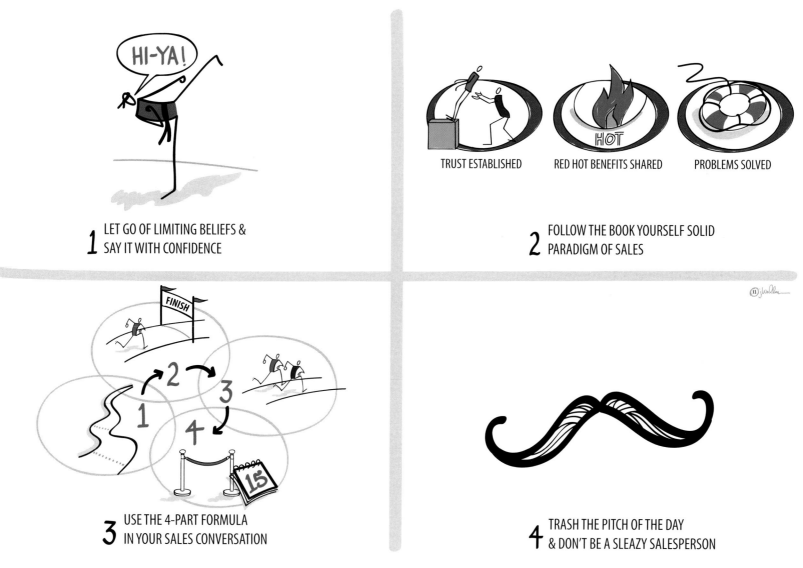

1 LET GO OF LIMITING BELIEFS & SAY IT WITH CONFIDENCE

TRUST ESTABLISHED   RED HOT BENEFITS SHARED   PROBLEMS SOLVED

2 FOLLOW THE BOOK YOURSELF SOLID PARADIGM OF SALES

3 USE THE 4-PART FORMULA IN YOUR SALES CONVERSATION

4 TRASH THE PITCH OF THE DAY & DON'T BE A SLEAZY SALESPERSON

CRUISING ALTITUDE

So far you have done a systems check on the ground with Module One—Your Foundation. Then you helped your business take off from the runway by putting all of your horsepower into Module Two—Building Trust & Credibility. Module Three, Perfect Pricing & Simple Selling, took you to full throttle, where you gave it all she's got.

Just like flying an airplane, the aim of your business is to get it to a cruising altitude, where you can go a greater distance, at a higher speed, while consuming less fuel.

Self-promotion is the fuel that propels your entire business, but it needs the other three modules to be in place in order to stay at cruising altitude. When you can get your marketing system on autopilot, you'll have more clients than you can handle.

A word to the wise: High mindedness, the sensibility that you are above marketing and selling and that you shouldn't have to do those "salesy" things, is small thinking. This is due to two conflicting intentions: the intention to be great at what you do rather than great at marketing, and the intention not to sell out or compromise your integrity. As you'll see, the two aren't mutually exclusive.

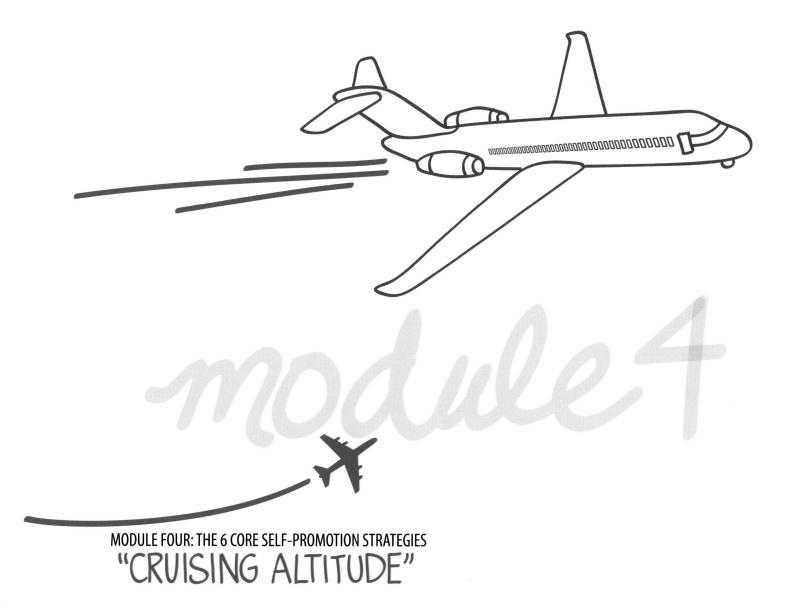

MODULE FOUR: THE 6 CORE SELF-PROMOTION STRATEGIES
"CRUISING ALTITUDE"

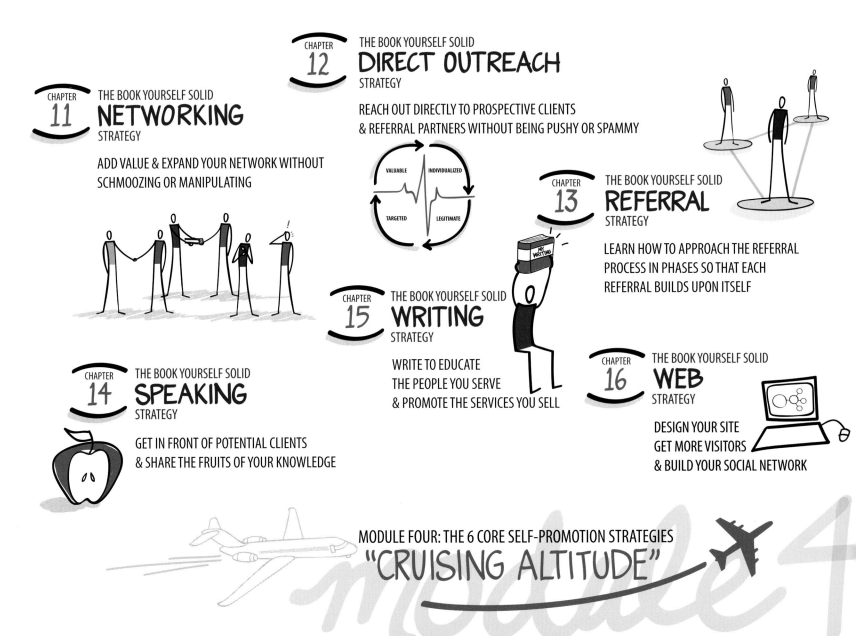

CHAPTER 11

THE BOOK YOURSELF SOLID
NETWORKING
STRATEGY

ADD VALUE & EXPAND YOUR NETWORK WITHOUT
SCHMOOZING OR MANIPULATING

CHAPTER 12

THE BOOK YOURSELF SOLID
DIRECT OUTREACH
STRATEGY

REACH OUT DIRECTLY TO PROSPECTIVE CLIENTS
& REFERRAL PARTNERS WITHOUT BEING PUSHY OR SPAMMY

VALUABLE   INDIVIDUALIZED

TARGETED   LEGITIMATE

CHAPTER 13

THE BOOK YOURSELF SOLID
REFERRAL
STRATEGY

LEARN HOW TO APPROACH THE REFERRAL
PROCESS IN PHASES SO THAT EACH
REFERRAL BUILDS UPON ITSELF

MY WRITING

CHAPTER 15

THE BOOK YOURSELF SOLID
WRITING
STRATEGY

WRITE TO EDUCATE
THE PEOPLE YOU SERVE
& PROMOTE THE SERVICES YOU SELL

CHAPTER 14

THE BOOK YOURSELF SOLID
SPEAKING
STRATEGY

GET IN FRONT OF POTENTIAL CLIENTS
& SHARE THE FRUITS OF YOUR KNOWLEDGE

CHAPTER 16

THE BOOK YOURSELF SOLID
WEB
STRATEGY

DESIGN YOUR SITE
GET MORE VISITORS
& BUILD YOUR SOCIAL NETWORK

MODULE FOUR: THE 6 CORE SELF-PROMOTION STRATEGIES
"CRUISING ALTITUDE"

module 4

The 6 Core Self-Promotion Strategies

MODULE FOUR

Watch out, because you're not only on your way to liking marketing and selling, but you are now dangerously close to loving both. Just like any new love affair, you want to give yourself time to absorb the newness of it all. Don't let the multitude of strategies in Module Four overwhelm you. Pick the strategies that are most aligned with your strengths and run with them—you don't need to execute all of them. Only three of the strategies are mandatory, whereas three of them are optional. Can you guess which are mandatory and which are optional?

You might have guessed that speaking and writing strategies are optional, but are you surprised to hear that the web strategy is also optional? Yes, having a professional web site that effectively starts conversations with potential clients is probably a very good idea, but beyond that, you need not learn or use any of the additional web strategies.

The only possible mistake you can make is to try all of these strategies at once. You run the risk of watering down your efforts, becoming frustrated, or worse, quitting before you see any results. I suggest that you use the four mandatory strategies and pick one of the optional strategies to start.

module 4

MODULE FOUR: THE 6 CORE SELF-PROMOTION STRATEGIES
"CRUISING ALTITUDE"

CHAPTER 11
The Book Yourself Solid
Networking Strategy

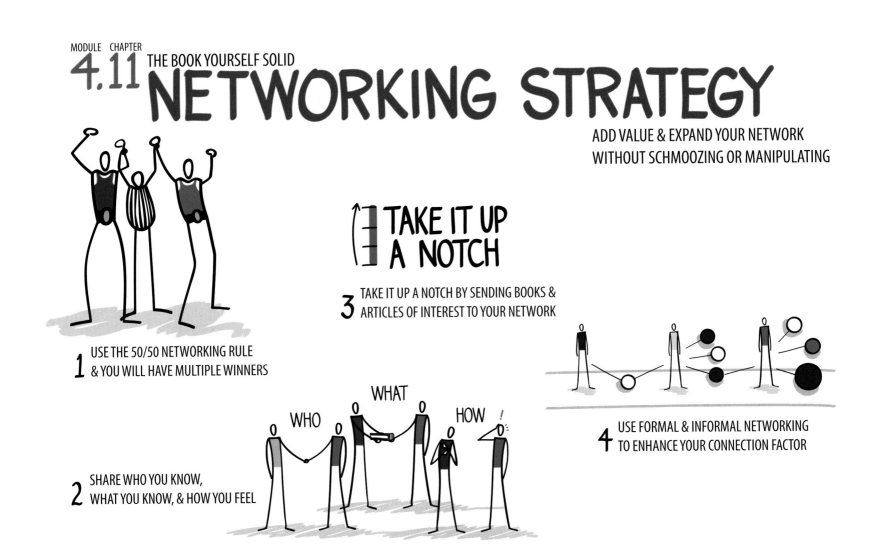

MODULE   CHAPTER
4.11   THE BOOK YOURSELF SOLID
NETWORKING STRATEGY

ADD VALUE & EXPAND YOUR NETWORK
WITHOUT SCHMOOZING OR MANIPULATING

TAKE IT UP
A NOTCH

3 TAKE IT UP A NOTCH BY SENDING BOOKS &
ARTICLES OF INTEREST TO YOUR NETWORK

1 USE THE 50/50 NETWORKING RULE
& YOU WILL HAVE MULTIPLE WINNERS

WHO   WHAT   HOW !

2 SHARE WHO YOU KNOW,
WHAT YOU KNOW, & HOW YOU FEEL

4 USE FORMAL & INFORMAL NETWORKING
TO ENHANCE YOUR CONNECTION FACTOR

4.11 THE NETWORKING STRATEGY

Some cause happiness wherever they go; others, whenever they go.

—Oscar Wilde

When most service professionals hear the word networking, they cringe and think of the old-school business mentality of promotional networking at meet-and-greet events where everyone is there to schmooze and manipulate one another in an attempt to gain some advantage for themselves or their business.

Who wouldn't cringe at the thought of spending an hour or two exchanging banalities and sales pitches with a phony smile plastered on your face to hide your discomfort? If it feels uncomfortable, self-serving, and deceptive, chances are all those business cards you collected will end up in a drawer of your desk never to be seen again because you'll so dread following up that you'll procrastinate until they're forgotten.

Take heart, because it doesn't have to be that way. The Book Yourself Solid Networking Strategy teaches you to shift your perspective from one of scarcity and fear to one of abundance and love.

No Wrestling Required

Do you believe networking is like pro wrestling? You know, world domination, flexing muscles, and striking fear in your opponents? There is an old-school business mentality of scarcity and fear that asks:

- How can I push my agenda?
- How can I get or keep the attention on myself?
- What can I say to really impress or manipulate?
- How can I use each contact to get what I want or need?
- How can I crush the competition?
- How can I dominate the marketplace?

The Book Yourself Solid Networking Strategy (one of abundance and love) asks:

- What can I give and offer to others?
- How can I help others to be successful?
- How can I start and continue friendly conversations?
- How can I put others at ease?
- How can I best express my sincerity and generosity?
- How can I listen attentively so as to recognize the needs and desires of others?
- How can I provide true value to others?
- How can I fully express myself so I can make genuine connections with others?

When we use the word networking let's think of connecting, instead. A connection with another human being means that you're in sync with, and relevant to, each other. Let that be our definition of networking. Does that help you fall in love with the concept of networking? We don't get contacts, we don't find contacts, we don't have contacts; we make connections with real people.

When people ask me what is the most important factor in networking success, I always have a two-word answer: other people. Your networking success is determined by other people—how they respond to you.

If you keep asking yourself the preceding value-added questions and follow the Book Yourself Solid Networking Strategy, you'll create a large and powerful network that is priceless and will reap rewards for years to come. Old-school networking tries to body slam the competition—but networking the Book Yourself Solid way will build compassion, trust, and integrity.

REAL NETWORKING ISN'T ABOUT TRYING TO CRUSH THE COMPETITION.

The Book Yourself Solid 50/50 Networking Rule

The Book Yourself Solid Networking Strategy employs the 50/50 networking rule, which requires that we share our networking focus evenly between potential clients and other professionals. Most people think of networking as something you do primarily to try to reel in clients. That's not so. The 50/50 rule makes room for multiple winners.

While the Book Yourself Solid Networking Strategy adds value to the lives of people who could become your clients, you'll also want to spend 50 percent of your networking time connecting with other professionals. Networking with other professionals provides you with an opportunity to connect and share resources, knowledge, and information. Bear in mind that working solo does not mean working alone. You can create so much more value when other talented people are involved.

HAVE YOU GOT ANY SOUL?

The absolute best education I have ever received on the concept of networking was from Tim Sanders in his book, *Love Is the Killer App: How to Win Business and Influence Friends*.

Tim Sanders's message is that being a love cat is the key to business success, and it's at the heart of the Book Yourself Solid Networking Strategy. He quotes philosopher and writer Milton Mayeroff's definition of love from his book *On Caring*: "Love is the selfless promotion of the growth of the other." Tim then defines his idea of business love as "the act of intelligently and sensibly sharing your intangibles with your biz partners."

What are those intangibles? According to Tim, they are your knowledge, your network, and your compassion. They are the three essential keys to networking success.

Networking requires that you consciously integrate each of these intangibles until they become a natural part of your daily life, everywhere you go, and in everything you do. Yes, I said daily life. Networking isn't something you do only at networking events. It's an ongoing process that makes it a win for both you and your connections.

WHEN YOU SHARE YOUR
NETWORKING FOCUS,
THERE ARE MANY WINNERS.

Share Who You Know, What You Know, & How You Feel

We said that to be truly connected with another human being is to be in sync with, and relevant to, one another. There are three things we can do to help us with that aim.

1. **SHARE WHO YOU KNOW.** This is everyone you know. It's as simple as that. Whether family, friend, or business associate, everyone in your network is potentially a good connection with someone else, and you never know whom you might meet next who will be the other half of a great connection.

2. **SHARE WHAT YOU KNOW.** This means everything you've learned—whether through life experience, observation, conversation, or study—and everything you continue to learn.

3. **SHARE HOW YOU FEEL.** This is all of your compassion, the quality that makes us most human. It's our ability to empathize with others. Sharing your compassion in every aspect of your life will bring the greatest rewards, not only for your bottom line, but also in knowing that you're operating from your heart and your integrity in all your interactions.

NOTE: Give each of these three intangibles freely and with no expectation of return. After all, that's how love is meant to operate, too. While it may seem calculated to plan a strategy around them, the fact remains that when you're smart, friendly, and helpful, people will like you, will enjoy being around you, and will remember you when they or someone they know needs your services.

WHO

WHAT

HOW

SHARE WHO YOU KNOW.

SHARE WHAT YOU KNOW.

SHARE HOW YOU FEEL.

Share Who You Know

I will do anything I can to support the people I like and respect. I go out of my way to serve the people who serve me. Do you?

Think about it: Whom do you want to give your business to or recommend to other members of your network? It's the people who have served you in some way; the people who are friendly, nice, smart, and helpful; the people who will go the extra mile, give that little bit more than anyone expects, and who genuinely strive to provide the best service they can with integrity. It's the people who are upbeat, always have a ready smile, and from whom you walk away feeling supported and energized.

WHO

SHARE WHO YOU KNOW.

If you are that person in each and every interaction you have with others, whether business or personal, your network is going to grow exponentially, and those people are going to remember you and want to do business with you. They're going to link you with others in their network with whom you can make beneficial connections, and they're going to refer you to everyone they know who could possibly use your service or products.

I can think of scores, if not hundreds, of friends and colleagues I have who are like this. There is one who comes to mind as the ideal example of what it really means to share your network openly, without reservation, and without expecting anything in return.

Caroline Kohles, of NiaNewYork.com, is a fitness, health, and wellness expert. She is one of the most authentic and talented people I have the pleasure of knowing, and I will do anything for her any chance I get. Why? Because she constantly sends me clients, connects me with people who I can partner with, gives me opportunities to market my services, and constantly shares things she's learned or heard about that she thinks will help me personally or professionally. The most remarkable thing about Caroline is that she expects nothing in return.

There is one thing that is essential to consider with respect to sharing your network. You must do what you say you're going to do—always. And if you don't, apologize and make it right. If you make commitments and don't fulfill them, you'll damage your reputation and close doorways that were once open to you. If you don't make commitments to connect, no one will do it for you. These habits of commitment making and fulfilling are essential to developing yourself into a masterful connector who truly and meaningfully adds value to the lives of others.

Each business day, introduce two people within your network who do not yet know each other but you think might benefit from knowing each other. This is not a referral for a specific work opportunity but rather a way to connect two people who may find some benefit in knowing each other. Maybe they are both in the same field or share some business connection. Maybe they are both into martial arts or golf. Or, maybe they just live in the same town. Either way, all you're doing is creating an opportunity for connection. If they're the kind of people who value meeting others, then something special might happen. Hey, you never know . . . you might be introducing two people who are going to save the planet from climate calamity or fall in love and get married.

I created a software program that helps you do this. It's called solid.ly, and each day the system suggests possible connections based on your contacts' hobbies, locations, professions, and more. You pick one of the suggested connections and connect. The system then tracks all the connections you've made ensuring that you never reconnect the same people. It also spaces out the connections so you are never too helpful (which can overwhelm your contact). Furthermore, the system manages your follow-up with each person so you continue to develop and nurture the relationship. You can learn more about how it works, see a demo, and get your reader's bonus extended trial at www.solid.ly.

Written Exercise 11A

SHARE YOUR NETWORK

Use the visual worksheet on the next page for the following exercise.

1. List five people in your network who consistently support you by sending referrals, giving you advice, or doing anything else that's helpful.

2. Identify someone in your network for each of these five people whom you could connect them with. Whom do you know who will add value to their work or life? Is it a potential client, a potential business partner, a potential vendor?

BOOKED SOLID ACTION STEP: Try it now. Go through your address book and find two people who share something in common, something that each one of them will find relevant about the other and introduce them to each other.

The people you listed in this written exercise and the people you connected in the Booked Solid Action Step are going to appreciate the opportunity to connect or the recommendation that you make, and when someone they know needs your service or product, they'll be more likely to remember you and to reciprocate.

SHARE YOUR NETWORK

THINK OF PEOPLE WHO SUPPORT YOU WITH REFERRALS & ADVICE
AND CONNECT THEM WITH THOSE WHO COULD BRING THEM VALUE

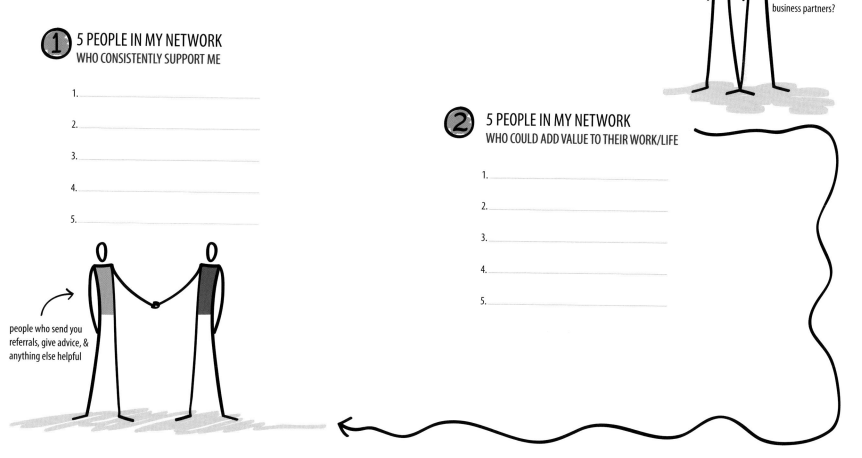

YOU →

← potential clients?

vendors?

business partners?

1 5 PEOPLE IN MY NETWORK
WHO CONSISTENTLY SUPPORT ME

1. _____

2. _____

3. _____

4. _____

5. _____

2 5 PEOPLE IN MY NETWORK
WHO COULD ADD VALUE TO THEIR WORK/LIFE

1. _____

2. _____

3. _____

4. _____

5. _____

people who send you
referrals, give advice, &
anything else helpful

Written Exercise 11B

The six degrees of separation theory says that you are only six people away from the person or information you need. (In your field, your degrees of separation from anyone you need or want to connect with are even fewer.)

Everyone you meet has the potential to connect you (through his network and his contacts' networks) to someone or some piece of information that you need. So step out of your comfort zone and make a sincere effort to connect with people you might not normally interact with. The more diverse your network of connections, the more powerful and effective your network becomes. It opens doors that might otherwise remain closed.

EXPAND YOUR NETWORK

Use the visual worksheet on the next page for the following exercise.

1. Think of the types of people or professions that are not represented in your current network. List five that would expand and benefit your network.

2. Next, list ideas for where you might find them. What industry conferences might they attend? Of what organizations might they be members? Are they findable in an online social network? Which ones? Who do you know who could connect you with someone in that profession?

EXPAND YOUR NETWORK

STEP OUT OF YOUR COMFORT ZONE
& CONNECT WITH NEW PEOPLE, GROUPS, & PROFESSIONS

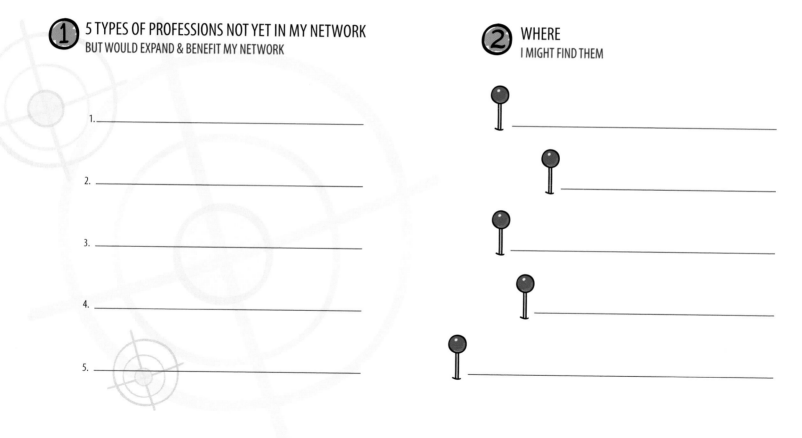

1 5 TYPES OF PROFESSIONS NOT YET IN MY NETWORK
BUT WOULD EXPAND & BENEFIT MY NETWORK

1. _____

2. _____

3. _____

4. _____

5. _____

2 WHERE
I MIGHT FIND THEM

Your World Is Bigger Than You Think

Every once in a while I get some push-back about sharing your network that goes something like this: "But, Michael, I don't know that many people, so this won't work for me." Not so fast, my big thinking friend. Criss Ittermann, a business owner who took one of my courses, showed me how you can create 45 connections from a network of only 10 people. Bump it up to 20 people and you've got 190 connections. It seems like funny math but it's not. It's factorial math (whatever that is).

Here's how it works for just 10 people.

Introduce person 1 to persons 2 to 10.

That's 9 connections.

Person 2 has met person 1, but needs to meet persons 3 to 10.

That's 8 connections.

Person 3 has now met persons 1 and 2 and needs to meet persons 4 to 10.

That's 7 connections.

Person 4 has now met persons 1 to 3 and needs to meet persons 5 to 10.

That's 6 connections.

Person 5 has now met persons 1 to 4 and needs to meet persons 6 to 10.

That's 5 connections.

Person 6 has now met persons 1 to 5 and needs to meet persons 7 to 10.

That's 4 connections.

Person 7 has now met persons 1 to 6 and needs to meet persons 8 to 10.

That's 3 connections.

Person 8 has now met persons 1 to 7 and needs to meet persons 9 to 10.

That's 2 connections.

Person 9 has now met persons 1 to 8 and needs to meet person 10.

That's 1 connection.

That's a total of 45 connections created out of only 10 people.

If you start with 20 people, you end up with 190 connections because $19 + 18 + 17 + 16 + 15 + 14 + 13 + 12 + 11 + 10 + 9 + 8 + 7 + 6 + 5 + 4 + 3 + 2 + 1 = 190$.

Your world is much bigger than you might think. If your eyes gloss over with this math stuff, no worries. The Book Yourself Solid® software will do this funny factorial math for you. Find out more at www.solid.ly.

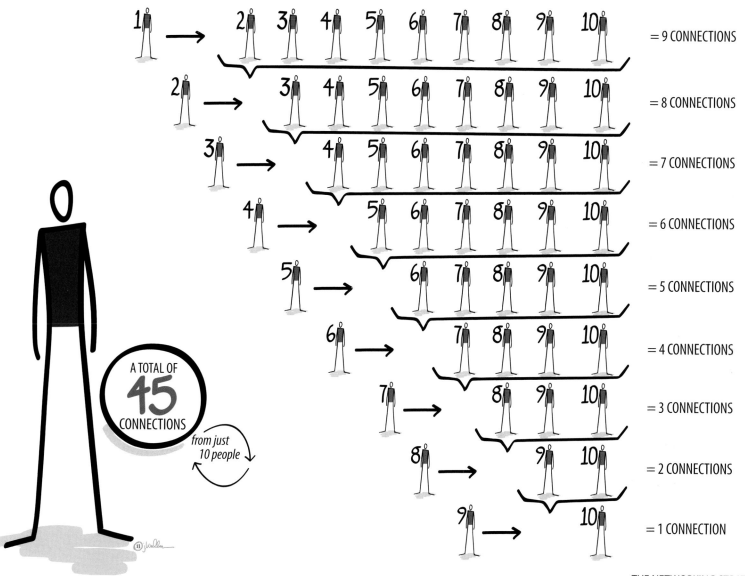

1 → 2 3 4 5 6 7 8 9 10 = 9 CONNECTIONS

2 → 3 4 5 6 7 8 9 10 = 8 CONNECTIONS

3 → 4 5 6 7 8 9 10 = 7 CONNECTIONS

4 → 5 6 7 8 9 10 = 6 CONNECTIONS

5 → 6 7 8 9 10 = 5 CONNECTIONS

6 → 7 8 9 10 = 4 CONNECTIONS

7 → 8 9 10 = 3 CONNECTIONS

8 → 9 10 = 2 CONNECTIONS

9 → 10 = 1 CONNECTION

A TOTAL OF 45 CONNECTIONS

from just 10 people

Share What You Know

I recommend books all the time, and I'm often asked, "How do you read so much?" which always makes me smile because, when I was a kid, my father was worried that I wasn't going to amount to much because he couldn't get me to read beyond the Hardy Boys. But now I read about two books per month. What changed? I realized that the answers to most of my questions are offered in books. Even better, I get to choose what I learn and from whom. Then armed with this information, I am in a great place to share it with others.

You may be thinking, "But if I'm always referring to other people's work, won't they just forget about me and get everything they need from the book or resource I referenced?" Good question. First of all, if they love the book or information that you referred them to, it's highly likely they'll associate much of that value with you. They will feel connected to you because you helped them achieve a goal or change their life or simply learn something new, the value of which is not to be underestimated. The more knowledgeable you are, and are perceived to be, the more trust and credibility you'll build in your network. Reading books is, by far, the best and most efficient way to increase your knowledge.

Reading a book on a topic that is related to the services you provide offers an easy way to start a conversation with potential clients or contacts. In fact, they may start the conversation with you instead with one simple question, "What are you reading?" Think about it; you're constantly bumped, pushed, and shoved by people you don't know. If you have a book in your hand, what do you think this conversation is going to be about? You guessed it—the book. And what better way to get into your Book Yourself Solid Dialogue than to explain why you're reading the particular book you're holding in your hand.

Of course, this doesn't just apply to New York subway cars. Everywhere you go you're running into, meeting, and connecting with other people. What if you always had a book in your hand that allowed you to share what you know about your particular area of expertise, for the betterment of the person you're talking with? I know that not every person you meet or run into is a member of your target market, or at first thought, can send you clients, but it doesn't matter. You're just finding opportunities to add value to those you meet by sharing what you know—as long as it's relevant to them.

BOOKED SOLID ACTION STEP: Try it with this book. Carry it wherever you go. I know the book is huge but it'll build up your muscles, so suck it up and explain to people why you're reading it. You'll have the opportunity to talk about the Book Yourself Solid philosophy of giving so much value that you think you've gone too far and then giving more, and how it's in sync with your values and what you do as a service provider. You'll then be able to get into your Book Yourself Solid Dialogue with ease.

Ask yourself what knowledge, once acquired, would add the greatest value and make you more attractive to potential clients and business partners, and then go after learning it. Your investment in books—buying them and reading them—will pay dividends you can't even imagine.

SHARE WHAT YOU KNOW.

Written Exercise 11C

GET KNOWLEDGE, SHARE KNOWLEDGE

List five books you've read that you know are must-reads for your target market. Think about and jot down the names of any specific people who come to mind for each book.

RECOMMENDED READS THAT ADD VALUE TO YOUR PEEPS

List five books that have been recommended to you as must-reads or that you know contain information that would add value to your target market. Then go out and make the investment in at least one this week.

MUST-READ BOOKS FOR MY TARGET:

1. _____
2. _____
3. _____
4. _____
5. _____

WHO THIS BOOK MIGHT HELP:

_____

_____

_____

_____

_____

RECOMMENDED BOOKS FOR ME TO READ:

1. _____
2. _____
3. _____
4. _____
5. _____

IF I READ IT, WHO I CAN HELP:

_____

_____

_____

_____

_____

IKEBANA

Books aren't our only source of knowledge. Our life experience, observations, and conversations are as well. Think about the many areas in which you're knowledgeable and list a minimum of five. Have fun with this. If you know a lot about skydiving, or ikebana (the Japanese art of flower arranging), include them! You never know what subject might help make a connection.

AREAS IN WHICH I AM KNOWLEDGEABLE: **WHO THIS MIGHT HELP:**

1.

2.

3.

4.

5.

I Saw This Article & Immediately Thought of You

Let's take it up a notch. Once per week, send a book to someone with whom you'd like to develop a meaningful business relationship. Include a nice card with a note about why you're sending them the book—what it's meant to you and why you think it'll be valuable to them. Follow up three weeks later by phone to see how they're enjoying the book. This strategy is especially beneficial for those who are not particularly comfortable with small talk because now you've got something to talk about.

Now, let's take it up one more notch. Sharing magazine, journal, and newspaper articles can work even better than books because the recipient of the information can consume it so quickly. Each day, send personally or professionally relevant articles to three people in your network. I know what you're thinking, Michael, c'mon, how much time is that going to take? What do you think, I'm just sitting around with nothing to do? No, of course not. I know how busy you are. That's why the Book Yourself Solid® marketing software is so valuable.

For example, if you've tagged Bob as someone who owns a small engineering business and focuses on high technology, and Monday morning the *New York Times* publishes an article about the state of the high-tech engineering industry, you'll be able to send the article to Bob before he even turns on his computer. Your e-mail will include a link to the article and a little note that says, "Good Morning, Bob. I saw this article and immediately thought of you. Wonder if you've seen it? Pretty interesting when the author says that. . . ." You might just make Bob's day by sharing some very relevant and timely information that he might have otherwise missed. Not to mention, that Bob is going to feel so fortunate you're out in the world thinking about him and his needs. Of course, you can do this the old-fashioned way and just read the relevant publications on your list each day and then decide to whom you are going to send various articles and then make note of it in your address book. Doing this with three different articles for three different people manually usually takes about an hour. Doing it with www.solid.ly usually takes about 10 minutes.

BOOKED SOLID ACTION STEP: Try it now. Go to your favorite online publication, browse through today's articles and when you find one that is relevant to someone in your network, send it to them with a note as suggested earlier. Or, go set up your www.solid.ly account now, and let the program do it for you.

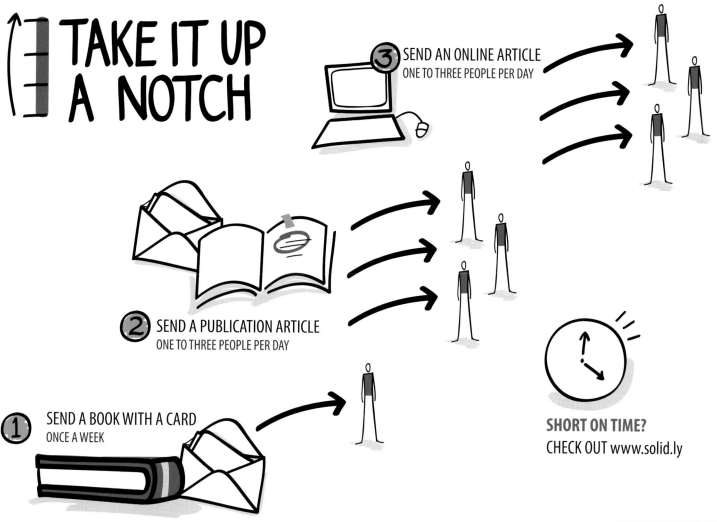

TAKE IT UP A NOTCH

3 SEND AN ONLINE ARTICLE
ONE TO THREE PEOPLE PER DAY

2 SEND A PUBLICATION ARTICLE
ONE TO THREE PEOPLE PER DAY

1 SEND A BOOK WITH A CARD
ONCE A WEEK

SHORT ON TIME?
CHECK OUT www.solid.ly

Share How You Feel

In a business like yours that is based on service, people will generally not hire you unless they feel you have compassion for what they're going through. Expressing that compassion is the first step to a successful working relationship. How do you do that? Listen attentively. Be fully present when making connections, smile as often as possible, make eye contact, and ask engaging, open-ended questions that express your curiosity and interest.

Take the time to add value to the person you're connecting with by offering information or resources that speak to her needs. If you don't have what she needs, think about who in your network would meet her needs and how to go about acting as the link for them. Remember, this is done with no expectation of any immediate return.

BOOKED SOLID ACTION STEP: Note a recent situation, business or personal, when someone else expressed compassion for you. Think about how you felt following the interaction. How do you feel about that person because of the compassion she showed for you?

Can sharing your compassion be a marketing tactic? Absolutely. Do you do it manipulatively or to try to gain some favor? No, that is not the Book Yourself Solid way. You can be deliberate and developmental in the way that you share your compassion—that's not manipulative!

At least once per week, send a card or e-mail to someone in your network just to share your compassion. If you know he's going through a difficult time, send a note expressing sympathy. If he's just been honored with an award, shower him with praise. If he recently experienced a family triumph, like the marriage of a child, congratulate him. These simple, yet powerful, gestures make people thankful to know you. It keeps you at the top of their mind. And, most important, you're making other people feel better about who they are and what they do.

These Booked Solid Action Steps are your new daily and weekly networking activities and you don't even need to leave the house to get them done.

- You'll share your network by introducing two people each day who may benefit from meeting each together. You'll come across as a real connector, someone who thinks about the needs of others, and that's an amazingly attractive quality.

- You'll share what you know by sending one book per week, and three articles per day, to important networking partners. It'll make you look like a smartypants, give you something to talk to them about, and in the process build your relationship.

- You'll share your compassion with one person in your network each day, making her feel better about herself and in the process thankful that she knows you.

These simple, yet meaningful, networking strategies will get, and keep, you booked solid for many years to come. You just have to do it—each and every business day.

SHARE HOW YOU FEEL.

The Possibilities Are Endless

The possibilities for meeting people are endless. Any time you're sharing your connections, knowledge, and compassion, you're networking. Any time you're learning more about what others do and know, you're networking. Anytime you link or connect two people you know, you're networking.

INFORMAL NETWORKING

These are the ones that we might not think of as networking but that we can't afford to overlook. We have dozens of these every day:

- Casual chat in line at the grocery store.
- While checking out videos at your local video store.
- Speaking with your neighbor while walking your dog.

Let's take the neighbor you see while walking your dog as an example. Every day you walk the same path with your dog. Each time, you smile and chat with your neighbor as your dogs sniff each other. After a while you begin to greet one another by name, and you know enough about him to ask after his family. He mentions he was looking forward to a special evening out with his wife the following night for their anniversary but then sighs and says, "But our babysitter canceled at the last minute. I wish [one of the phrases to always be listening for] that I knew of a good backup to call." You recall that your friend Sally seems to know every sitter in town. You pull out your phone, look up her number, and give her a call. "Sally, meet Bob. He's looking for a great sitter for tomorrow night, and you know everyone, so of course I thought you might be able to help," you say as you hand your cell phone to Bob.

Now this exchange has absolutely nothing to do with business, or does it? On the surface it has nothing to do with business. However, who do you think Bob is going to call when he, or someone he knows, needs your services? Bob is thrilled with you because you've saved his special night out. And Sally is pleased too because you've given her high praise and allowed her to show off her knowledge of who's who in the world of local babysitters. Both of them feel better following their interaction with you, and that makes you memorable. And most important, you've increased your connection factor with each of them. Your connection factor is how much trust you've built with each person in your network. The more value you add to a person's life, the more she is going to trust you.

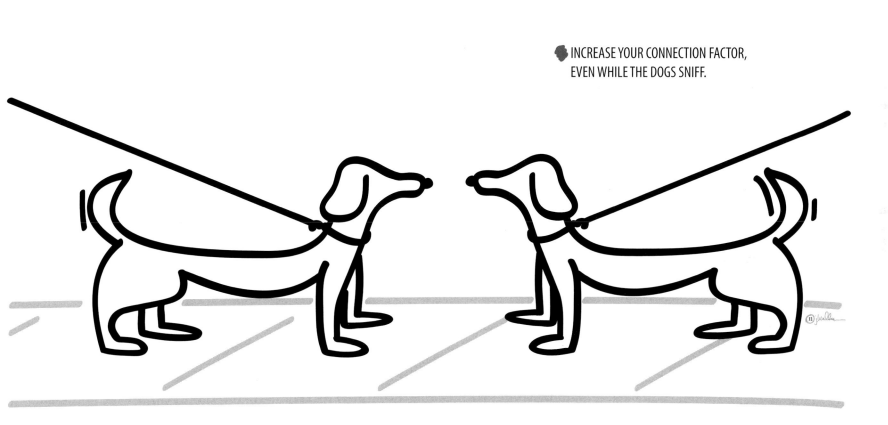

INCREASE YOUR CONNECTION FACTOR,
EVEN WHILE THE DOGS SNIFF.

Written Exercise 11D

INFORMAL NETWORKING

Think for a moment: Have you recently missed any opportunities for making a deeper connection with someone? Using the visual worksheet on the next page, list five informal connections that would have been made if you had just shared your knowledge, your network, or your compassion.

Do you see any patterns? I'm guessing there are places you go and people you see on a regular basis, but you haven't been in the mind-set of intentionally connecting in this way. When you do, you'll add value and watch your network grow.

FORMAL NETWORKING

These are the more formal, business meet-and-greet opportunities that can be fun and enjoyable and offer great rewards:

- Toastmasters International.
- Chamber of Commerce meetings.
- Networking or leads groups—for example, Business Network International.
- Trade association meetings.

Do some research and come up with five business networking opportunities like the ones I've listed that you can attend with the intention of adding value to others as well as enhancing your network.

INFORMAL & FORMAL NETWORKING

LIST OPPORTUNITIES FOR CONNECTIONS IN BOTH INFORMAL
& FORMAL SETTINGS THAT WILL ADD VALUE & ENHANCE YOUR NETWORK

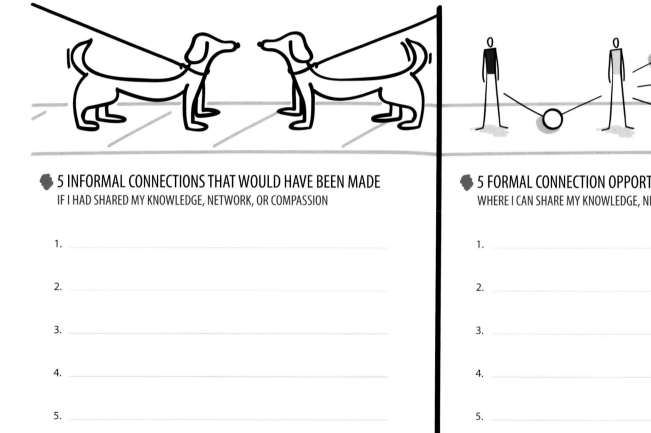

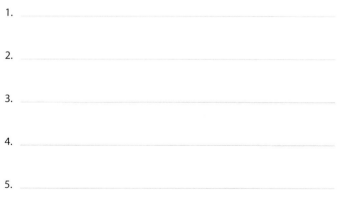

5 INFORMAL CONNECTIONS THAT WOULD HAVE BEEN MADE
IF I HAD SHARED MY KNOWLEDGE, NETWORK, OR COMPASSION

1.

2.

3.

4.

5.

5 FORMAL CONNECTION OPPORTUNITIES
WHERE I CAN SHARE MY KNOWLEDGE, NETWORK, OR COMPASSION

1.

2.

3.

4.

5.

Networking Events—What to Do

- **RELAX AND BE YOURSELF.** Contrary to conventional wisdom, you don't have to fit in. It may sound trite, but be yourself, unless when you're being yourself you end the evening with your tie wrapped around your head doing a nosedive into the shrimp salad. Seriously, people want to meet the person who is out in front, who is writing the rules and taking the lead, not the one who is following the pack. So don't be afraid to be fully self-expressed. If you are, you'll be more memorable.

- **FOCUS ON GIVING.** If your focus is on giving of yourself, you're going to get returns in spades. If you focus on what you can get, you will be much less successful.

- **INTRODUCE YOURSELF TO THE PERSON HOSTING THE EVENT.** This person may be a very valuable addition to your network. Never forget to say, "Thank you."

- **PREPARE FOR THE EVENT.** Learn the names of the organizers and some of the key players. Identify what and how you can share with others at the function: who you know (without being a name dropper), what you know (without being a know-it-all), and what you can share from your heart (without making assumptions) with the people who will be at this particular event. You never know what might change someone's life.

- **INTRODUCE YOURSELF TO THE BIGWIG.** If there's someone you want to meet at a big seminar or event, someone famous in your industry, do you go up to her and say, "Here's what I do and here's my business card"? No! You start by offering praise. You say, "I just want to tell you your work had a great effect on me," or "Your work inspired me to do this or that." Then the next time you are at the same event, you can say, "I'd love to assist you in some way that adds value to your life or your work. I know I would learn a lot from you in the meantime."

- **OFFER PRAISE OR SHARE HELPFUL INFO.** When first meeting someone, whenever possible, offer praise, compassion, or a connection. When you can say, "I know someone you have to meet," or "There's a great book I think may offer the solution to your problem," he is going to see you very differently from the person who shoved a business card in his face and said, "Let's stay in touch, dude." If you can leave him feeling even better, more uplifted, and energized after his interaction with you, he's going to remember you.

- **START CONVERSATIONS BY ASKING QUESTIONS.** This is a great approach, especially if you're nervous. It takes the spotlight off you and allows the other person to shine. It allows you to learn something new at the same time.

- **TAKE THE INITIATIVE.** Go up to people and make friends. People love to be asked about themselves, their hobbies, or their family. This is the time to get to know a few personal tidbits that will give you the opportunity to find a common interest that makes connecting easier and more natural.

- **BE INCLUSIVE.** Ask others to join your conversations; this is very important. Don't monopolize people, especially those who are in high demand, like the speaker from the event. It makes the speaker uncomfortable. Remember, she's there to meet lots of people too. It also annoys others who want to meet the person you're trying to keep to yourself. Tip: If you want to be helpful, ask the speaker if there is anybody you can introduce her to, or simply be sure to keep including people in your conversations with her. This way, you'll be seen as a very generous and open person by the others at the event, and the speaker will remember you as someone who helped her easily network and navigate the event.

- **ASK FOR A BUSINESS CARD AND THEN KEEP IN TOUCH.** It's your responsibility to ask for a card if you want one, and it's your responsibility to follow up. Quality, not quantity, counts when making genuine personal connections. If you race through an event passing out and collecting business cards from anyone and everyone as though there were a prize for the most cards gained at the end of the event, you'll do yourself a huge disservice. And remember, just because someone gives you his business card does not mean you have permission to add him to your mailing list or e-zine list. You do not. You can certainly send a personal e-mail as a follow-up, and you should, but you should not and cannot add him to your list. You don't have permission to do so.

Networking Events—What Not to Do

- **DON'T TRY TO BE COOL.** And don't overcompensate for your nervousness by bragging about your success; this is a major turnoff.

- **DON'T LET "WHAT DO YOU DO?" BE THE FIRST QUESTION YOU ASK.** Let it come up naturally in conversation. Instead, ask them why they decided to attend the event. Then ask questions that will draw out their story. For example, "What made you decide to get into the _____ business?"

- **DON'T SIT WITH PEOPLE YOU ALREADY KNOW FOR MOST OF THE EVENT.** While it may be more comfortable to sit with the people you know, it becomes too easy to stay with them, and if you do, you'll defeat the purpose of being there. Step out of your comfort zone and get to know new people.

- **DON'T JUGGLE MULTIPLE ITEMS.** Travel light to eliminate the necessity of juggling your coat, purse, briefcase, drink, or buffet plate. Keep that right hand free for handshakes and for jotting down quick notes on business cards.

- **DON'T COMPLAIN ABOUT NETWORKING OR THE EVENT YOU ARE ATTENDING.** While complaining is an icebreaker, it's not an attractive one. Change the subject—for example, "Have you tried the shrimp?"

- **DON'T DRINK TOO MUCH.** Some drink one too many in hopes they will gain some courage, but slurring while you hiccup through your introduction won't make the best first impression. Opt for a lemon water and you'll be glad you did.

DON'T TRY TO BE COOL, DRINK TOO MUCH, OR JUGGLE MULTIPLE ITEMS.

So You've Got Spinach in Your Teeth

I've given you a lot of techniques in this chapter about what to do, what not to do, and how to interact with others when you're networking, but there's a big difference between techniques and principles, and it's the principles that are most important to remember and begin implementing. If you can incorporate the principles, you'll naturally do well.

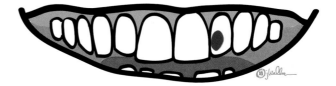

For example, everyone says when you meet people at a networking event you're supposed to look that person in the eye, give them a firm handshake, smile, and nod your head, but if you do that and don't take the giver's stance, it won't matter how slick you are. However, if you always take the giver's stance and share who you know, what you know, and how you feel, even if you have spinach in your teeth and your palm is sweaty, you'll be fine, because people are going to respond to who you are as a human being. In fact, they'll share their compassion with you by gently letting you know about the large piece of spinach entrenched between your teeth.

You Are Always Networking

Profits will come from connections with people who can send you business—whether that's by way of a satisfied client who refers others to you; or another professional who has the ability to book you for speaking engagements, write about you, or partner with you; or the manager at the video store who appreciates your big, friendly smile each weekend and the recommendation you made for a great babysitter when he desperately needed one.

With the Book Yourself Solid Networking Strategy, the prospect of creating a phenomenal network of connections doesn't have to be overwhelming or intimidating. We all connect constantly, with everyone, every day. Now we just need to do it consciously, with greater awareness, until doing so becomes a natural and comfortable part of our daily lives.

Then follow up. Keep in touch. It is imperative that you get every one of your connections into your database and act on each connection. If the contact isn't in your database or you don't take the action necessary to keep in touch, your networking is pointless.

So what do you think? Are you ready to network your way to more clients, more profit, and deeper connections with people? Sharing your knowledge, your network, and your compassion will bring you one step closer to being booked solid.

1 USE THE 50/50 NETWORKING RULE & YOU WILL HAVE MULTIPLE WINNERS

2 SHARE WHO YOU KNOW, WHAT YOU KNOW, & HOW YOU FEEL

TAKE IT UP A NOTCH

3 TAKE IT UP A NOTCH BY SENDING BOOKS & ARTICLES OF INTEREST TO YOUR NETWORK

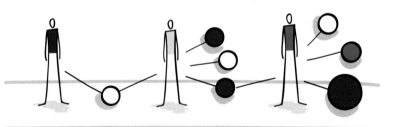

4 USE FORMAL & INFORMAL NETWORKING TO ENHANCE YOUR CONNECTION FACTOR

MODULE FOUR: THE 6 CORE SELF-PROMOTION STRATEGIES
"CRUISING ALTITUDE"

CHAPTER 12

The Book yourself Solid Direct Outreach Strategy

4.12 DIRECT OUTREACH STRATEGY

REACH OUT DIRECTLY TO PROSPECTIVE CLIENTS & REFERRAL PARTNERS WITHOUT BEING PUSHY OR SPAMMY

1 DON'T BE THE NOISE THAT INTERRUPTS THEIR QUIET

2 AVOID SENDING AN OUTREACH MESSAGE THAT BREAKS DOWN

3 USE THE VITL OUTREACH APPROACH TO ENSURE YOUR MESSAGES ARE ACTED UPON

VALUABLE   INDIVIDUALIZED

TARGETED   LEGITIMATE

4 CREATE YOUR BYS LIST OF 20, REACH OUT, TRACK YOUR EFFORTS, & FOLLOW UP

4.12 THE DIRECT OUTREACH STRATEGY

You miss 100 percent of the shots you don't take.

—Wayne Gretzky

As a business owner, you'll need to proactively reach out to potential clients, marketing partners, and other decision makers to create business opportunities.

In fact, the most important direct outreach you do will be to network, cross-promote, and build referral relationships with other service professionals and associations.

You will find yourself using the Book Yourself Solid Direct Outreach Strategy time and time again when you want to reach out to:

- An ideal client or a referral partner within your target market
- The decision maker at an organization or association to cross-promote, secure speaking engagements, submit articles for publication, and more
- The press
- And a myriad of other business development opportunities

Spam Is the Noise That Interrupts Their Quiet

As you know, spam is not the Book Yourself Solid way. It never has been and never will be. Before the advent of the Internet, direct outreach was a very common marketing strategy. I suppose it's no less common today, but unfortunately, it is often perceived as spam. You must be very careful and discerning with respect to how you contact others.

Spam has typically been considered unsolicited mail or e-mail, sent, without permission, to mailing lists or news groups. However, I think the way people now see spam has grown in scope and definition. Today, there are many more ways you can be labeled a spammer—even when you think you're standing in the service of potential clients or business associates.

YOU CAN NOW BE LABELED A SPAMMER IF YOU:

- Send an unsolicited e-mail directly to a potential client that contains any kind of sales message or promotional or business offer.

- Cold call. Many people just consider that another kind of spam, since it's unsolicited.

- Use social media. Even direct outreach to an individual through Facebook, Twitter, LinkedIn, and other social media platforms can get you pegged as irrelevant or worse, a spammer. Posting comments on a blog or other social media site, yes, even your friends' Facebook pages, can get you called out for spamming if they smack of self-promotion.

YOU DON'T FIND THEM—THEY NOW FIND YOU

Clients now find you. That doesn't relieve you of your marketing responsibilities. You need to create awareness for what you offer so that when potential clients go looking for the kind of services you offer they find you. Google has changed the way customers and businesses interact. When people go searching online they're willing to wade through junk in search of what they want because they feel in control of the process. When they find what they want, and if it's you, they'll give you permission to market to them.

WE HAVE TO EARN THEIR ATTENTION, NOT DEMAND IT

My colleague Seth Godin, the father of Permission Marketing, puts it this way, "Go ahead and make what you want, as long as you stand behind it and don't bother me. If you want to sell magnetic bracelets or put risque pictures on your web site, it's your responsibility, your choice. Want to find a web site featuring donkeys, naked jugglers, and various illicit acts? It's junk, sure, but it's out there. You just have to go find it. Junk turns into spam when you show up at my doorstep, when your noise interrupts my quiet."

This is why, even though it's easier than ever to make noise and get noticed, direct outreach has become trickier than ever. When you reach out, unsolicited, to a potential client or business associate about a business opportunity, their default assumption is that you're a spammer interrupting their peace and quiet. Is it fair? Doesn't matter. Until there's a cure for selfishness, one that eliminates spammers and their spam, it's the reality that you and I have to deal with. Don't make noise that interrupts others' quiet.

THEY WON'T LISTEN TO UNSOLICITED OUTREACH

Do I Know You?

Sometimes the easiest way to understand a concept is to see real examples of what works and what doesn't. I don't want to scare you off from doing direct outreach. Just the opposite—I want to encourage you to do more of it, but in a way that will make sure you come across as a thoughtful, considerate, empathetic, relevant, and high integrity professional with value to add.

To make sure you're always perceived this way, I'm going to show you a series of direct outreach messages sent to me that went terribly wrong. I've changed the names of all involved to protect the innocent, but the following are actual messages from real people. In fact, I'm pretty sure they were sent by decent, hard-working professionals. Unfortunately, they haven't yet learned how to do direct outreach and, as a result, their messages broke down like a stockcar that missed a pit stop.

Let's start with this broken-down attempt, which landed in my LinkedIn inbox.

DIRECT OUTREACH (BAD) EXAMPLE #1

LinkedIn Recommendations

Maria Venter is requesting an endorsement for work.

Dear Michael,

I'm sending this to ask you for a brief recommendation of my work that I can include in my LinkedIn profile. If you have any questions, let me know. Thanks in advance for helping me out.

—Maria Venter

Endorse Maria Venter. It only takes a minute. Your endorsement can help Maria Venter:

- Hire and get hired
- Win customers and partnerships
- Build a stronger professional reputation

This e-mail was sent to you by Maria Venter (email@website.com) through LinkedIn because Maria Venter entered your e-mail address. If you have any questions, please contact customer_service@linkedin.com.

WHY MARIA'S REQUEST IS PROBLEMATIC:

1. Let's start with the fact that I don't know her.

2. If I don't know Maria, why would I recommend she get hired, win customers and partnerships, and build a stronger professional reputation?

3. To send it, all she had to do was enter my e-mail address. Clearly no effort was demonstrated on her part.

4. My LinkedIn profile states that I don't check e-mail at LinkedIn. Rather, I request that people e-mail me at a public e-mail address, which I list.

WHAT SHOULD MARIA HAVE DONE INSTEAD?

1. She could have started by giving me a recommendation first, if she thought I deserved one. Always better to offer something before asking for something.

2. If it was important to her that we connect, she could have attempted to meet me at an event, if it was convenient for her.

3. She could have commented on my blog posts or notes on my LinkedIn profile or Facebook Fan Page. This would have been noticed and appreciated.

4. She could have sent me an e-mail to my public e-mail address expressing some appreciation for my work or find some other way of making a personal connection through any number of other activities that don't ask for anything in return and don't make any assumptions.

My suggestions have nothing to do with professional status. I would approach anyone this way. Of course, if the person you're reaching out to is already familiar with your work or your name, the connecting process usually speeds up. And, if you're thinking that it's just novice business owners whose direct outreach goes wrong, think again.

YOUR OUTREACH MESSAGES WILL BREAK DOWN IF YOU TAKE THE WRONG APPROACH.

Form Letters Will Crash and Burn

This next e-mail is from a publicity and promotions manager at a marketing firm that represents authors and large publishing houses. I don't know the sender or the author and have no connection to the publisher of the book. Again, I've changed the names of all parties involved.

What's so bad about a PR or marketing firm reaching out to an author to see if he'll help promote another author? Nothing. Nothing at all. In fact, one of the primary ways authors get noticed is through promotion from other authors.

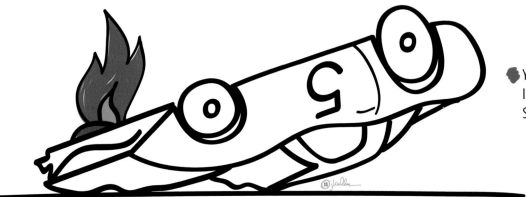

YOU'LL CRASH AND BURN IF YOUR FIRST OUTREACH SMACKS OF SELF-PROMOTION.

DIRECT OUTREACH (BAD) EXAMPLE #2

Dear Mr. Port,

I have not heard back from you on my e-mail below. This is a great opportunity to get your products out in front of a huge audience looking for this kind of material (our previous book campaign was seen by over 5 million people)! Not only will you be offering your subscribers an incredible package, you will also be directing more traffic to your web site and building your own mailing list. Remember, there is no cost involved.

Click on the link below to view a previous campaign we put together for John Smith's *New York Times* bestselling book, XXXXXX:

http://www.longurltoasalespage.com

Please let me know right away if you would like to participate or if you have any questions.

Thank you,

Andrea Tiffonelli

Assistant Publicity and Promotions Manager

Progressive Marketing Firm, Inc.

A Better Way to Make First Contact

Now, let's show you what that better alternative looks like. Notice in the example at right, she keeps her first letter brief. Hallelujah! I might actually read it if it's short. Next, notice how Andrea tells me who she is right away? Very clear. I don't have to work to figure out who she is, what she does, or whom she represents.

In her second paragraph, Andrea includes a personal message indicating to me that 1) she isn't sending me a spammy form letter; 2) she has read at least some of my work, and she knows why I do what I do.

Lastly, Andrea doesn't ask me for anything in her first correspondence. She just introduces herself and asks if she can do anything for me. Home run, Andrea.

WHEN YOUR FIRST OUTREACH
FOCUSES ON THEM IN A PERSONAL WAY,
IT'S A MUCH SMOOTHER RIDE FOR EVERYONE.

DIRECT OUTREACH: THE BETTER ALTERNATIVE FOR EXAMPLE #2

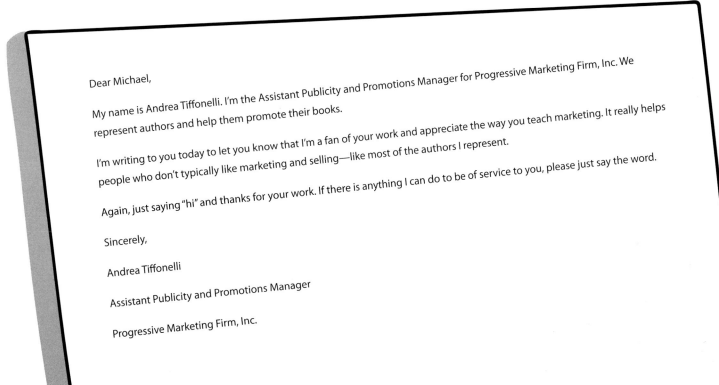

Dear Michael,

My name is Andrea Tiffonelli. I'm the Assistant Publicity and Promotions Manager for Progressive Marketing Firm, Inc. We represent authors and help them promote their books.

I'm writing to you today to let you know that I'm a fan of your work and appreciate the way you teach marketing. It really helps people who don't typically like marketing and selling—like most of the authors I represent.

Again, just saying "hi" and thanks for your work. If there is anything I can do to be of service to you, please just say the word.

Sincerely,

Andrea Tiffonelli

Assistant Publicity and Promotions Manager

Progressive Marketing Firm, Inc.

Don't Be a Poser

Imagine this. A guy named John calls you, and he's done a little homework about you. He seems to know what you do and what you stand for. After a little small talk, he implies he is interested in your services, and asks if you would be willing to meet for coffee so that he could learn more. You say sure, and arrange the time and place.

You arrive, get a cup of joe, and after a little chit-chat you ask, "Well, John, what questions do you have for me?"

Then he proceeds to go into a sales pitch about his own business, and claims that you need what he sells.

Excuse me?

This is not direct outreach the Book Yourself Solid way. If you think all you need to do is get in front of a person and then you'll "close the sale," you are sorely mistaken. Don't mislead or pose as someone who is interested in another's services, when you are only interested in your own.

THE COFFEE GETS COLD FAST IF YOU LIE ABOUT WHY YOU WANTED TO MEET.

Avoid Desperate Outreach Measures

There are lots of different tools that you can use to reach out to other people. You can write e-mails, letters, or postcards. You can reach out to people through social media sites including, but not limited to, Facebook, Twitter, and LinkedIn. You can use the phone. And you can do what I call the whatever-it-takes direct outreach, as long as it doesn't get you arrested; like parachuting into the backyard of the CEO of Google because you think you have a great service to offer his company. It will get you noticed but not in a good way.

● SOME STUNTS WILL GET YOU NOTICED, BUT NOT ALWAYS IN A GOOD WAY.

These tools can be instruments with which you can make beautiful music or they can be weapons of mass destruction. It just depends on how you use them. My mantra is Winston Churchill's quote: "It is a mistake to look too far ahead. Only one link of the chain of destiny can be handled at a time." Keep that on the top of your mind as you progress through the direct outreach process and you'll be able to avoid desperate direct outreach measures. You'll build trust over time instead and end up swimming in success.

When reaching out to others, you'll go through multiple stages of relationship development. At each stage of the process you'll, hopefully, build more trust and earn more credibility with your new friend, much like the Book Yourself Solid Sales Cycle Process that you learned in Chapter 6. And, just like the sales cycle, no relationship will develop in the exact same way. There isn't a secret formula that will guarantee everyone will love you and do exactly as you wish but there is a way to know whom to contact when, how to make contact, and whether to do it again—and the method requires a well-developed social intelligence.

You Will Connect More When You've Got the Skinny

It doesn't matter if you are prospecting, door knocking, outreaching, introducing, or just plain canvassing. If you do any or all of these without knowing the person or business you are contacting, you'll find yourself winded, your time wasted, or your wares unwanted. No one wants to feel like a cheesy, shady, pushy, or unprepared salesperson.

So, you say you want to create a never-ending pool of heartwarming and bank account–filling clients? You want to get booked solid? Then, do me a favor. Show up front, center, and in the know with all the people you want to know. There's no minimizing your overall effectiveness and confidence when you're packin' preparation. So find out ….

1. **WHAT MOTIVATES THE PERSON?** What really gets the person's juices flowing? What makes his eyes sparkle? It might be business, family, or hobbies. Look at the photos, books, and other things sitting on or near his desk or on his web site or social media pages. What is he reading, referring to others, or genuinely interested in?

2. **WHAT HAS THE PERSON ACCOMPLISHED?** Do an online search. Go to her site and do a Google Image search if you don't know what her smiling face looks like yet. Who is singing her praises? Has she won awards, received acknowledgments, public recognition, or publication announcements?

3. **WHAT COMMON INTERESTS MIGHT YOU HAVE?** How have your paths crossed? Express your compassion, enthusiasm, and understanding for these shared interests. Keep your focus coming back to the person. Use these common interests as a starting place to learn more about how they feel and think about the world.

4. **WHO ARE THE PERSON'S PEERS?** Do you have any mutual friends or social circle overlap? Do you have common Facebook friends or Twitter followers? And, are you involved in these circles? Be informed and stay connected.

5. **WHAT UNIQUE BENEFITS DO YOU OFFER?** What do others love about the way you do business? Be easy. Know your strengths. Show up as the kind of person people love being with and want to do business with.

6. **WHAT EXCITES YOU ABOUT KNOWING OR WORKING WITH THIS PERSON?** We all want to feel appreciated, acknowledged, and respected. Share how the person's work and opinions have influenced or affected you. Stay positive, be yourself, and be complimentary.

7. **WHAT DO YOU BELIEVE IS POSSIBLE FOR THE PERSON?** No matter how confident or successful we appear, all of us have limiting beliefs. Can you see areas of business or life where the person has been holding back? Describe in detail (but keep it to yourself, for now) the true potential you see for the person based on what they want and need. As you get to know each other, you may decide to share what you see.

8. **WHAT IS YOUR CURRENT STATUS OR ROLE IN THE PERSON'S LIFE?** Don't overrate or exaggerate who you are or why the person should work or connect with you. Be realistic about what you bring to the table and how you see the relationship unfolding. The best relationships grow slowly and with a foundation of trust.

9. **HOW CAN YOU BECOME AN INDISPENSABLE ASSET TO THE PERSON?** Do you truly know how and why the person should know or work with you? Do you believe that her life will be happier, easier, fuller, richer, or just plain better with the benefit of you and your services?

YOU'LL BE GIVING HIGH-FIVES IF YOU SHOW UP PREPARED.

Doors Will Slam if You Spam

Sales aren't always sensible. Connecting isn't always cool. Even if your proposition seems picture perfect . . . life, decisions, and relationships are always wrapped up in underlying influences. Some of these foundational influences we can see quickly at first glance, while others take a bit more time.

But, when you show up knowledgeable and prepared, you address the human needs of the people you want to serve, and you are closer to meeting both the other person's needs and your own. You might have a shot at getting what you ask for. Plus, aren't conversations just easier and more fun when you know and share these commonalities? Doors stop slamming. People start playing and they start paying, too.

When initiating your direct outreach strategy, please make sure that your efforts are targeted, individualized, valuable, and legitimate so they are not perceived as spam and are instead appreciated and acted upon.

Using the Book Yourself Solid Direct Outreach Strategy is all about making personal connections. Whichever of the following direct outreach tools you employ, you should be reaching out to others from the heart, in a way that is genuine and authentic for you.

When I was an actor (that was my first career) I had a modicum of success. I appeared in *Sex and the City*, *Third Watch*, *Law & Order*, *All My Children*, *The Pelican Brief*, *Down to Earth*, and many other shows. I also did hundreds of television commercials and voice-overs, but hung up my hat for what I thought was the meaning and stability of a career in the corporate world. Boy was I wrong about the "meaning" thing. Anyhow . . . in my acting days, I recall blowing auditions because I was trying to knock it out of the park. Instead of focusing on getting the callback, I was focusing on getting the part. What I should have done was focus on getting the callback. Then, once I had the callback, work on getting the second callback. Then, once I had the second callback, work to get the producer's meeting. Once I had the producer's meeting, work to get the screen test, and so on. I want you to do the same thing with your direct outreach. Take it one step at a time and you'll do fine, and it will feel more authentic to you.

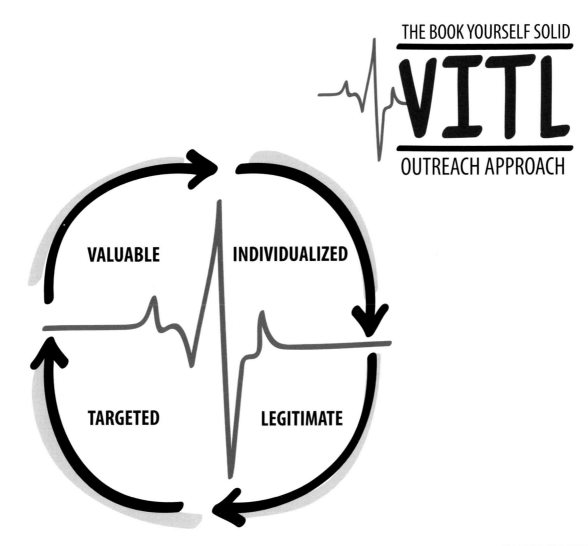

THE BOOK YOURSELF SOLID

VITL

OUTREACH APPROACH

VALUABLE

INDIVIDUALIZED

TARGETED

LEGITIMATE

Social Intelligence: Look Inward, Look Outward

When I'm asked, "What are the best marketing and sales books ever written?" my answer is always the same: "Besides my books?" Kidding. In all seriousness, my answer is, just one: *Social Intelligence: The New Science of Human Relationships*, by Daniel Goleman, a popular science writer. We absolutely need to draw on social neuroscience research to learn how to market and sell professional services. At its core, social intelligence is a person's ability to understand his or her environment and react in a way that creates successful relationships. And successful relationships ensure successful direct outreach.

You may or may not like this concept, depending on your interpretation of self, but your ability to succeed in many entrepreneurial endeavors is, in large part, based on your self-awareness and social savvy. Being able to understand yourself and what's going on with others and then skillfully responding to them is a question of social intelligence, not how many different clever pitches you've memorized or methods you've got on hand to impress.

According to Goleman, humans are wired to connect, neurologically speaking. Holy rapid-fire synapses, Batman! That means you are wired to market and sell!

But the news gets even better. Goleman believes that the ability to connect can be learned, if worked on and developed. Darn-tootin' right, my sharp, big thinker. There's nothing mystical about your direct outreach success. To enhance how you connect with real people in the real world, increase your social intelligence. With diligence, reflection, and the commitment to improve, set aside time to study your:

- **SELF-AWARENESS.** The ability to read your own emotions and recognize their impact on others while using gut feelings to guide decisions.

- **SELF-MANAGEMENT.** Involves controlling your emotions, impulses, and the ability to adapt to changing circumstances.

- **SOCIAL AWARENESS.** Your ability to sense, understand, and react to others' emotions while comprehending social networks.

- **RELATIONSHIP MANAGEMENT.** The ability to inspire, influence, and develop others while managing conflict.

If you want to be more socially intelligent, develop the ability to scan your environment and react in a way that builds relationships. This brand of intelligence is the most important component of your direct outreach strategies.

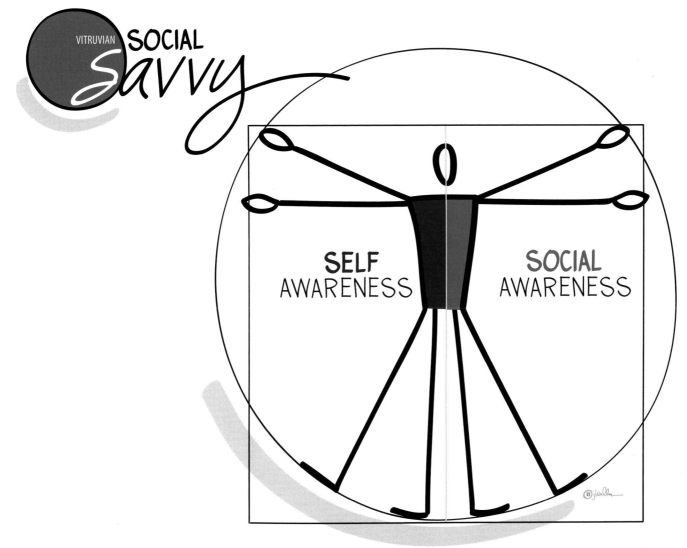

VITRUVIAN SOCIAL *Savvy*

SELF
AWARENESS

SOCIAL
AWARENESS

Written Exercise 12A

THE BOOK YOURSELF SOLID LIST OF 20

The list never leaves your side. It sits on your desk. It lives on your computer and travels with you when you're on the road. Your success is, in large part, determined by the people within your industry who are willing to refer others to you or to put you in front of your ideal clients or endorse you, so you need to keep these people at the top of your mind. Keeping this list by your side will ensure that you're thinking of them and, if you do, you'll begin to notice opportunities to connect with them and get to know them. Twenty is a good number because it's a large enough number to keep your focus expansive but narrow enough that you won't be overwhelmed.

Using the visual worksheet on the next page:

STEP 1: Identify a minimum of three and a maximum of 20 people you'd like to reach out to directly and personally, to develop a professional relationship.

THESE ARE PEOPLE YOU DO NOT YET KNOW, INCLUDING:

- Influencers in your target market
- Prospective clients
- Decision makers at an organization or association
- The press, online and offline publications contacts

At this moment, you might not think you can fill out your list of 20, but now that you know what you need to do, you'll start to take notice of the people you should add to this list. You'll see in a minute how your list will grow far beyond just 20 people.

BOOKED SOLID ACTION STEP: Reach out to the first person on your list of 20 and then add her to your follow-up system. Then add a new person to your list of 20.

BYS LIST OF 20

LIST 20 PEOPLE YOU DO NOT YET KNOW
WHO CAN HELP YOU GET BOOKED SOLID

#	NAME	#	NAME
1.		11.	
2.		12.	
3.		13.	
4.		14.	
5.		15.	
6.		16.	
7.		17.	
8.		18.	
9.		19.	
10.		20.	

Track Your BYS List of 20

In the Book Yourself Solid® marketing software at www.solid.ly, there is a special section for your BYS List of 20. Here's what the software will help you do with your list. (If you're not using the software, make sure you find another way to track this process and create an accountability structure of some sort to make sure you get it done.)

- Each day, the system will prompt you to reach out to the person at the top of the list, giving you options on exactly how to connect with him.

- After you've reached out to this person, the system will place this person in the twentieth spot on the list and prompt you to connect with him again after 20 business days, which is about one month.

- Now that this person has been moved to the end of the list, the person who was Number Two on the list becomes Number One and each other person on the list moves up one spot. This way your list of 20 always stays at 20.

This direct outreach activity occurs every day. You'll reach out to one new person, each and every day, and you'll follow up with people you've already reached out to, each and every day. This is critical. Dedicated, disciplined, and determined action is key to your direct outreach success. Remember, the Book Yourself Solid List of 20 is your wish list. Your list of 20 people who could have a significant impact on your business through their referrals, introductions, and advice. Do this daily and you'll be booked solid in no time flat.

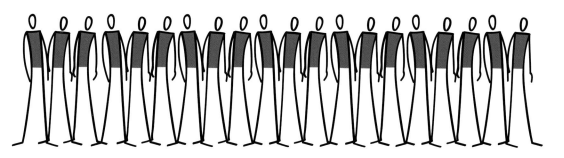

Making Your Case

When you get to the point in a relationship at which it's time to make your case for something you want, usually after the initial courtship, the next step is to expand upon your reason for contacting her and make your case. To do this, there are three things that others take into account, whether consciously or unconsciously, when they consider a proposal you make:

1. Is it going to be successful?

2. Is it worth doing?

3. Is this person able to do what she says she can?

If you get a resounding "Yes!" for each question, you're in. If your reader raises an eyebrow at even one of the questions, you've probably gone as far as you're going to go with this person. For your direct outreach to be effective, all the questions must be answered in the affirmative.

Also, to make sure all your bases are covered, before you make any calls or send out any letters or e-mail, ask yourself the following questions:

- Do I connect with the reader about one of her accomplishments?

- Do I indicate that I will follow up?

- Do I know how I'm going to follow up?

- Am I being direct without pushing?

- Am I being real in the message?

- Am I clear about the next steps?

Whatever-It-Takes Direct Outreach

You can do a lot to grab attention, but attention is only valuable if it shows you off in a light that's flattering. If you're a creative soul with a strong and developed sense of play, you'll have a lot of fun conceiving of and executing no-rules attention-grabbing direct outreach campaigns. Because, yeah, there may be a time when someone you really want to connect with is just not paying attention.

Years ago, when I was a vice president at an entertainment company, I had a boss who swore, literally, every which way till Sunday that I had to get a particular executive at a big cosmetics firm to agree to sponsor one of our programs. The only problem was that the executive wouldn't take my calls. I tried to explain to my boss that I didn't think they were the right fit for us, but he disagreed and directed me to make it happen.

After a few more weeks of trying to get a meeting with the executive, I was about to give up when his assistant, the toughest gatekeeper I'd ever encountered, let slip that the executive was at lunch when I called. Just making pleasant conversation, I asked, "Oh, yeah? What'd he go for today?"

"Chinese, it's his favorite . . ." she replied, without thinking much about it. "Okay, thanks. Have a nice day!" I said and hung up.

The next day I had a great big order of Chinese food delivered to him at that exact same time. Inside the order was the proposal for the project. Twenty minutes after the food had arrived, I called him. This time I was put right through. I said, "Will you take a look at my proposal now?" "No," he answered. "Why not?" I asked. "Because I don't like any of the dishes you sent over." "What do you like?" I asked. He told me. I said, "If I send these over tomorrow, will you read my proposal and take a meeting with me?" He said, "No, but I will read your proposal. If I like it, then I'll take a meeting with you." I said, "Great. When would you like me to follow up?" He told me and we said good-bye.

He did like the proposal and subsequently took a meeting with me, but we never actually made a deal. It turned out that our companies really weren't a good fit, just like I was telling my boss. But we became friendly, and he introduced me to one of my first clients after I had left the corporate world and started my own business. You just never know.

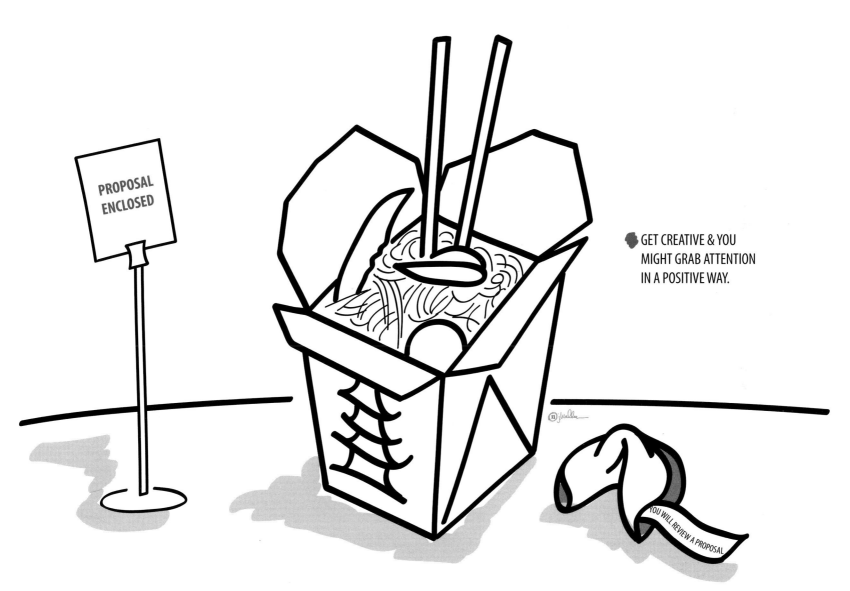

GET CREATIVE & YOU MIGHT GRAB ATTENTION IN A POSITIVE WAY.

Written Exercise 12B

WILD AND WACKY WAYS TO MAKE A CONNECTION

One of my clients was trying to connect with a meeting planner at a large multinational corporation and couldn't get the planner to give him the time of day. After all his other direct outreach attempts had failed, he sent her a coconut with a note that said, "You're a tough nut to crack. How about it?" She was still laughing when she called him to schedule an appointment.

Think creatively about what kind of fun, outrageous, no-rules attention-grabbing direct outreach strategies would work for you. Really let loose and let the ideas flow freely.

STEP 1: List three wild, wacky, and unique ways to make a personal connection, especially with anyone you've been unsuccessful connecting with in the more traditional ways.

WACKY WAYS TO REACH OUT
LIST UNIQUE WAYS TO MAKE
A PERSONAL CONNECTION

① ② ③

The Direct Outreach Plan

There are many ways to connect with potential clients and customers, but none of the concepts I laid out are effective without a plan. After you have identified a person or organization you'd like to reach out to, what do you do? Do you create a plan and then execute the plan? No? Well, that's okay because now you will and you'll be delighted with the success your new plan will bring. Each day, when working with your BYS List of 20, here's how to keep it simple.

1. Identify the individual you're going to reach out to.

2. Choose the steps you'll take to connect with her.

3. Create a schedule for your initiatives.

4. Execute the plan.

5. Evaluate the plan.

PATIENCE AND PERSISTENCE PAY OFF

Remember that there is no trick to direct outreach. The magic formula to direct outreach, if there is one, is a consistent and open course of action throughout the life of your business. Direct outreach, like networking and keeping in touch, is something that must become a part of your regular routine. It takes time, but if you're patient and persistent, you will book yourself solid.

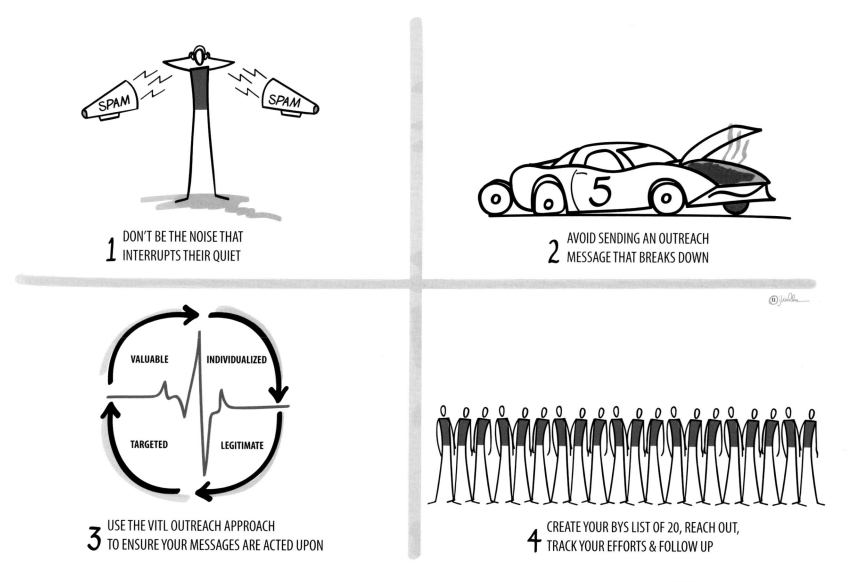

1 DON'T BE THE NOISE THAT INTERRUPTS THEIR QUIET

2 AVOID SENDING AN OUTREACH MESSAGE THAT BREAKS DOWN

VALUABLE INDIVIDUALIZED

TARGETED LEGITIMATE

3 USE THE VITL OUTREACH APPROACH TO ENSURE YOUR MESSAGES ARE ACTED UPON

4 CREATE YOUR BYS LIST OF 20, REACH OUT, TRACK YOUR EFFORTS & FOLLOW UP

MODULE FOUR: THE 6 CORE SELF-PROMOTION STRATEGIES
"CRUISING ALTITUDE"

CHAPTER 13

The Book Yourself Solid Referral Strategy

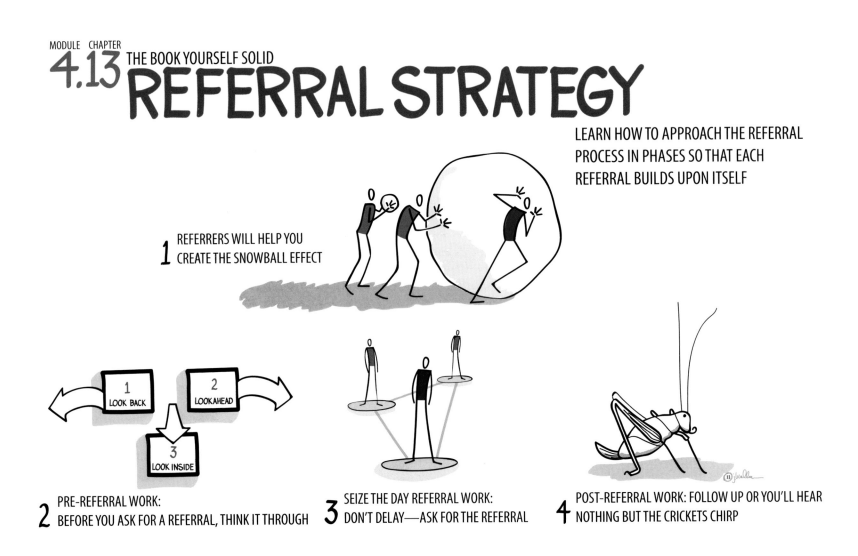

REFERRAL STRATEGY

LEARN HOW TO APPROACH THE REFERRAL
PROCESS IN PHASES SO THAT EACH
REFERRAL BUILDS UPON ITSELF

1 REFERRERS WILL HELP YOU
CREATE THE SNOWBALL EFFECT

1 LOOK BACK

2 LOOKAHEAD

3 LOOK INSIDE

2 PRE-REFERRAL WORK:
BEFORE YOU ASK FOR A REFERRAL, THINK IT THROUGH

3 SEIZE THE DAY REFERRAL WORK:
DON'T DELAY—ASK FOR THE REFERRAL

4 POST-REFERRAL WORK: FOLLOW UP OR YOU'LL HEAR
NOTHING BUT THE CRICKETS CHIRP

4.13 THE REFERRAL STRATEGY

For it is in giving that we receive.

—Saint Francis of Assisi

Imagine enjoying deeper relationships with every client you work with while attracting three or four times as many wonderful new clients as you have right now. It's not only possible but simple and inexpensive. The key lies in generating client referrals. By starting an organized referral program, you can immediately and effortlessly connect with an increasing number of potential new clients.

Referral-generated clients are often more loyal, consistent, and better suited to you than any other category of potential clients you could find.

To do this, the Book Yourself Solid Referral Strategy has four phases:

1. Pre-Referral Work
2. Seize the Day Referral Work
3. Post-Referral Work
4. Ongoing Referral Work

Create the Snowball Effect

Because your clients enjoy and respect working with you, they will be eager to recommend your services and products to their clients, friends, and family. In fact, the vast majority of your new clients already come to you as a result of word-of-mouth referrals, either directly or indirectly.

If I had to, I'd guess that you don't have a program in place to benefit from all the word-of-mouth promotion that you could be receiving. How many referrals do you get without a referral system right now? Now triple or quadruple that number. That is the potential increase in clients you could be working with as early as next month.

The Book Yourself Solid Referral Strategy teaches you how to create this kind of snowball effect through those who know you and believe in you. Rather than leave it to chance, you can be intentional so that your referral quotient builds upon itself, like making a giant snowball.

YOUR REFERRERS WILL HELP YOU CREATE THE SNOWBALL EFFECT IF THEY BELIEVE IN YOU.

Pre-Referral Work: Think Before You Leap

Most small business owners don't put much thought or effort into the pre-work phase of their referral methods. Without this pre-work phase, you could:

- Miss opportunities to identify the right referrers.

- Fail to follow up if you don't have a system to track the referral activity.

- Receive referrals that don't fit your target market or ideal client, which wastes time for everyone.

- Run the risk of damaging the relationship you have with your referrer if you request a referral without thinking it through.

It is simple to increase your referral quotient exponentially, with the Book Yourself Solid Referral Strategy.

The Pre-Referral Work phase of this strategy includes:

1. Look Back: Past Referrals Analysis.

2. Look Ahead: Referral Opportunities Tracking Log.

3. Look Inside: See It From Your Referrer's Point of View.

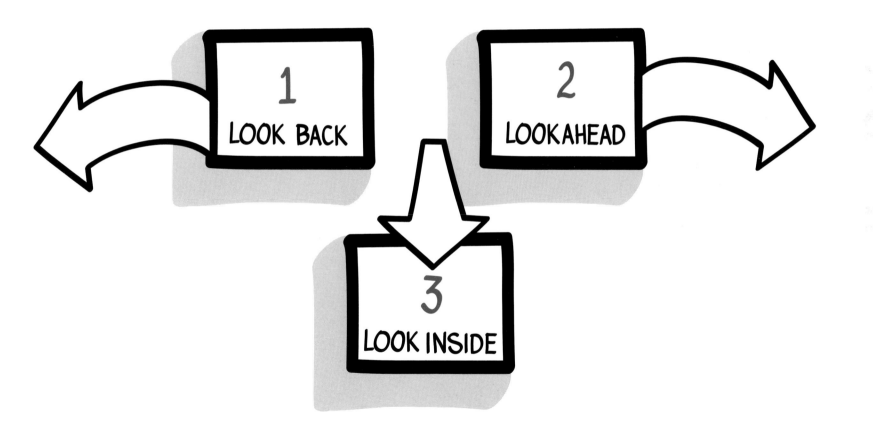

Written Exercise 13A

LOOK BACK: PAST REFERRALS ANALYSIS

Let's look at how you've already received referrals. By identifying a situation in the past where a client or colleague, or someone else altogether, referred a client to you, you will recognize patterns that will help you consistently produce the results you desire.

Use the visual worksheet on the next page for this written exercise. Start by remembering the last time a quality referral came to you:

1. From whom did the referral come?

2. What was the referral for, specifically?

3. Did the referral need your services immediately?

4. How were you contacted—by the person making the referral or the potential client?

5. Had you educated the referrer about your services before he made the referral?

6. How did you accept the referral and follow-up?

7. Is that new referral a continuing client today?

You may have already noticed some of your strengths in generating referrals, or perhaps parts of the process need a little of your attention. Either way, we're creating an easy and profitable process.

REFERRALS—LOOK BACK
ANALYZE PREVIOUS REFERRALS TO DETERMINE BETTER WAYS
TO CONSISTENTLY RECEIVE MORE REFERRALS IN THE FUTURE

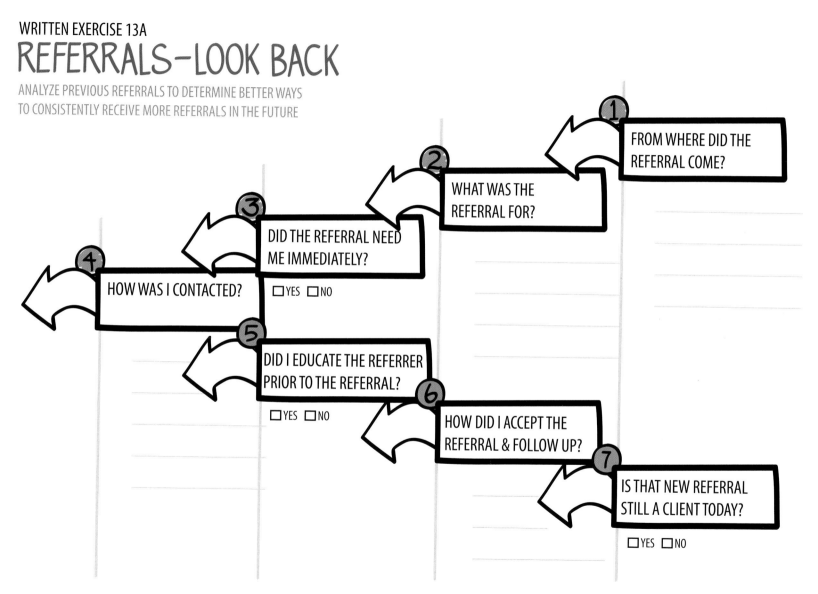

① FROM WHERE DID THE REFERRAL COME?

② WHAT WAS THE REFERRAL FOR?

③ DID THE REFERRAL NEED ME IMMEDIATELY?
☐ YES ☐ NO

④ HOW WAS I CONTACTED?

⑤ DID I EDUCATE THE REFERRER PRIOR TO THE REFERRAL?
☐ YES ☐ NO

⑥ HOW DID I ACCEPT THE REFERRAL & FOLLOW UP?

⑦ IS THAT NEW REFERRAL STILL A CLIENT TODAY?
☐ YES ☐ NO

Written Exercise 13B

LOOK AHEAD: REFERRAL OPPORTUNITIES TRACKING LOG

Referral opportunities are all around you, but most are slipping through your fingers right now because you either aren't noticing them or you aren't acting on them. Start by choosing one day of the week that you can focus on where and when you could be asking for referrals. Don't get nervous yet! You are simply increasing your awareness of potential referral opportunities. Pay close attention and mentally seek out every possible situation in which you could see yourself asking for referrals.

Use the visual worksheet on the next page for this written exercise:

STEP 1: Create a referral tracking log based on the seven questions in the preceding written exercise and begin to track daily referral opportunities.

STEP 2: Over time, take note of what works and doesn't work. Study the interactions and learn from them. Then adjust what you do and say to increase your referral quotient.

Your referral tracking log should focus on the details of your referral interactions so that you can better see what works and what doesn't work in the referral process. If you study these interactions, you can learn from them and adjust your behavior accordingly while significantly increasing your referral quotient. You're going to be pleasantly surprised at the plethora of untapped referral opportunities that are appearing before you every day.

REFERRALS—LOOK AHEAD

GOING FORWARD, LOG ACTIVITY AS NEW REFERRALS COME
TO CONSISTENTLY RECEIVE MORE REFERRALS IN THE FUTURE

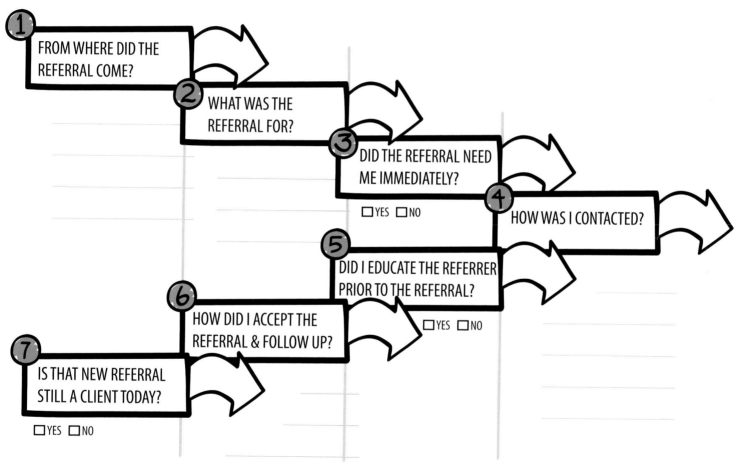

1 FROM WHERE DID THE REFERRAL COME?

2 WHAT WAS THE REFERRAL FOR?

3 DID THE REFERRAL NEED ME IMMEDIATELY?
☐ YES ☐ NO

4 HOW WAS I CONTACTED?

5 DID I EDUCATE THE REFERRER PRIOR TO THE REFERRAL?
☐ YES ☐ NO

6 HOW DID I ACCEPT THE REFERRAL & FOLLOW UP?

7 IS THAT NEW REFERRAL STILL A CLIENT TODAY?
☐ YES ☐ NO

Written Exercise 13C

LOOK INSIDE: SEE IT FROM YOUR REFERRER'S POINT OF VIEW

The following four steps help us take a look inside, from the perspective of the referrer.

STEP 1: IDENTIFY YOUR CLIENT'S BENEFITS & WHY THEY WOULD GIVE A REFERRAL

As you prepare to ask for a referral, create a list of benefits your clients experience when they work with you. These are the same benefits a referral would experience if they worked with you also. What are the emotional, social, and professional benefits that go along with being someone who refers people in need to those who can help?

STEP 2: IDENTIFY THE TYPES OF REFERRALS YOU SEEK

Remember your Red Velvet Rope Policy of working only with ideal clients with whom you do your best work? Write down the types of people who make great referrals. They may have no idea whom to refer to you, so make it easy for them to send the right people your way.

STEP 3: IDENTIFY THE PLACES WHERE YOUR REFERRERS MEET IDEAL REFERRALS

Write down the places where your referrers would meet or connect with good referrals for you. Your goal here is to help your clients and other acquaintances understand who in their lives will benefit most from and where they cross paths with these people.

STEP 4: CLARIFY AND COMMUNICATE HOW YOUR REFERRERS MAKE A REFERRAL

Let's empower your referrers to have a simple conversation with a potential referral who will effectively connect them to you and what you do. You can't leave this to chance. You must be able to articulate what you do in a way that truly connects you to the people you're meant to serve. It's essential for booking yourself solid.

Write down how you'd like your referrers to refer their contacts to you. What do you want them to say? How do you want them to talk about what you do? What specific words and phrases do you want them to use? Get very specific. You decide how you want people to talk about you.

REFERRALS—LOOK INSIDE

LOOK INSIDE FROM THE PERSPECTIVE OF THE REFERRER TO IDENTIFY
WHY, WHO, WHERE, AND HOW THEY MIGHT REFER IDEAL CLIENTS TO YOU

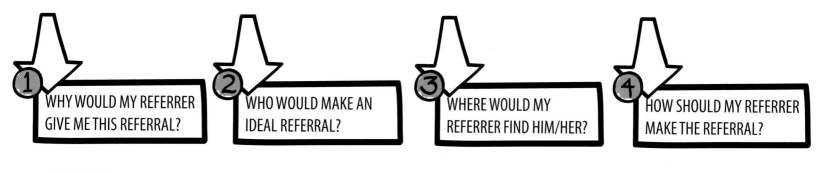

1 WHY WOULD MY REFERRER GIVE ME THIS REFERRAL?

2 WHO WOULD MAKE AN IDEAL REFERRAL?

3 WHERE WOULD MY REFERRER FIND HIM/HER?

4 HOW SHOULD MY REFERRER MAKE THE REFERRAL?

Seize the Day Referral Work: Go For It

1. ASK FOR REFERRALS

If you want to increase your referral quotient by 50 percent, the best strategy is to ask for referrals. This is the simplest part of the Book Yourself Solid Referral Strategy, as well as the most important. The preceding and following exercises will help you ask effectively. Please make sure to complete these exercises thoughtfully before you run off and just ask for referrals willy-nilly. What you can start with today is seeking out opportunities for referral conversations.

NOTICE NATURAL SITUATIONS FOR REFERRALS WHEN YOUR IDEAL CLIENT:

- Thanks you for a great session or work well done.
- Asks you for more services.
- Asks for clarification on a process or concept.
- Describes a past problem that you helped fix or goal you helped her achieve.
- Mentions a friend or business associate who's been facing the same challenges your client has faced.
- Mentions she is going to an industry conference for a few days (and you serve businesses or individuals within that industry).

YOU CAN CREATE THE OPPORTUNITY FOR A REFERRAL CONVERSATION BY:

- Thanking clients for their energy and enthusiasm during your session or project.
- Clarifying their goals or making a suggestion to work on their own.
- Asking clients how they are feeling about the work you're doing together or about past challenges.
- Complimenting clients on their progress—always.

Once you get clients talking, ask them about the value they get from your sessions. Use this as an open door to have them talk about how your services could benefit other people or organizations they have relationships with.

BOOKED SOLID ACTION STEP: Make the commitment to ask for referrals every day for five days straight.

2. FACILITATE THE REFERRAL CONNECTION

Offer to meet, consult with, or advise anyone who is important to your clients. Let them know that you want to help educate their friends about the benefits of your services.

Hand out a card or send an e-mail that clients will pass on to friends and family. Or better yet, ask them to make the introduction today. There are times when you can take the burden of calling or sending the e-mail off of your referrer. Not because your referrer doesn't want to make the referral happen but because life gets in the way. People are busy and they can get distracted by other tasks on their to-do list. If you actually make the connection and do the follow-up, it's sure to happen.

The same is true any time you personally meet potential clients. They say they're going to call you, and even if they have the best of intentions, things come up that get in the way, and you don't get a call. So I suggest that when you meet someone you really connect with and who has expressed interest in your services, you call him.

Post-Referral Work: Don't Wait While the Crickets Chirp

1. FOLLOW UP WITH THE REFERRAL

This is a no-brainer, right? You *must* follow up. After the introduction has been made, don't wait for the referral to make the next move. If you sit around and wait for the call, you'll be hearing nothing but the crickets chirping. This not only means you miss the opportunity, but you could also hurt your relationship with the referrer.

So contact the new referral and introduce them to what you have to offer—in a meaningful, connected, and helpful way. This is where your always-have-something-to-invite-people-to offer comes into play. It gives you a really easy way to start a conversation with the potential client and extend a no-risk, no-barrier invitation that is compelling and attractive. All you have to do is make a generous invitation and you've started the Book Yourself Solid Sales Cycle.

When beginning a relationship with potential clients, consider the following:

- Hold private meetings or demonstrations to eliminate any fear or embarrassment they may have about trying something new.

- Learn about any past experience with your type of services or products that they may have had and, most important, what they hope to achieve.

- Tell them what to expect, how you work, and the benefits they will experience.

- Include administrative details too: what to have available, if anything. Help clients feel as comfortable and prepared as possible.

- Provide third-party articles and facts that support your analysis in describing benefits they will achieve.

- Invite clients to work with you, and remember the Book Yourself Solid Super Simple Selling System. Offer a specific date and time that suits their schedule.

IF YOU DON'T FOLLOW UP,
ALL YOU'LL HEAR IS THE
CRICKETS CHIRPING.

Post-Referral Work: Show & Share, and Circle Back

2. SHOW & SHARE YOUR REFERRAL PRESENTATION

- Speak with lots of expression, get excited, and show the passion you have for the benefits your services can offer.
- Smile.
- Make eye contact.
- Be confident.
- Open your heart.

When your potential client starts speaking, hush up and listen.

3. CIRCLE BACK WITH THE REFERRER

It sounds so simple, but I can't stress this enough. Tell your referrer the status of the referral they gave you! If they have to ask you how it went, you've missed the boat. Your referrer wants to see you succeed, so if they took the time to help you, please take the time to follow up and also thank them. Nurture the relationships you develop with those who refer others to you.

CIRCLE BACK TO YOUR REFERRER,
SHARE HOW IT WENT,
& SAY THANKS.

More Referral Ideas

SERVICE PROFESSIONALS WITH COMPLEMENTARY OFFERINGS

Other professionals who offer services and products that are complementary to your own, and work with your target market, are ideal sources of referrals. When you operate from a perspective of abundance and cooperation, rather than from scarcity and competition, it becomes easy to reach out to others to develop relationships that can be mutually beneficial.

The more you refer to others, the more they'll be inspired to refer to you. Many service professionals have a formal referral group with five or six other professionals who serve the same target market but offer complementary services and products. Each member of the group works to send referrals to each other member of the group. If you join a high integrity referral group, you'll greatly extend your referral reach. You'll also build your reputation by having others talk about you and your services.

AFFILIATE FEES AND REWARDS PROGRAMS

Create rewards for those who refer others to you. A reward could be anything from a formal affiliate program, through which you pay cash for referrals, to coupons for discounts on your services, products, or programs.

Some professionals worry about losing money by paying affiliate fees. The numbers tell a different story. Say you charge $500 per month for your services and you currently have 10 regular clients. You're currently earning $5,000 a month. Suppose each one of your 10 clients refers one more client to you at $500 per month. That's another 10 clients for another $5,000 a month. If you give a referral fee of 10 percent, you'll be paying a total of $500 in referral fees. Would you spend $500 for a profit of $4,500 and a new monthly income of $9,500, almost double what you were making? I would. And think about what this means if you are currently making $40,000 or $50,000 per month.

A word to the wise. It's rare that someone will refer simply because you're offering a referral commission or reward. They'll do it because they believe in you and what you stand for.

Strike While the Iron Is Hot

While some of your clients, friends, family, and colleagues may refer others to you without your having to ask, many won't. As I mentioned earlier, it isn't that they don't want to; they're just busy with their own lives and it hasn't occurred to them. While it may feel awkward at first to ask for referrals, give it a try. You'll be surprised at how willing they are to do so once you've brought it to mind. Certainly, if they've worked with you, they'll want their friends, family, and business associates to experience the same great benefits they have. And they'll enjoy being able to help you as well. When someone has a positive effect on one's life, even in small ways, it feels good to give something back, and referrals are a great way to do it.

Are you as excited as I am about the dozens of potential clients you're going to meet? Just think about all those potential clients who have been searching and waiting to be introduced to an expert like you. I hope and expect that you will serve your potential clients and community by immediately starting to ask for client referrals. Once you start speaking with your potential clients on a deep and personal level, they will see you as far more than just your title. They will see you with more value, dimension, and a higher level of respect. This meaningful connection is the key to achieving a greater level of prosperity and personal satisfaction. It's the Book Yourself Solid way.

Before you know it, you'll be booked solid.

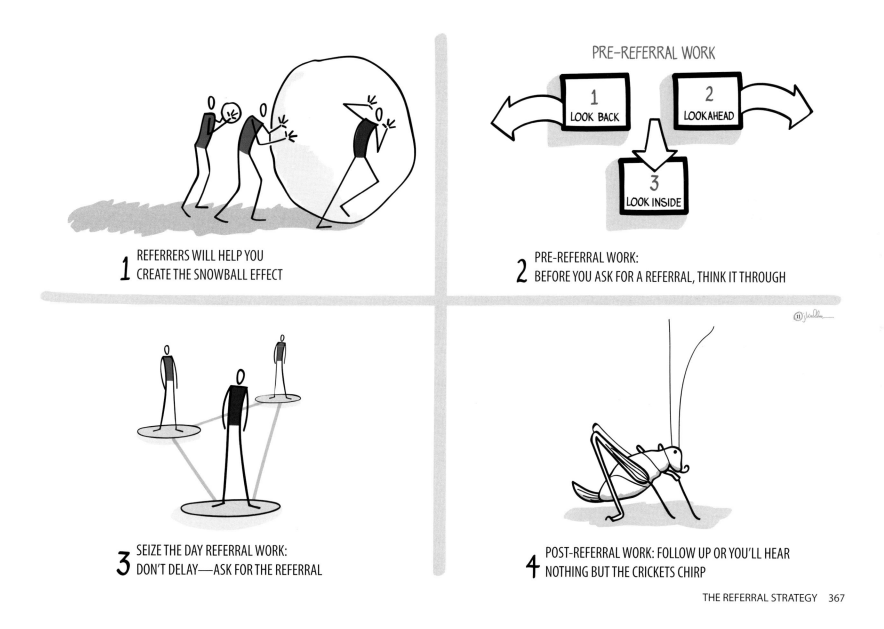

PRE-REFERRAL WORK

1 LOOK BACK

2 LOOK AHEAD

3 LOOK INSIDE

1 REFERRERS WILL HELP YOU CREATE THE SNOWBALL EFFECT

2 PRE-REFERRAL WORK: BEFORE YOU ASK FOR A REFERRAL, THINK IT THROUGH

3 SEIZE THE DAY REFERRAL WORK: DON'T DELAY—ASK FOR THE REFERRAL

4 POST-REFERRAL WORK: FOLLOW UP OR YOU'LL HEAR NOTHING BUT THE CRICKETS CHIRP

module 4

MODULE FOUR: THE 6 CORE SELF-PROMOTION STRATEGIES
"CRUISING ALTITUDE"

CHAPTER 14

The Book Yourself Solid Speaking Strategy

4.14 THE BOOK YOURSELF SOLID
SPEAKING STRATEGY

**GET IN FRONT OF POTENTIAL CLIENTS
& SHARE THE FRUITS OF YOUR KNOWLEDGE**

1 SPEAK TO SELF-PROMOTE
& SHARE THE FRUITS OF
YOUR KNOWLEDGE

6 STEP GUIDE
TO ORGANIZING YOUR PRESENTATION

3 USE THE 6 STEP GUIDE TO
ORGANIZING YOUR PRESENTATION

the
HIERARCHY
OF ASSOCIATIONS & ORGANIZATIONS
WHO SERVE YOUR TARGET MARKET

2 GET BOOKED TO SPEAK
BY IDENTIFYING THE
ORGANIZATIONS WHO SERVE
YOUR TARGET MARKET

4 DELIVER YOUR MESSAGE
& MAKE IT SIZZLE

4.14 THE SPEAKING STRATEGY

It usually takes me more than three weeks to prepare a good impromptu speech.

—Mark Twain

The Book Yourself Solid Speaking Strategy can be used by virtually any service professional to get in front of potential ideal clients based on your knowledge, talents, and strengths.

The wonderful thing about sharing your knowledge is that it's rewarding for both you and your audience. They will leave your presentation or event a little smarter, thinking bigger, and with an action plan that will help them implement what you've taught them. You will benefit because you'll know you've helped others, which is the reason you do what you do. And at the same time, you'll increase awareness for your services and products.

Just Show Up and Shine

SELF-PROMOTION

To get in front of your target market you can promote yourself or have others promote you. When you promote yourself, you're inviting your target market to something that is going to help them solve their problems and move them toward their compelling desires. When you are promoted by others, they put you in front of your target market. You may want to travel both routes. I do.

First, let's look at pure self-promotion, such as inviting your target market to events that you produce—not necessarily big workshops or conferences but simple, community-building, meaningful, enlightening events at which you can shine, show off your products and services, and build your reputation and credibility in your marketplace. These types of speaking and demonstrating events might fall into the category of an always-have-something-to-invite-people-to offer or they may be one-off events.

CONFERENCE CALLS

Start a monthly or weekly call for clients to learn the benefits of working with you. Prepare a new, timely, and relevant topic every time. Pick up a magazine in your industry and use one of the articles to inspire your topic, invite guests to discuss their area of expertise, and ask your clients to tell you what they'd most like to hear about. The rest of the call will naturally flow into a Q&A session. Here are a few ideas to get you started and to spark your inspiration and creativity for your own unique ideas:

- **FINANCIAL PLANNERS** can offer weekly conference calls on the best strategies for building wealth using the products they sell.

- **INTERNET MARKETING CONSULTANTS** can offer web conferences giving updates on search engine optimization and other web traffic generation strategies.

- **PERSONAL COACHES** can offer conference calls on their area of expertise: reducing anxiety, increasing focus, setting boundaries.

If you're doing a conference call, or teleseminar, as it's often called, it won't cost you a dime. There are hundreds of companies that provide these types of services for free, and others that charge nominal fees, but provide additional features. Record each call and link to it from your web site—all these services have conference recording built in. Those who couldn't make the actual call will still have the opportunity to listen to it and benefit from it. Archiving the calls on your web site or blog is also a wonderful way of immediately establishing trust and credibility with new web visitors.

NO PLANNING NECESSARY.
JUST SHOW UP AND SHINE.
AND IT WON'T COST YOU A DIME.

Demonstrations and Educational Events

These opportunities are similar to conference calls except that they're conducted in person. Demonstrations and educational events are an excellent way to reach potential ideal clients if your services are physical or location-based or if the people you serve are all located in the same town or city. This approach is also a great alternative if you feel that a conference call doesn't speak to your strengths.

Holding an educational event is another opportunity to get creative and share the fruits of your knowledge. For example, you could create some excitement with an open house or outdoor demo at a park or at any other venue. Don't just invite your potential clients but also your current clients, friends, or colleagues who know the value of your services and are willing to talk about their experiences. Some ideas:

- **FITNESS PROFESSIONALS** can offer a weekly physical challenge for clients and potential clients. Ask clients to bring a new friend every week. Each week a new type of workout would be planned with a social event afterward.

- **REAL ESTATE AGENTS** can offer weekly real estate investor tours in which they fill a van or tour bus with active real estate investors and scour the neighborhood hotspots.

- **PROFESSIONAL ORGANIZERS** can offer a monthly makeover in which they go to a potential or new client's office or home, along with a small group of 10 or 15 people (it's not bad to have a waiting list for these types of offerings), and the professional organizer reorganizes the space and teaches the guests the basics of how to be more productive and effective through an organized office.

- **HAIR STYLISTS** can do something similar with the monthly makeover concept. Offer a contest or raffle each month, and the winner would get the makeover.

Introduce these offerings at the end of your Book Yourself Solid Dialogue. Add, "I'd like to invite you to... " or, "Why don't you join me and my clients for a fun, playful..." Try out different venues and topics until you discover the one that works for you. Remember, the difference between the typical client-snagging mentality and the Book Yourself Solid way is that the typical client-snagging mentality plays it safe so as not to look foolish. The Book Yourself Solid way asks, "How can I be unconventional and risky so as to create interest and excitement for my services?"

You will never be at a loss for different things to try or experiences to create for your clients and potential clients. You want to invite as many people as possible to these events for three important reasons:

1. **YOU WANT TO LEVERAGE YOUR TIME.** so you're connecting with as many potential clients as possible in the shortest amount of time.

2. **YOU WANT TO LEVERAGE THE POWER OF COMMUNITIES.** When you bring people together, they create far more energy and excitement than you can on your own. Your guests will also see other people interested in what you have to offer, and that's the best way to build credibility.

3. **YOU'LL BE VIEWED AS A GENEROUS CONNECTOR.** If you're known in your marketplace as someone who brings people together, it will help you build your reputation and increase your likability.

SHARE THE FRUITS
OF YOUR KNOWLEDGE.

Written Exercise 14A

When you promote yourself, you're inviting your target market to something that is going to help them solve their problems and move them toward their compelling desires. So let's make it a reality for you. Take the ideas and get creative with them. Apply them to your own business strategy and you'll be booked solid in no time.

ADD VALUE BY WAY OF INVITATION

Use the visual worksheet on the next page for the following exercise.

STEP 1: Review the different ideas we have discussed for inviting your target market to something that allows you to shine and show off your products and services. Which of these ideas do you feel most driven to do? Circle two or three of them on the visual worksheet.

STEP 2: For each of the invitation types that you circled, expand on the idea. Who might you invite? What might you share that would add value? What logistics and planning might you need to consider?

STEP 3: Pick one of the ideas you've been working on and jot down a few next steps to help you get it started.

BOOKED SOLID ACTION STEP: As you develop your always-have-something-to-invite-people-to event, integrate the Book Yourself Solid Keep in Touch Strategy from Chapter 7. How will you collect people for your database and then connect with them after the event is over? Be intentional about this, or you will miss opportunities.

Now you are well on your way to using the Book Yourself Solid Speaking Strategy to share knowledge with those you are meant to serve, while also bringing awareness about the products and services you offer.

Well done!

ADD VALUE BY WAY OF INVITATION

BRAINSTORM IDEAS FOR INVITING YOUR TARGET MARKET TO SIMPLE EVENTS
WHERE YOU CAN PROMOTE WHAT YOU OFFER & SHARE YOUR FRUIT OF KNOWLEDGE

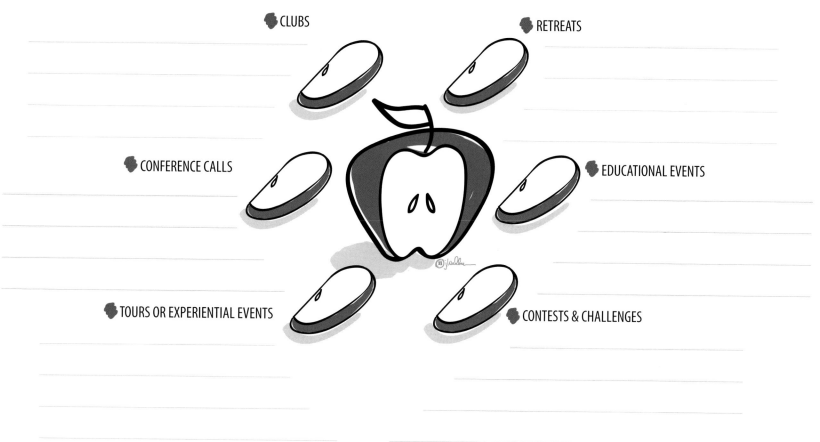

CLUBS

RETREATS

CONFERENCE CALLS

EDUCATIONAL EVENTS

TOURS OR EXPERIENTIAL EVENTS

CONTESTS & CHALLENGES

Getting Promoted by Others

Now let's address the second approach—getting promoted by others to speak or demonstrate. I won't address the details of being a professional speaker, someone who makes a living speaking to associations and organizations, but rather how you can use public speaking to create awareness for what you have to offer and get booked solid.

If you're speaking for exposure, you probably won't be paid up front for most of the speaking and demonstrating you do, except possibly an honorarium and travel costs. You're doing it for the opportunity to address potential clients and to interest them in your offerings.

There's an assumed trade involved. You receive marketing opportunities, and the association or organization that brings you in to speak or demonstrate gets great content that serves their constituents. The key is to balance the two. If you are invited to speak and you spend 90 percent of your time talking about what you have to offer, you won't be well received and you certainly won't be invited back. However, if you don't make any offers at all, you'll be sure to miss great opportunities for booking yourself solid.

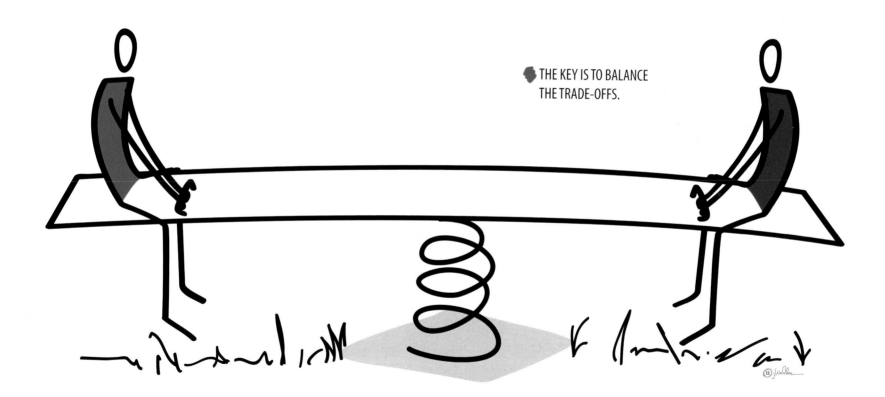

THE KEY IS TO BALANCE
THE TRADE-OFFS.

Booking Your Way Up

If you would like to be promoted by others, you need to develop trusting relationships with decision makers at associations and organizations that serve your target market. In the business world, these people are often called meeting planners. At your local associations, these people may be called communication or education directors or something different altogether. Bottom line: They are the people who can get you in front of your target audience.

There are thousands of associations and organizations that serve your target market. For example, colleges and universities all across the country sponsor executive extension courses, community learning programs, and all kinds of management and small business seminars and workshops. And to create comprehensive programs, the colleges and universities will often invite guest experts, like you, to make a presentation on their area of expertise. Trade associations and networking groups all need speakers to address their memberships, and this phenomenon has spread into for-profit companies as well.

The most potentially rewarding venues will offer:

- Large audiences.
- Audiences that include potential buyers for your products and services.
- Name recognition that is prestigious.
- The opportunity to sell products at the event (books and CDs, for example).

There is a hierarchy of associations and organizations that can sponsor you and your services. I start the list with the lower-level organizations and associations and work up to the highest-level organizations and associations. The lower-level organizations are usually smaller and less prestigious, but don't let the hierarchy fool you. You can fill your practice by speaking in front of members of the lowest-level associations and organizations, but you don't necessarily have to start with the lowest and work your way up. It may help to have previous speaking experience with some of the lower-level associations and organizations for you to get booked with the higher-level associations and organizations.

the HIERARCHY

OF ASSOCIATIONS & ORGANIZATIONS
WHO SERVE YOUR TARGET MARKET

4 NATIONAL & INT'L
TRADE ASSOCIATIONS;
LARGE CORPORATIONS

3 LOCAL & REGIONAL
TRADE ASSOCIATIONS; SMALL BUSINESSES

2 FOR-PROFIT BUSINESS GROUPS,
LEARNING PROGRAMS, & SCHOOLS

1 NON-PROFIT ORGANIZATIONS
& COMMUNITY GROUPS

Written Exercise 14B

LEVEL 1: NON-PROFITS & COMMUNITY GROUPS

Your entry point to speaking and demonstrating is with local not-for-profit community groups or organizations like the community center, churches, YMCA and YMHA, service clubs, or political action groups and chambers of commerce. Some of these groups serve a particular target market, but most are made up of individuals who share similar interests. They're good places to find potential clients and great places to work on your material and practice speaking and demonstrating in front of other people.

WRITTEN EXERCISE: Identify several Level One groups or organizations that you can contact.

LEVEL 2: FOR-PROFIT BUSINESS GROUPS & LEARNING PROGRAMS

Seek out local for-profit business groups, learning programs, and schools, including schools of continuing education and networking groups like The Learning Annex, Business Network International, colleges, and others.

These organizations are higher up the value scale for you because they serve more targeted groups of people who are really there to learn what you have to offer. Furthermore, they tend to be slightly more prestigious than the local not-for-profit community groups.

WRITTEN EXERCISE: Identify several Level Two groups or organizations that you can contact.

LEVEL 3: LOCAL & REGIONAL TRADE ASSOCIATIONS

There are more local and regional trade associations than you can count or ever speak to in a lifetime. Do a quick search on Google to find them. Local and regional trade organizations are excellent opportunities because you know the exact makeup of your audience.

Another avenue to consider, depending on your target market and the kind of services you provide, is businesses, both large and small. I put the smaller businesses on Level Three and the larger corporations on Level Four. Many companies offer educational workshops, programs, and conferences just for their employees.

WRITTEN EXERCISE: Identify several Level Three local or regional trade associations or small businesses that you can contact.

LEVEL 4: NATIONAL & INTERNATIONAL TRADE ASSOCIATIONS

From here you're just going to keep moving up the trade association ladder, from local and regional trade associations to national trade associations and then to international trade associations. There's even a Federation of International Trade Associations (FITA).

Also think about the larger corporations who may bring in a speaker for a lunchtime session. Other times, the setup is more formal, and you'll speak to large groups of people at a conference center. Just be clear on why you're targeting a particular business. Know what you have to offer them that will serve their needs and what opportunities the business or the individuals who make up the business offer you.

WRITTEN EXERCISE: Identify several Level Four national or international trade associations or large corporations that you can contact.

Written Exercise 14C

HOW TO FIND YOUR AUDIENCES

Most of the information you'll need about associations and organizations that serve your target market is on the Internet. It can sometimes be difficult to identify from a web site whom to contact, but it's the best and cheapest way to start. If you're serious about using the Book Yourself Solid Speaking Strategy as your go-to marketing strategy, pick up a copy of the *NTPA: National Trade and Professional Associations of the United States*. It contains the name of every trade association, its president, budget, convention sites, conference themes, membership, and other pertinent information. You might also consider referencing the *Directory of Association Meeting Planners and Conference/Convention Directors* and the *Encyclopedia of Associations* at your local library.

STEP 1: From the previous written exercise, pick one or two of the organizations from each level you identified, and write them in the spaces provided for this exercise.

STEP 2: Identify the decision makers for the organizations you chose.

STEP 3: Go through your network to see who you know who might be able to connect you with these decision makers or someone else who might know them.

STEP 4: This is where www.solid.ly comes in handy again. It'll help you identify who you know, and who might know them. And then, of course, you'll use your BYS List of 20 to reach out to them and manage your follow-up.

BOOKED SOLID ACTION STEP: After reading this chapter and doing your homework, contact these decision makers using your newfound direct outreach strategies and begin getting booked to speak.

FIND YOUR AUDIENCES

IDENTIFY THE ORGANIZATIONS & DECISION MAKERS
WHO COULD BOOK YOU FOR A SPEAKING ENGAGEMENT

4 NATIONAL & INT'L
TRADE ASSOCIATIONS;
LARGE CORPORATIONS

ORGANIZATION: _____

DECISION MAKER: _____

3 LOCAL & REGIONAL
TRADE ASSOCIATIONS;
SMALL BUSINESSES

ORGANIZATION: _____

DECISION MAKER: _____

2 FOR-PROFIT BUSINESS GROUPS,
LEARNING PROGRAMS, & SCHOOLS

ORGANIZATION: _____   ORGANIZATION: _____

DECISION MAKER: _____   DECISION MAKER: _____

1 NON-PROFIT ORGANIZATIONS
& COMMUNITY GROUPS

ORGANIZATION: _____   ORGANIZATION: _____

DECISION MAKER: _____   DECISION MAKER: _____

Get Booked to Speak

Meeting planners and their respective counterparts get lots of offers from people like you to speak to their constituents. That's why it's critical that you follow the Book Yourself Solid system. You will not only get all the clients you want, but you'll also earn the respect of the decision makers at the associations and organizations for whom you'd like to speak if you:

- Have a strong foundation and a trust and credibility strategy in place for your business, so you understand why people buy what you're selling;

- Know how to talk about what you do, have identified how you want to be known in your market, and know how to have a sales conversation; and,

- Are a likable expert within your field, and have created brand-building self-expression products.

Do your homework. If you're going to contact a meeting planner or education director, make sure you know as much as you possibly can about their organization. You'd be surprised at how many people overlook this step and cold-call these meeting planners without having done their homework. The meeting planner knows it within the first few minutes of the conversation.

Talk to organization members first, if possible. Learn about their urgent needs and compelling desires. They know best what they need, so learn it from them and then reach out to the decision makers. You'll get booked a lot faster that way. Even better, have a member or board member refer you. How much do we love it when other people talk about us so we don't have to? So much!

Send an e-mail or appropriate materials first and follow up with a call. And as always, be friendly, be relevant (meaning that you offer your services only if you can really serve the group), have empathy (step into the shoes of the meeting planner), and be real (no big sales pitch).

WHAT YOU NEED TO PRESENT TO GET BOOKED

Each meeting planner, depending on the organization and type of event she's planning, will ask you to submit different materials in order to be considered. If you're trying to get booked at the local community center, a simple phone conversation may do the trick. If you're trying to get booked to speak at the largest conference in your industry, more is expected. You may be asked for a video, session description, learning objectives, speaking experience, letters of recommendation, general biography, introduction biography (which is what is used to introduce you right before you present), and more. Even if five organizations ask for the same materials, it's likely each one will ask for them in their own special way. Here's a word to the wise: Make sure you follow instructions. People, especially meeting planners, like that.

YOUR INVITATION TO SPEAK

When invited to speak or present a program, a preliminary meeting or phone call usually sets the stage for further interaction with the person responsible for the program. During the initial contact, you and the meeting planner can usually nail down the topic to be covered and the length of time expected for the presentation.

CONTACT INFORMATION

From the time you receive your invitation to the time you write thank-you notes, knowing the key players and how to contact them is vital. Things have a way of changing, however. If you stay on top of your follow-up schedule, you won't get blindsided at the last minute.

- Who is in charge of the event.
- Who will introduce you.
- Land line and cell numbers.

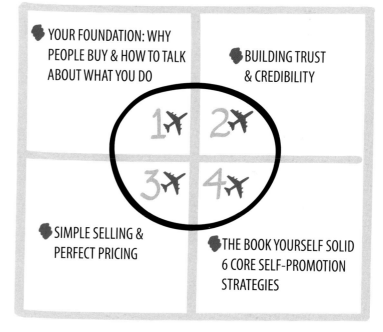

FOLLOW THE BYS SYSTEM

YOUR FOUNDATION: WHY PEOPLE BUY & HOW TO TALK ABOUT WHAT YOU DO

BUILDING TRUST & CREDIBILITY

1 | 2
3 | 4

SIMPLE SELLING & PERFECT PRICING

THE BOOK YOURSELF SOLID 6 CORE SELF-PROMOTION STRATEGIES

Preparation Makes Perfect

KNOW YOUR AUDIENCE

Start by considering your audience. Do as much research as you can on the people who will be attending your presentation so that your learning objectives can be directed right at their needs and desires. Work to understand the culture of the group you're speaking to so you can understand how to best communicate with them. Your audience will influence your choice of vocabulary (technical jargon) and may even influence how you dress. Knowing your audience well will also help you decide how much background material you need to deliver for you to effectively communicate your message.

Ask if you may have an opportunity to interview some of the leadership personnel (and even more exciting, some of those who will be attending the seminar or conference) to determine who they are along with their personal goals and agendas. Will they allow you to involve them in the presentation?

KNOWING YOUR AUDIENCE—QUESTIONNAIRE

Experience has shown that at this point it is appropriate to present a questionnaire that gives you background information specifically tailored to this particular audience. Developing various forms to help you present effectively and evaluate your performance give you the professional edge when talking with the person in charge of the program.

The kind of forms that you need include:

- Pre-Questionnaire—Know Your Audience in Advance

- Audience Evaluation Forms, Follow-Up Forms

- Testimonial Forms

- Contact Information Forms

BE PREPARED

Of course you will find out where your presentation is to be held and what audiovisual equipment will be available to you, if any. You don't need to use slides or any other visual aid if you prefer not to. Clarify how long you'll be speaking and what your audience will be doing before and after your presentation so you can incorporate that information into your planning. It's even a good idea to end a few minutes early. You'll find that, even when you bring down the house, your audience will appreciate a little extra free time.

Don't forget to remind the facilitator of your requirements closer to the presentation date. Remember, he is juggling a lot of information. Your presentation may be a small part of a larger conference.

KNOW YOUR SPEAKING VENUE

Ask to visit the speaking site. As a guest speaker, an appointment with the conference chair, facilitator, or meeting planner is important, as you probably will have only one chance to determine several factors:

- Room setup—time of access to facility and meeting room.
- Location of restrooms.
- Setup and breakdown time allowed for your presentation—staff help?
- Your technical and physical needs—who provides what?
- Back-of-room sales—permitted or not?
- Parking—free, reserved, access, permit required?

SPEAKING PREP **CHECKLIST** ✓ RESEARCH YOUR AUDIENCE ✓ GET FORMS ✓ NAIL DOWN LOGISTICS

The BYS Guide to Putting Your Presentation Together

Now that you're going to be booked to speak, you need to put together a presentation that rocks the house. Keep your presentation as simple as possible. To be an effective speaker, you need to either teach your audience something that they don't know or haven't yet fully realized—but will really value learning—or give them an experience that makes them feel great. Ideally, you want to do both.

When putting your program together, start by considering your venue, the primary learning objectives, and the amount of time you have with your audience. I know how much you have to offer, and I know you want to give so much value that you knock people right out of their chairs. Believe it or not, you'll do that by delivering a reasonable amount of content rather than an overwhelming amount of content. It's likely that your audience is going to be rushing from somewhere else and then rushing to somewhere else after you've finished. So simplicity and clarity is a winning approach. Again, it's important to never run over time—unless, of course, you get a standing ovation and they scream, "Encore! Encore!" Then, by all means, take a bow and carry on.

DEVELOP YOUR BIO AND INTRODUCTION

I've heard it said that the two most important ingredients in a good speech are respect from the audience and love for the audience. I'm sure you've got the love covered, but to get respect you must show respect—both toward yourself and toward your audience. So be sure to give yourself adequate time to develop a bio and introduction that says it the way you want it said. Salute your own accomplishments—not (just) to boost your ego but because you need the audience to respect you before you set foot on the stage. And, of course, make sure the bio articulates what you do for them. From the questionnaire you have sent out and received back, you know the profile of your audience and what they expect of you.

WHEN YOU BEGIN A PRESENTATION, THE AUDIENCE OFTEN WONDERS:

- Why have you been asked to present?
- Who recommended you?
- What is your reputation in the company or community?
- Why are you considered an expert in your field?
- Why do you get up every day to do the work you do?

Make sure your introduction bio covers all these details. If it does, the audience is much more likely to offer you its respect right from the get-go.

WHO WILL INTRODUCE YOU?

- Send your introduction in advance but take at least two copies with you, as it will probably have been lost amid all the conference preparation papers.

- Go over the introduction with the facilitator in advance and ask if they plan on adding anything extra. If yes, ask how it will integrate in the introduction.

- Be sure the person introducing you knows how to pronounce your name correctly and that any other information is clearly understood. Writing your name phonically in your introduction and asking the presenter to say it out loud a couple of times is a sensible precaution to take. Take this seriously even if you think you have a name that is easy to pronounce. I've been introduced more than once as Michael Porter, the esteemed author and Harvard Business School professor. The person introducing you may be a sponsor or some other VIP, and until you become better known, may not know you from Adam. My name, by the way, is Michael Port.

TO GET RESPECT YOU MUST SHOW IT — TO YOURSELF & TO YOUR AUDIENCE.

Plan Your Presentation

I once heard it said that experts don't necessarily know more than others, but their information is better organized. There may be some truth to that. Knowing how to organize your information is the key to success when you're making any kind of presentation.

CHOOSE YOUR ROLE

I've already suggested that one of the steps you take when you're developing the content for your information product is to choose the role you will play as the author of the information product. The same is true when you're creating the content for your presentation: Choose the role you're taking as the presenter. Choosing your role can help you shape the way that you prepare and present the content of your presentation.

DEFINE YOUR MESSAGE

To make your speech compelling, you must have something to say. It's rare that everybody in your audience will agree with your message or opinions.

However, if you have a strong and clear message, and you are respectful of other viewpoints, even people who don't agree will listen with interest. Your entire presentation should focus on delivering the takeaway message in a clear and convincing way.

DEVELOP YOUR PRESENTATION TITLE

Another nugget from Jan Leaton, a Certified Book Yourself Solid Coach, who describes developing a message as follows:

"I like to think of any presentation title as the gift card on a stupendous gift basket I'm presenting to my audience. How I address my gift card and wrap my package is every bit as important as the gift itself. It provides the 'Wow, I can hardly wait to open this present' moment. Your presentation title has to say it all. It has to personalize, tantalize, build expectation, and motivate action."

PERSONALIZE, TANTALIZE, BUILD EXPECTATION, & MOTIVATE ACTION.

Fill Your Presentation Basket

Writing your script can be a lot easier if you know where you're going before you launch. Still using the basket analogy—the first handle on your presentation basket will be your conclusion—or takeaway point, which tells the audience where you're going. Next, balance the basket by grabbing the second handle that sets your stage and creates interest in exploring the basket content. When you have balanced the basket, you can now fill it with all the motivating goodies, concepts, and tools you have that make your audience want to carry the basket away with them.

Having a well-organized presentation can determine how well you're received. When considering your material, ask yourself, "What are the steps an audience member will need to take in order to understand the information I'm presenting?"

The following 6-step guide will help you organize your information so you're well prepared for any speaking or demonstrating situation.

STEP 1: To design your presentation, start by setting your main objective for the presentation. What would you like your audience to take away from the presentation? What idea, concept, or strategy do you want them to learn, understand, or benefit from?

STEP 2: Prepare your opening. It should include:

- The purpose of the presentation—your objective.
- The process of the presentation—what you're going to do.
- The payoff of the presentation—what they're going to get.
- The presenter of the presentation—a few words about why you're the one to make this presentation, including your web site and your always-have-something-to-invite-people-to offer.

STEP 3: Deliver the content of your presentation by expressing the key points of the presentation in the appropriate order. Keep it simple.

STEP 4: Summarize your key points—what you just taught your audience or demonstrated for your audience.

STEP 5: Offer Q&A—or mix it throughout, whichever is more appropriate for your situation.

STEP 6: Close by thanking them and your host and remind them how they can continue to connect with you through your always-have-something-to-invite-people-to offer.

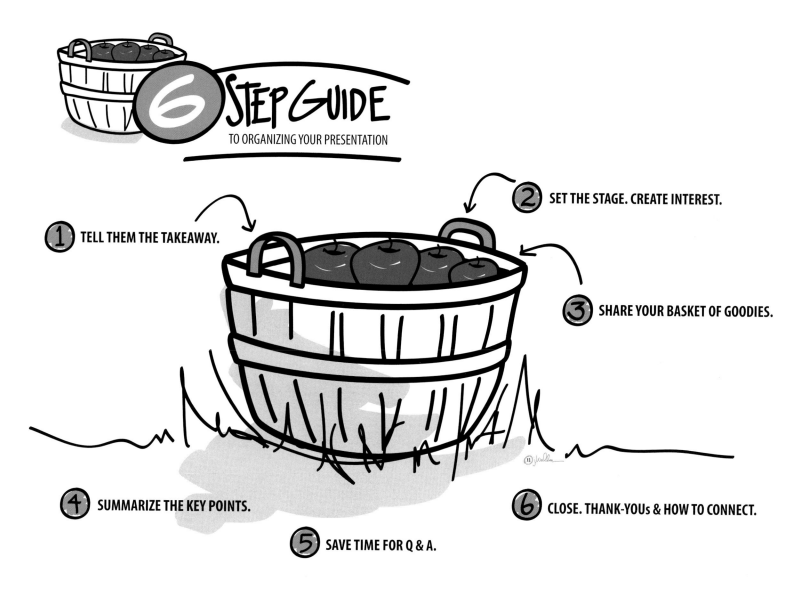

6 STEP GUIDE

TO ORGANIZING YOUR PRESENTATION

1. TELL THEM THE TAKEAWAY.

2. SET THE STAGE. CREATE INTEREST.

3. SHARE YOUR BASKET OF GOODIES.

4. SUMMARIZE THE KEY POINTS.

5. SAVE TIME FOR Q & A.

6. CLOSE. THANK-YOUs & HOW TO CONNECT.

Deliver Your Message & Make It Sizzle

When preparing your presentation, remember that people basically learn in one of three ways—although, of course, there will be overlap along the way. Some learn by hearing, some by seeing—PowerPoint or whiteboard illustrations, for example, and some by a touchy-feely atmosphere that is more experiential—sensory word pictures that bring in feeling, texture, smelling, and tasting. A good speaker will attempt to add a little spice by combining all three ways of learning into a presentation so that at some point the whole audience is engaged in the presentation. Use few, but appropriate, materials to support your points. And that means no bullets on PowerPoint presentations. Seriously. Most slide presentations actually detract from your message. For a great guide on giving presentations take a look at either *Beyond Bullet Points* by Cliff Atkinson or *Presentation Zen* by Garr Reynolds.

What do people see when they hear you? The speaker's own body language also sends a message to the audience. Some speakers make a special study of how body language influences their audience. A speaker who understands this skill also has an advantage when watching the audience.

HOW TO MAKE YOUR PRESENTATION SIZZLE

- Practice, practice, practice.
- Stage your presentation.
- Love your audience.
- Dress appropriately—for your audience.
- Market yourself as an expert while staying on topic.
- Use mics, props, and handouts effectively.
- Videorecord your presentation so it can be leveraged into information products, marketing tools, and more.

KNOW YOUR MATERIAL

The best way to give the impression that you know what you're talking about is to really know what you're talking about. You must understand your subject very well and be able to answer related questions. On the other hand, it is impossible to know everything. If you're asked a question for which you don't know the answer, there is no shame in answering, "I don't know, but I'll find out and get back to you." Or you might ask if someone in the room knows the answer. Very often you'll find that someone will.

In preparing your presentation, take the time to survey friends, clients, and others in your network who represent the kind of people you'll be speaking to. Learn as much as you can about what others are saying about your topic and make sure that your presentation passes the "so what" test. Deliver it to a test audience and make sure they don't say, "So what?" at the end of the presentation.

WRAP-UP AND FOLLOW UP

Be sure those participants have your contact information and that you have contact information for participants where possible. Your follow-up strategy will also include thank-you notes to those who helped make your presentation a success: the person or organization that invited you to speak, the facilitator who introduced you, anyone who helped with room preparation, and so on. Of course, a survey at the end of your presentation that asks for their contact information and permission to e-mail them additional information would be ideal.

You may want to remind the organization of the availability of follow-up materials as part of your keeping-in-touch plan. Make notes of what you learned so that you can apply it to future presentations and particularly to the current organization, should you be asked back again.

MAKE YOUR PRESENTATION SIZZLE AND GIVE IT A LITTLE SPICE.

To Speak, or Not to Speak, That Is the Question

It's important to be aware of what your talents are and to not use the speaking strategy if public speaking isn't one of your strengths. You have to be clear about that, which isn't to say you can't get better at public speaking and performing—you can. I'm better at giving presentations now than I was when I started. You learn by integrating your first presentation into your second, and so on. However, I wouldn't suggest using the speaking and demonstrating strategy as one of your primary marketing strategies if you really aren't comfortable speaking in public or just don't want to.

Having said that, I'd like to make a key distinction: Even if you're feeling stage fright at the thought of speaking, that doesn't mean you don't have the ability to be a good speaker. I'm nervous before almost every single speech I make. I'd be worried if I weren't, because it's natural to feel nervous. If you're drawn to speaking and demonstrating and would like to give it a try, then by all means, go for it! Practice in front of a group of supportive friends or associates, or start by giving a telephone seminar, which may feel more comfortable. Then gradually work your way up as your comfort level and confidence increase.

No one likes to be told that they didn't do a good job, and I'm no exception. Early in my career, in spite of receiving positive feedback about my presentation from many who attended, I was mortified, crushed, by the negative feedback from one or two. I ran into my biggest fear—that people would think I was stupid, that they wouldn't like what I had to say. That's my biggest conflicting intention about being a public speaker—that people will think I'm stupid. But I remind myself of the founding principle of the Book Yourself Solid way: If you feel called to share a message, it's because there are people in the world who are waiting to hear it.

The Book Yourself Solid Speaking Strategy is a great way to get your message out to the world in a bigger way, allowing you to reach more of those you're meant to serve.

1 SPEAK TO SELF-PROMOTE
& SHARE THE FRUITS OF YOUR KNOWLEDGE

2 GET BOOKED TO SPEAK BY IDENTIFYING THE
ORGANIZATIONS WHO SERVE YOUR TARGET MARKET

3 USE THE 6 STEP GUIDE TO
ORGANIZING YOUR PRESENTATION

4 DELIVER YOUR MESSAGE
& MAKE IT SIZZLE

MODULE FOUR: THE 6 CORE SELF-PROMOTION STRATEGIES
"CRUISING ALTITUDE"

CHAPTER 15

The Book Yourself Solid Writing Strategy

4.15 THE WRITING STRATEGY

Words are the most powerful drug used by mankind.

—Rudyard Kipling

In this chapter I'm going to teach you the 3-part Book Yourself Solid Writing Strategy. To help you learn the parts, I give you visuals that look like books on a shelf, one shelf for each part of the strategy. And while you can use this strategy to write a book, I want you to learn and apply it in multiple ways. So we will start by writing articles to post online, one of the most effective ways to generate traffic to your web site.

I'll also teach you how to analyze the different off line writing markets and the steps to get editors to publish your articles. Writing articles and publishing them online and off line will help you establish your reputation as an expert while generating interest in your products, programs, and services. By publishing online and off line, you will imprint your position as a category authority as widely as possible.

The 3-part Book Yourself Solid Writing Strategy

IF YOU CAN SPEAK, YOU CAN WRITE!

If you consider yourself a writer, you're going to say, "Yes, this Book Yourself Solid self-promotion strategy is for me and I'm going to jump on this right now!" If you don't picture yourself as a writer, you might be inclined to skip over this chapter, but please don't! Take it from me, even nonwriters can learn to write effective articles.

My fourth-grade teacher said I had the worst spelling she had ever seen in her 25-year career in teaching. Many years later, when I told one of my childhood friends that I had sold a book to a big-time publisher, he questioned how I could do that without his help. He still had an impression of me as the kid who didn't even like to write five paragraphs for a high school essay. But I wound up writing a lot more than five paragraphs—and good ones, too!

The point is that I don't want you to miss out on this important self-promotion strategy simply because you think you can't write. If you can speak, you can write. Even if writing isn't one of your natural talents, it's a skill that can be learned well enough for you to master the Book Yourself Solid Writing Strategy and can be improved upon through practice.

Article writing is an exciting self-promotion strategy. Remember, we like to think big but start small, and to help us do that we'll work on this strategy in three parts:

PART 1: PLAN IT

1.1 Decide the Subject

1.2 Choose an Ideal Topic

1.3 Clarify the Objective

PART 2: CREATE IT

2.1 Create an Attention-Grabbing Title

2.2 Write the Introduction

2.3 Write the Body

2.4 Write the Conclusion

PART 3: SHARE IT

3.1 Get Published on the Web

3.2 Get Published in Print

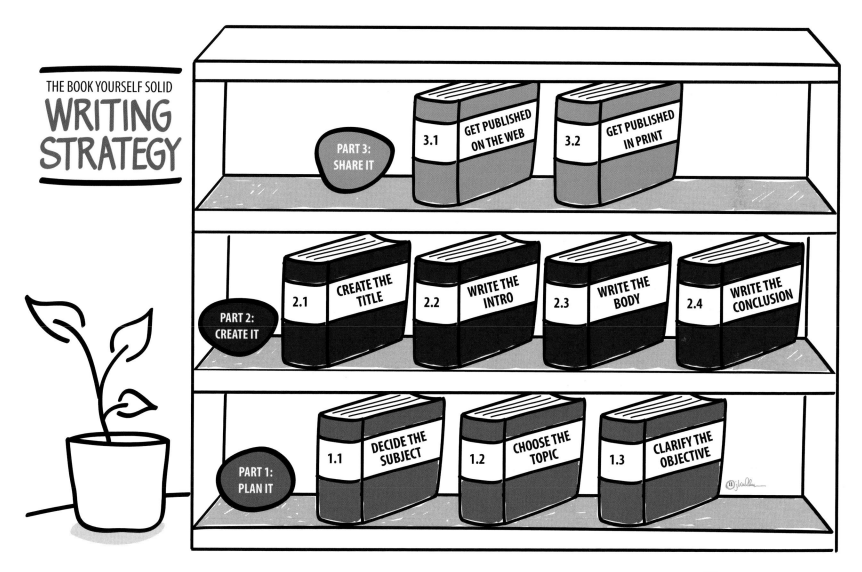

How to Get Out of Writing & Still Be an Author

Does the thought of having to write an article still make you cringe? If so, don't worry. There are two other ways to gain the benefits that article writing provides without going anywhere near a keyboard:

1.   Hire a ghostwriter.
2.   Collaborate with a writer.

Ghostwriters are professional writers who will custom write an article for you on the subject of your choice, for a fee. Your name and business information appear in the byline and in the author's resource box at the end. Sure, it costs a little, but it's still a comparatively inexpensive marketing tool. And once you have it, you can use it in many different ways:

•   Distribute it to online article directories.
•   Send it to related web sites and newsletters that accept submissions.
•   Publish it in your own electronic newsletter (e-zine).
•   Upload it to your own site and announce it to your mailing list.
•   Submit it to print publications that cater to your area of expertise.

You can get a lot of mileage out of one article, especially if it's of professional quality.

Collaborating with a writer is another easy way to get the word out about your services. If you know someone who can write well, maybe someone whose articles you've read and admired, consider pitching a joint venture to this person. You provide the expertise, and she provides the writing skills to prepare an article based on your supplied information. Then both of your names and web site addresses appear together in the author's box at the end.

This sort of collaboration is a great way to solve the I-dislike-writing problem while effectively promoting two businesses at once.

● YOU CAN GET A LOT OF MILEAGE
OUT OF ONE ARTICLE.

Part 1: Plan It

This is the ever-so-important, pre-work part of writing. In this phase you will brainstorm possible subjects for your work, and understand the difference between your subject and your topic. Once you have a few possible subjects about which you may like to write, you will develop more narrowed topics that fall under that subject. All of these subjects and topics, of course, are ideal for you and ideal for the people you serve.

PART 1: PLAN IT

1.1 Decide the Subject

1.2 Choose the Topic

1.3 Clarify the Objective

To get clear on your objective, you will ask yourself a series of questions about what role you want to play as a writer and how you want to be known. You will also reexamine your target market, to ensure that what you write about serves a common need or a compelling desire.

Are you ready to work on the plan for your writing? Here we go.

Written Exercise 15A

DECIDE THE SUBJECT

A subject is a broad category of knowledge, such as dancing, boating, fashion, business, society, and recreation. It's possible you already know a great deal about the subject of your article, or maybe you're curious about a new subject and want to expand your knowledge of it. To help identify a direction for your writing, ask yourself these questions:

- What am I passionate about?
- What interests me on a personal level?
- What is the scope of my expertise?
- What life lessons have I learned?
- What is my target audience interested in learning?

Just remember the golden rule of writing: Write what you know. If you feel stuck, consider a subject that relates to your products, programs, and services.

Don't forget to explore your personal interests as well. Consider subjects based on hobbies, family, community involvement, or charity work. Your life experiences can provide endless ideas for article writing.

WRITING STRATEGY PART 1.1

Use the visual worksheet on the next page for the following exercise.

STEP 1: Reflect on your passions, your personal interests, your areas of expertise, the life lessons you've learned, and what your target market is interested in learning.

TIP: Flip back to the work you did on Written Exercise 2B: Your Passion, Talent, Know-How. That exercise helped you identify your target market, but the same applies here as well.

STEP 2: Based on your reflections from Step 1, list five subjects you would feel comfortable writing about. The visual worksheet on the next page gives you a fun tool for brainstorming. Go ahead, write a different subject next to the numbers in the visual.

Once you've chosen a subject area to write about, you're ready to narrow it down to an ideal topic.

DECIDE THE SUBJECT

LIST 5 POSSIBLE SUBJECTS FOR YOUR WRITING BY REFLECTING ON
WHAT FITS YOU & WHAT FITS YOUR TARGET MARKET

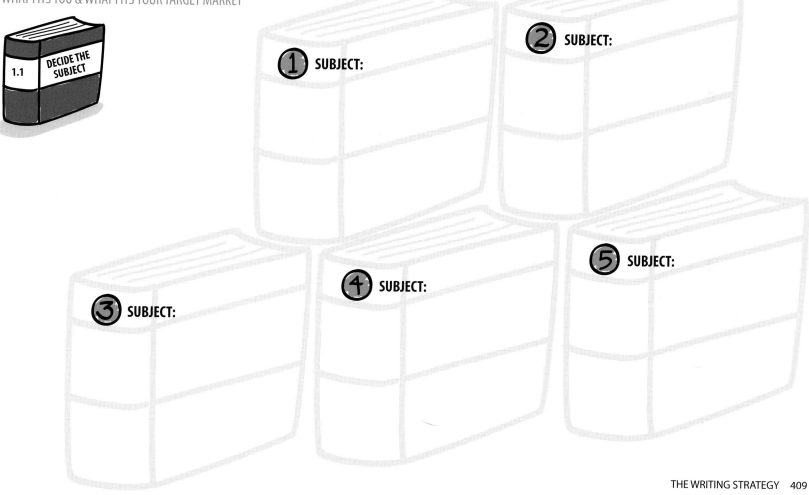

1.1 DECIDE THE SUBJECT

① SUBJECT:

② SUBJECT:

③ SUBJECT:

④ SUBJECT:

⑤ SUBJECT:

Written Exercise 15B

CHOOSE AN IDEAL TOPIC

A topic is a specific, narrow focus within your subject area. Subjects such as dancing, boating, and fashion are too broad to write about, especially since article pieces are usually between 500 and 3,000 words. Have you ever noticed that most articles and books (other than reference materials) are focused on a narrow topic? The reason is simple—it makes the writing (and reading) more manageable.

Let's say you're writing about dancing. You might choose a topic like how modern dance evolved from folk dance, how dancing contributes to heart health, comfortable clothes to wear while dancing, or the growing interest in a certain style of dance.

The following examples demonstrate how to narrow a broad subject area to reach a focused topic.

Dancing ⇢ Dancing for Men ⇢ *Smooth Moves for the Dancing Don Juan*
Dancing ⇢ Dancing for Couples ⇢ *Ballroom Dancing for Latin Lovers*

Boating ⇢ Water Sports ⇢ *Water Skiing Safety Tips*
Boating ⇢ Angler Fishing ⇢ *Hot Bait for the Angler Catching Weakfish*

Fashion ⇢ Seasonal Trends ⇢ *Top 10 Looks for Fall Fashion*
Fashion ⇢ Teens ⇢ *Prom Night: Get the Red Carpet Look for Less*

WRITING STRATEGY PART 1.2

Use the visual worksheet on the next page for the following exercise.

STEP 1: Take the five subjects you chose from Exercise 15A and write them next to the numbers on the visual worksheet for Exercise 15B.

STEP 2: For each subject, list a focused topic you would feel comfortable writing about.

CHOOSE THE TOPIC

LIST FOCUSED TOPICS FOR EACH SUBJECT
THAT FIT YOU AND YOUR TARGET MARKET

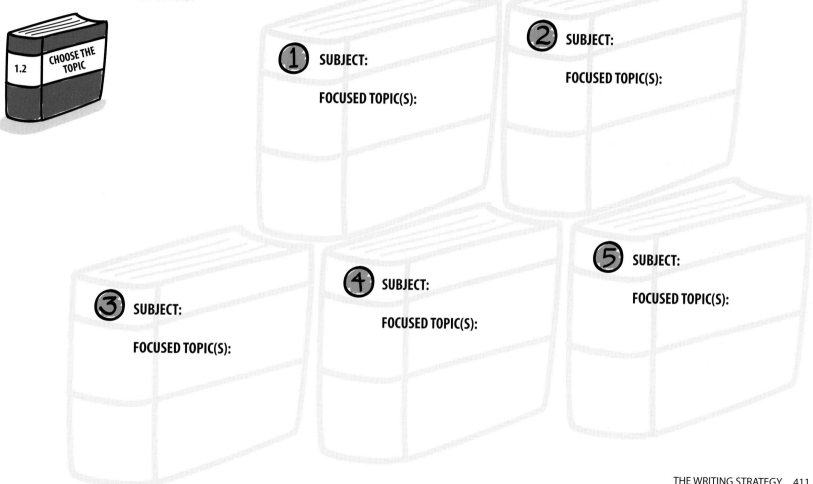

1.2 CHOOSE THE TOPIC

① SUBJECT:

FOCUSED TOPIC(S):

② SUBJECT:

FOCUSED TOPIC(S):

③ SUBJECT:

FOCUSED TOPIC(S):

④ SUBJECT:

FOCUSED TOPIC(S):

⑤ SUBJECT:

FOCUSED TOPIC(S):

Determine & Clarify Your Objective for Writing

Now that you've chosen a focused topic for your article, you need to establish a clear purpose or objective. Are you writing to inform, persuade, explore new territory, or to express your personal opinion? Knowing your objective will help you zero in on the content of your article.

WRITING STRATEGY PART 1.3

To help determine your objective, ask yourself these questions:

- What do I want to teach the reader?
- What life experience do I want to share?
- Do I want to venture into new territory?
- How do I want to be known?

Let's examine these questions in more detail. One of the most popular types of article is the how-to article, in which you teach your readers something. This is a great place to start, especially for new writers, because you can simply tap in to an area of expertise you already have, cutting out the need for hours of research. Likewise, sharing an experience that taught you a life lesson is another straightforward way of telling a story that can really affect people.

Or you can do the research on a brand new topic, educating yourself and your readers at the same time. This keeps the writing process fresh and interesting for you.

Deciding now what sort of expert you want to be known as will help you determine the objective of your articles. Let's say you have a home-based accounting business. Writing a series of articles on tax tips for people who work at home is a great way to tap in to your existing knowledge base while establishing a reputation for yourself. And that kind of credibility can drive new business to your door without your spending a cent on advertising.

UNDERSTAND YOUR TARGET AUDIENCE. In Chapter 2 we worked to identify our target market and understand their urgent needs and compelling desires. These needs must be kept in mind, so refer back to the written exercises you did in Chapter 2 as you clarify your objective for writing. What problem does your target audience need to solve right away? What do they want to move toward? Digging deep to ponder questions about your readers will help you develop a mental picture of their lives and their needs.

Part 2: Create It

Get ready to write! We are going back to the basics, because let's face it, they work. But we will do it in a way that helps you see how each step builds upon itself and utilizes what you wrote in the previous steps.

PART 2: CREATE IT

2.1 Create an Attention-Grabbing Title

2.2 Write the Introduction

2.3 Write the Body

2.4 Write the Conclusion

This isn't your typical sit down with a blank piece of paper, scribble something down, and roll it up in a ball to miss the trash can kind of work—Just follow the process. It's easy, and dare I say—FUN.

Written Exercise 15C

CREATE AN ATTENTION-GRABBING TITLE

I discussed in Chapter 8 how the title of your information product can make a big difference in whether it sells. The same concept is true when creating attention-grabbing article titles. In fact, some writers say it's the most important part because without an arresting title, no one will bother to read the rest of your article. Here are some additional tips to help spark your creativity when you're writing attention-grabbing titles:

- Select a few choice words that sum up the main point of the article.
- Tell the reader what he will learn. Use specifics: "95 percent of all …"
- Hint at the solution your article provides.
- Use questions in the title to involve the reader.
- Curiosity is a powerful tool, so consider a teaser title.
- Promise results. Explain how your article will solve a problem.
- Promise to teach them something using phrases like "How To" or "Five Steps to Improve."

OPTIMIZE YOUR TITLE. Do keyword research to determine the most likely phrases your readers would use. Search engines place a lot of emphasis on words they find in headings, so including your keywords here is vitally important to getting your article found on the web.

WRITING STRATEGY PART 2.1

STEP 1: Review Exercise 15B, choose your favorite three topics, and transfer them into the spaces provided in Exercise 15C.

STEP 2: Research several popular keywords for that topic.

STEP 3: Create attention-grabbing titles for each one based on your topic choices and popular keywords. Remember, titles need to summarize in a few words what your article is about and be intriguing enough to make people who are interested in that topic—and even those who aren't!—want to read more. If you can fit in your top keyword phrase, so much the better!

CREATE THE TITLE

CREATE ATTENTION-GRABBING TITLES
FOR YOUR TOPICS USING POPULAR KEYWORDS

2.1 CREATE THE TITLE

①

SUBJECT:

FOCUSED TOPIC(S):

POPULAR KEYWORDS:

ATTENTION-GRABBING TITLES:

②

SUBJECT:

FOCUSED TOPIC(S):

POPULAR KEYWORDS:

ATTENTION-GRABBING TITLES:

③

SUBJECT:

FOCUSED TOPIC(S):

POPULAR KEYWORDS:

ATTENTION-GRABBING TITLES:

Written Exercise 15D

WRITE THE INTRODUCTION

The introduction contains the nugget of your story, a short capsule that summarizes what's coming in the body of the article. It builds on the topic already presented in the title and explains why that information matters to the reader, which is why it's so important to know who your target audience is.

Some writers tend to back into their story by dropping their lead nugget down to the third or fourth paragraph, but this is a dangerous tactic. In nearly all cases, the first paragraph of your article should reflect the title, elaborate on it, and hint at all the juicy information to come.

Your introduction is also the place where you set the tone for the entire article, so be sure to speak directly to your readers using the words they use frequently. A casual style will endear you to your readers much more than an academic or technical style of writing. Above all, a strong introduction presents ideas that entice the reader to keep reading.

A compelling introductory paragraph answers everyone's most pertinent question: What's in it for me? Know how your information will benefit your readers and express that in your opening statement to them. If you can't imagine what benefit they will gain from your article, it may be wise to go back and refine your topic.

WRITING STRATEGY PART 2.2

STEP 1: Review Exercise 15C, choose your favorite subject and topic, and transfer the related information into the spaces provided in Exercise 15D.

STEP 2: Think about what the reader will gain from your article and write your ideas in the space. Here's where you get to appeal personally to the readers by telling them how you can help them learn something new, solve a problem, or simply entertain them for a short while.

STEP 3: Write your lead-in paragraph by presenting the most important information first. Remember to address the topic presented in your title and explain to your readers what they will gain from your article.

WRITE THE INTRODUCTION

WRITE A COMPELLING INTRODUCTORY PARAGRAPH
THAT TELLS THEM WHAT THEY WILL GAIN

2.2 WRITE THE INTRO

SUBJECT:

FOCUSED TOPIC:

ATTENTION-GRABBING TITLE:

WHAT THE READER WILL GAIN:

INTRODUCTORY PARAGRAPH:

Written Exercise 15E

WRITE THE BODY

The body of your article is where you fulfill the promise made in your title and lead-in paragraph by expanding on your theme. Here are a few tips to make the writing of this, the longest part of your article, easier:

- **USE CONCISE INFORMATION.** Try to stick to one idea in each sentence and two or three sentences in each paragraph. Concise bits of information are much easier for your readers to handle and are much less intimidating than long blocks of writing.

- **USE SUBHEADINGS.** These are like mini-titles that explain what's coming next and help break up the writing into manageable sections. Subheadings also help you organize the presentation of your information, somewhat like an outline. Put them in bold text or all capitals to make them stand out.

- **USE LISTS.** Giving your readers information formatted with bulleted lists, numbered lists, or any other visual device also makes the writing easier to read. The bottom line is that even the people who are very interested in your topic are in a hurry and want to get the goods fast.

- **BE CONSISTENT WITH YOUR LAYOUT.** If the first item on your list of bullet points starts with a verb, make sure the first word of every item starts the same way. For example, in this list of five points, each opening sentence—the one in bold red capitals—starts with the imperative form of a verb: use, be, optimize.

- **OPTIMIZE YOUR BODY COPY.** The keyword phrases you selected for your title must also appear throughout the body of your article if you want searchers to have a better chance of finding it. Repeating these phrases just often enough to be effective without going overboard is an art form, so aim for a level of keyword frequency that reads naturally.

Going to the trouble of optimizing your article's body is worth the effort for two reasons:

1. It helps your article get listed higher in the search engine results than other content, especially if other writers don't include relevant keyword phrases in their articles.

2. It will satisfy people doing the search because you've helped them find information that speaks directly to their needs. And people (you) who help other people (your readers) get what they need are often thought of very highly and remembered!

So you can see that adding relevant keyword phrases to the title and body of your article helps both you and your readers.

WRITING STRATEGY PART 2.3

I know you love the visual worksheets, but now it's time to get out your journal or your laptop and get cracking.

STEP 1: Review your work from Written Exercise 15D.

STEP 2: It is time to write the body of your article. You need to elaborate on and fulfill the promise made in your introduction by backing up your statements with facts. Refer back to the points listed earlier if you get stuck. And remember that you don't have to get all the words perfect in the first draft. Much of writing is about rewriting and editing. At this point, concentrate on the broad strokes and allow yourself to enjoy the process.

Written Exercise 15F

WRITE THE CONCLUSION

Have you said everything you wanted to say? Then it's time to wrap it all up—"bookend" style. For example, your introduction is one bookend, and your conclusion is the other.

The conclusion is easy because we pull the key points from everything you just wrote. The point is to leave your readers with an easy-to-remember summary of your main theme so that it is reinforced in their minds.

If you were simply to finish your article on point 9 of a list of tips, your readers would feel like books on a shelf with no bookend, nearly ready to fall. It's human nature to crave a satisfying ending to a story. You can leave them on an even sweeter note if you share with them how they can best use the information to their advantage, and you can offer a few words of encouragement.

WRITING STRATEGY PART 2.4

Use the visual worksheet on the next page for the following exercise.

STEP 1: Write the title of your article on the spine of the book.

STEP 2: From the introduction that you wrote in Exercise 15D, write some keywords or phrases that you might include in your closing.

STEP 3: Make a short, bulleted list of the key points from the body of your article.

STEP 4: Identify 1–3 possible ways your reader can best use the information you just gave them.

STEP 5: Now it's time to put it together. Pull the best of steps 1–4 and bookend your writing!

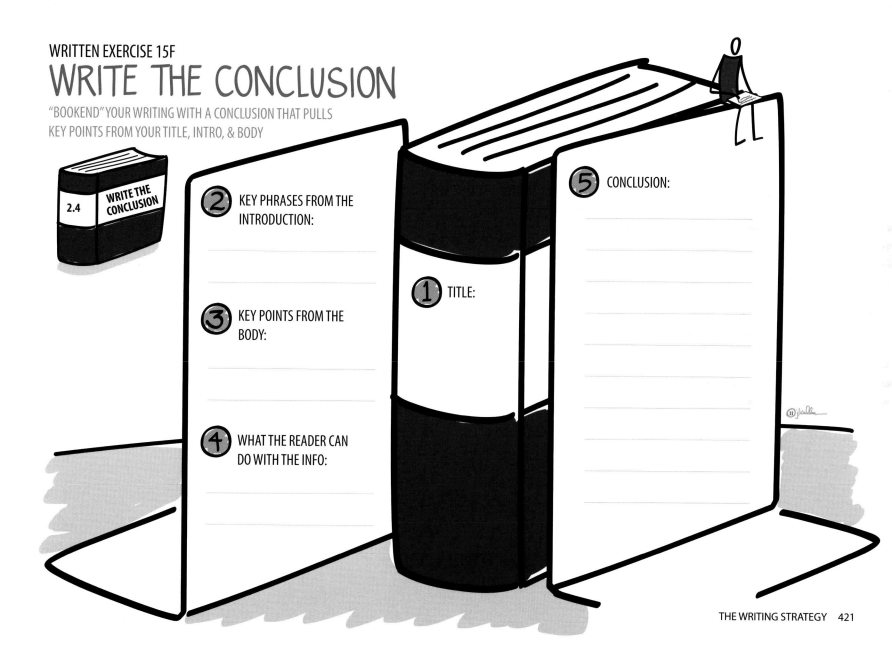

WRITTEN EXERCISE 15F

WRITE THE CONCLUSION

"BOOKEND" YOUR WRITING WITH A CONCLUSION THAT PULLS
KEY POINTS FROM YOUR TITLE, INTRO, & BODY

2.4 WRITE THE CONCLUSION

2 KEY PHRASES FROM THE INTRODUCTION:

3 KEY POINTS FROM THE BODY:

4 WHAT THE READER CAN DO WITH THE INFO:

1 TITLE:

5 CONCLUSION:

Written Exercise 15G

THE AUTHOR'S RESOURCE BOX

This is where you get to take a bow, share something pertinent about yourself or your business, and invite your readers to take an action. It's also an important opportunity to offer your services.

At the end of every article is a separate paragraph of about five or six lines (this depends on the guidelines of each publication, so check with them before submitting). This resource box or author's bio can be used in several ways.

THE KEY TO WRITING YOUR RESOURCE BOX. To make sure your resource box is effective, clearly invite action and explain why this action would benefit your readers. This applies to whether it's signing up for a free report, a complimentary consultation, a newsletter subscription, or simply a visit to your web site to learn more about your products, services, and programs or to read more of your scintillating articles!

WRITTEN EXERCISE

Use the visual worksheet on the next page for the following exercise.

STEP 1: Write 1–2 bullet points describing your area of expertise.

STEP 2: Briefly explain your business or a special offer.

STEP 3: Write a specific call to action.

STEP 4: Jot down your contact information, including web links.

STEP 5: Use what you wrote in Steps 1–4 to write a succinct, yet fluid, author's resource box.

THE AUTHOR'S RESOURCE BOX

WRITE A SHORT BIO YOU CAN INCLUDE AT THE END OF EVERY ARTICLE
THAT ALLOWS YOU TO PROMOTE YOUR BUSINESS & INVITE YOUR READERS TO TAKE ACTION

① AREA OF EXPERTISE:

⑤ BIO / RESOURCE BOX:

② BUSINESS OR OFFER:

③ CALL TO ACTION:

④ CONTACT INFO & LINKS:

Part 3: Share It

Now that you've got some great material written, what should you do with it? Why, share it! In this final phase of the Book Yourself Solid Writing Strategy, we uncover the places your writing can be shared.

PART 3: SHARE IT

3.1 Get Published on the Web

3.2 Get Published in Print

But we've got to be intentional and take the long view. Opportunities to publish are everywhere, and if you are not careful you could share your work in the wrong space. You want to publish on the web and in print with publications that serve your target market. Secondly, you want to increase your chances that they will want to include your work in their next issue.

There are many benefits to sharing your written work:

- Generate traffic to your web site
- Build credibility
- Increase visibility for your products, programs, and services
- Develop your own knowledge while you write
- Experience the joy of helping others through your writing

Get Published on the Web

This is when the fruits of your writing labor pay off. After you have completed writing your article, you'll want to search for the niche web sites that will help share your writing with the world. The Internet offers a number of unique environments:

- **ARTICLE ANNOUNCEMENT LISTS.** The intent of an article announcement list is to send out an e-mail announcing your article to web owners and electronic newsletter publishers who are seeking quality content.

- **NICHE WEB SITES.** The owner of a niche web site requires quality content written on a specific topic. The web owner's agenda is to keep their web site fresh with articles that cater to their targeted readers; they look to writers like you to supply them with this free content.

- **ELECTRONIC NEWSLETTERS (E-ZINES).** Electronic newsletters come in all shapes and sizes on varied topics. You write the content, share it with these publishers, and immediately gain access to their readers who are also your target audience. The publisher gains credible content without needing to write the articles, and you reach a larger group of prospective customers.

Where should you start? Consider your target audience and where they're most likely to spend their time online. However, before you start the submission process, there are a few more details you need to consider.

- **RESEARCHING RELEVANT ENVIRONMENTS.** Locate the specific environments that cater to your target audience, familiarizing yourself with the article submission guidelines.

- **CREATING AN ARTICLE SUMMARY.** Write a short synopsis of your article.

- **CHOOSING KEYWORDS AND KEYWORD PHRASES.** Make a list of your keywords and keyword phrases for the article directories that require them. (These should be the same keywords and keyword phrases you used to prepare your title and article copy for the search engines.)

- **PREPARING AN E-MAIL.** Write a letter to the e-zine publishers detailing what your article is about and why it would benefit the e-zine's readership. Insert a copy of your article into the body of the e-mail correspondence.

Written Exercise 15H

GET PUBLISHED ON THE WEB

Use the visual worksheet on the next page for the following exercise.

STEP 1: List five article directories that serve your target market.

STEP 2: List five e-zine publications that serve your target market.

BOOKED SOLID ACTION STEP 1: Compile all the accumulated elements of your research and writing to complete one article of 500 to 750 words on the topic of your choice, including the resource box. When it's polished to your satisfaction, share it with friends, colleagues, or a writing group to gain valuable insight on your writing progress.

BOOKED SOLID ACTION STEP 2: Submit your article to the article directories and e-zine publishers you identified.

GET PUBLISHED ON THE WEB

GENERATE TRAFFIC TO YOUR WEB SITE & BUILD CREDIBILITY
BY GETTING PUBLISHED ON THE WEB THROUGH ARTICLE DIRECTORIES & E-ZINES

**① ARTICLE DIRECTORIES
THAT SERVE MY TARGET MARKET**

1. _____
2. _____
3. _____
4. _____
5. _____

**② E-ZINE PUBLICATIONS
THAT SERVE MY TARGET MARKET**

1. _____
2. _____
3. _____
4. _____
5. _____

Get Published in Print

Consistency is the key to writing and publishing articles as a marketing tool. The idea is to saturate your target market so when a potential client is searching for valuable information, your name and articles come up again and again within the search engines' results.

Once you're comfortable with sharing your written work online, you might consider branching out and offering articles to print publications. Writing for the print market is a highly competitive process, but it's also very rewarding.

PLAN YOUR PRINT PUBLISHING STRATEGY:

1. Think big but start small.

2. Request the writing guidelines.

3. Analyze the contents.

4. Write a query letter.

5. Send an e-mail or letter.

6. Follow up with the editor.

Let's examine each step in more detail.

THINK BIG BUT START SMALL. Rather than going for the large mainstream magazines, shoot for the small, focused publications such as local newspapers and magazines, trade journals, or neighborhood community newsletters. These publications are more likely to accept your work and even help edit your articles for suitability.

Once you've been accepted to write in one of the smaller publications, you can build your portfolio of printed pieces and approach the larger markets. This is important because many large-publication editors won't consider your writing ability unless they can see you have been previously published. It's similar to when you're trying to break into the speaking circuit: You start at the local level, step up to the regional level, then to the national level, and finally to the international level. It's the same concept when you're trying to get your writing in print publications.

REQUEST THE WRITING GUIDELINES. Never submit articles without understanding what the publication is looking for and accepts. You need to be aware of word count, spacing format, style, and the type of information each publication is looking to include. For more detailed information on writing guidelines for thousands of print publications, pick up a copy of *Writer's Market* by Kathryn S. Brogan.

ANALYZE THE CONTENTS. From what I hear, nothing drives editors bonkers more than receiving articles that don't fit into the theme of their publication. Your chances of getting an article accepted for print will greatly improve if you take the time to become familiar with the publication. Either purchase a subscription or several back issues; then analyze the contents by looking at items such as article length, the tone of the writing pieces, the topics covered, the balance of short articles versus long, and how many illustrations or photos were used.

WRITE A QUERY LETTER. Now that you know which topics you want to write about and have identified the publications you want to write in, it's time to write a letter. A query letter is basically a one-page proposal that pitches your article idea. You can send a query letter about an article that has already been written or an article that hasn't yet been created, as a way to feel out the publication's enthusiasm for the concept.

Your query letter should follow the rules of a good business letter; it must immediately grab attention and convincingly (soft) sell your article idea. Use your business letterhead. If you don't own business letterhead, use white copy paper. Choose a simple font, point size 12, with single spaces. Use bullets to list key points for easier reading. Above all, be certain you spell the editor's name properly and use the correct address for the publication.

SUBMIT YOUR ARTICLE. Now it's time to send your e-mail or your letter.

FOLLOW UP WITH THE EDITOR. After sending your query letter and waiting the appropriate time for a response, follow up by telephone. Your objective is to inquire whether the editor is interested in your article and if she requires additional information. If the editor's response is no, don't be pushy and try to change her mind. Instead, ask her if there is a different slant to the article that might interest her or whether she knows someone else who might be interested in your piece.

Help Editors Help You

Every publication has an insatiable hunger for good content. They're looking for articles that will inform and entertain their readers—pieces that will help them improve their lives, whether it's how to save money, lose weight, build self-esteem, or build a shelving unit.

Most editors need good writers who also happen to be experts in their field—like you. They usually have to pay top dollar to staff writers or freelancers to provide it. So if you can give them good articles at no charge, the publication saves time and money, and you get great exposure.

A solid relationship with an editor can help you gain insight to:

- What type of information is being considered for future publications.

- What kind of story may be needed in the future.

- How to strengthen your chances of being interviewed to write a particular story.

Consideration goes a long way in the print publishing business. You'll discover that the most vital component for building relationships with editors is listening and providing the best information to meet their needs. If you stay in contact with them and consistently work to supply them with good stories, you'll successfully build relationships that will provide publicity for you and your business over time.

It's important to learn the art of delayed gratification. While it's natural to want instant results, this is a process, not a magic formula for overnight fame and fortune. One of the greatest mistakes I see service professionals make is giving up too quickly when their initial efforts don't produce immediate results. It's the cumulative effect that will pay off, so be consistent and be tenacious. Don't give up!

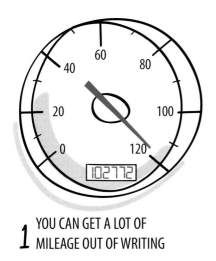

1 YOU CAN GET A LOT OF MILEAGE OUT OF WRITING

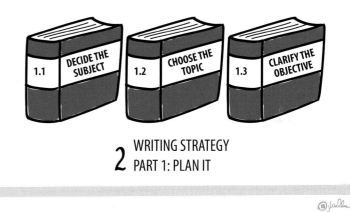

2 WRITING STRATEGY
PART 1: PLAN IT

1.1 DECIDE THE SUBJECT
1.2 CHOOSE THE TOPIC
1.3 CLARIFY THE OBJECTIVE

3 WRITING STRATEGY
PART 2: CREATE IT

2.1 CREATE THE TITLE
2.2 WRITE THE INTRO
2.3 WRITE THE BODY
2.4 WRITE THE CONCLUSION

4 WRITING STRATEGY
PART 3: SHARE IT

3.1 GET PUBLISHED ON THE WEB
3.2 GET PUBLISHED IN PRINT

module 4

MODULE FOUR: THE 6 CORE SELF-PROMOTION STRATEGIES
"CRUISING ALTITUDE"

CHAPTER 16

The Book Yourself Solid
Web Strategy

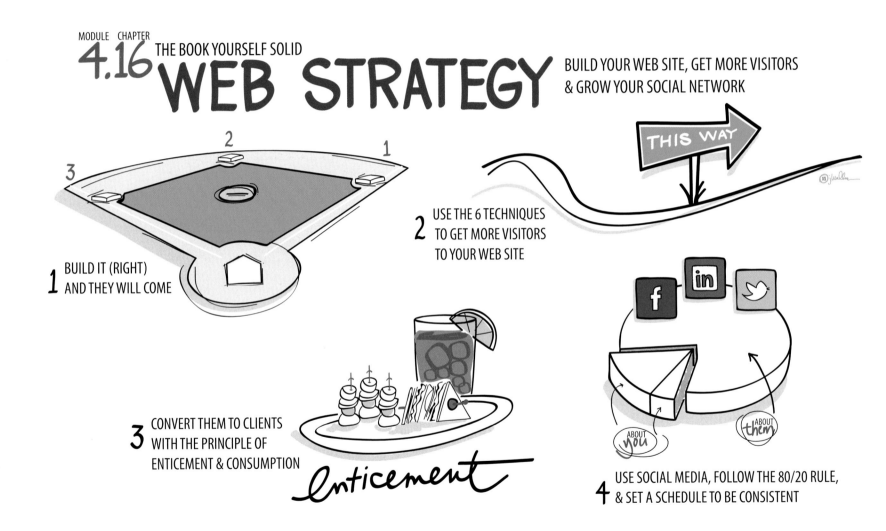

4.16 THE WEB STRATEGY

If you don't want to become an Internet marketing maniac, don't. Mastering tactics like search engine optimization, pay-per-click advertising, and the many other tools are for those who want to spend their time online. If that's not where your passion lies you'll quickly become overwhelmed. If you are simply not driven to spend your energy learning a new technology, but you still want to leverage the power of the Internet, hire or partner with others who have the skills, talents, and desires that you do not.

Either way, you need to know the fundamentals on how to:

- Build a great web site, and they will come.
- Get more visitors to your web site.
- Convert them into clients.
- Establish and grow your social media platform.

Guess What? You've Already Done Most of the Work

As challenging as the journey to web site success may seem right now, you might be pleasantly surprised that the work you've already done in this book has secretly set you up for success. Your web site is your opportunity to decide and control how you're known. Your tagline boldly expresses why you do what you do. Your site should speak to the values of your ideal clients and demonstrate how dedicated you are to your target market, their needs and desires, and the number one biggest result that you help them get, along with the financial, emotional, physical, and spiritual benefits they will receive from investing their time with you.

Your web site also demonstrates your platform and helps you build trust and credibility. Also, each of the 6 Core Self-Promotion Strategies can be integrated into the way you promote and use your site. Your web site can help you start a conversation with a potential client by offering free information products or experiences for new potential clients, and it's an effective way to introduce them to your sales cycle so you can build trust over time. Your site is an avenue through which you can offer various pricing incentives for your products and services, leading to super simple sales conversations with ideal clients.

Ideas of how to integrate the strategies right into your web site:

- **NETWORKING STRATEGY:** Invite people to join you on various social network platforms like Facebook, Twitter, LinkedIn, and so forth.

- **DIRECT OUTREACH STRATEGY:** Use direct outreach to get to know others in your field by commenting on their posts. Also, ask them if you can reprint some of their blog posts.

- **REFERRAL STRATEGY:** Write blog posts or articles that refer to another colleague who can help your clients with a particular problem they may be having, for which you are not the expert. Or, create a resource page in which you profile various referral partners. Your newsletter is another opportunity to offer referrals.

- **SPEAKING STRATEGY:** Advertise your teleseminars, classes, and events on your site. You can also do a podcast through your web site.

- **WRITING STRATEGY:** Integrate a blog into your site and have a page with articles that help position you as an expert in your field. Submit articles to article banks or directories that will help drive traffic to your site and enhance your status as an expert.

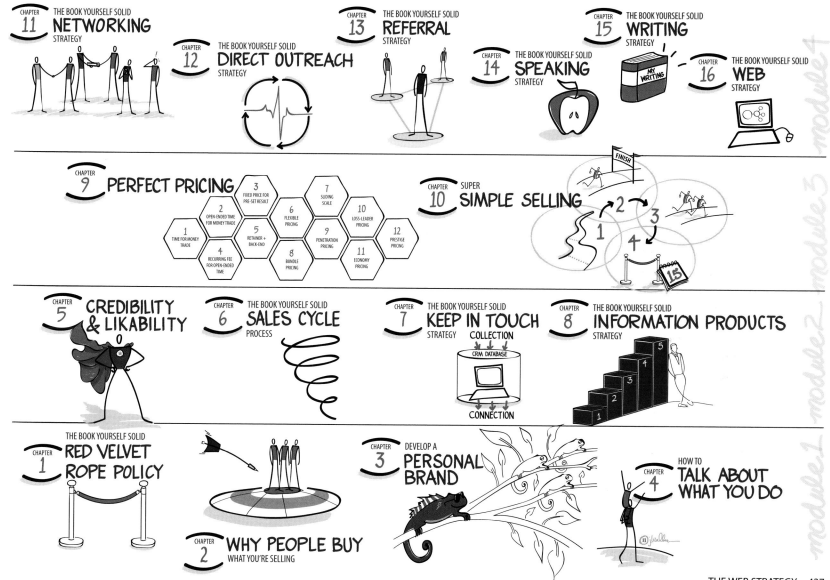

If You Build It (Right), They Will Come

Before we get into what makes a great web site, consider the biggest mistake most people make online: They don't know what they want their visitors to do when viewing the site and if they do know, they don't know how they're going to get the visitor to do it.

Most people consider a web site to be one thing. It's not. On the contrary, a web site is made up of a collection of pages that live on the same domain and are related to each other. For each page on your site, you should be able to answer the following three questions with complete clarity:

1. Who is coming to the page?
2. What do you want them to do?
3. How are you going to get them to do it?

Knowing the answer to these three questions will ensure that the content on each page of your site is perfectly designed for the type of person who visits the page. Why? Because you will consider what kind of story you're going to tell, and how you're going to tell it, to get your visitor to reach the goal you've set for that page. Your web site can be a remarkably effective tool for attracting and securing clients—if it's done right.

A pretty web site does not necessarily a good web site make. Sure, you may get a few calls because someone visited your site, or sell a few products, but the majority of the people who visit your site will not come back again just for the prettiness. Their behavior is not necessarily because they don't like what you have to offer, but people are busy and most don't even remember how they got to your site in the first place. Pretty is forgettable. Content that answers the needs of the visitor sticks in people's memories. And, ease of use allows them to consume the content.

As a successful online marketer, you will focus on attempting to convert the traffic that comes to your site into a potential client, someone who eagerly anticipates your marketing messages. These messages will come in the form of the next great service offering that will help her advance an aspect of her life. You might do this by giving these clients something of value, like a special report, free video lesson, or a big coupon, in exchange for permission to keep in touch with them. Remember how important building trust over time is. If your primary objective is to offer extraordinary value up front in exchange for an e-mail address and permission to follow up, then you can make relevant and proportionate monetized offerings later on, once you've built trust.

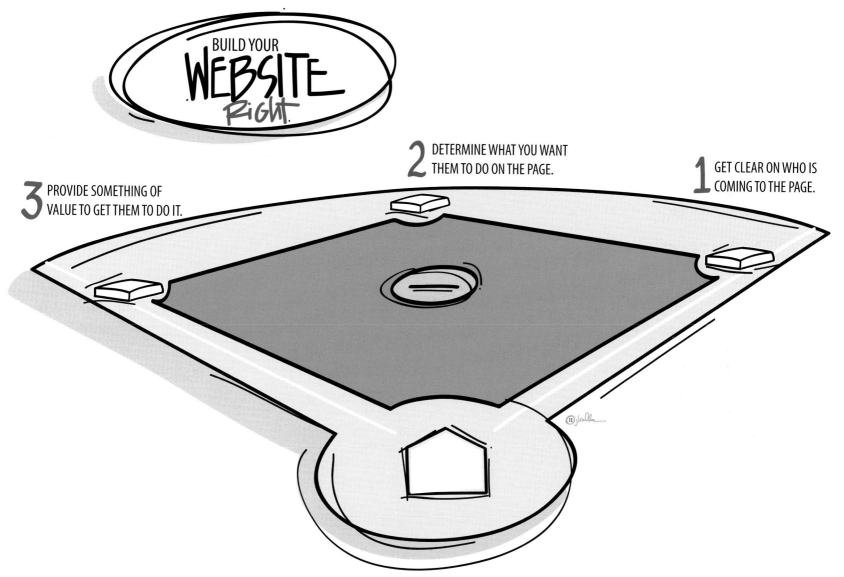

Written Exercise 16A

CONTENT AND STRUCTURE

The content and structure of your web site includes the information you wish to convey and how you organize and label it for easy navigation. Just as you can leverage the same content for an information product into several different formats, you can choose a variety of formats to lay out your web site content.

As you consider your content and structure, your focus should be on your target market. What do they want? What are their urgent needs and compelling desires? (You did this work in Chapter 2.) Design to meet their needs. The content has to be relevant to your target market and the layout should make it obvious where the visitor needs to go and what the visitor needs to do.

Visitors to your site want information and resources that will assist them in their work and their lives. If they can't find what they need, they'll get frustrated with your site and with you. The result is a lost connection. Make your site easy to navigate and easy to use, and you'll establish an immediate rapport with your visitors because they will feel that you already know and understand them.

Use the visual worksheet on the next page for the following exercise.

STEP 1: Consider the home page of your web site. Who is coming to this page? (That is, potential client, current client, past client, referral partner, or the press.)

STEP 2: What do you want the visitor to do? (That is, opt in to a newsletter so she can get access to a special report, sign up for a telephone conference that is your always-have-something-to-invite-people-to offer, and so forth.)

STEP 3: Now that you know what you want the visitor to do, how are you going to get them to do it? (That is, with a compelling story in your copywriting or in a video, or maybe an ethical bribe, and so on.)

STEP 4: Now repeat the previous three steps for each page of your web site. If you are in the process of building your web site, complete these exercises for each page of the site as you build it.

WEB PAGE CONTENT & STRUCTURE

BUILD A WEB SITE WITH PAGES THAT FOCUS ON YOUR TARGET MARKET,
WHAT ACTIONS YOU WANT THEM TO TAKE, & HOW YOU WILL GET THEM TO DO IT

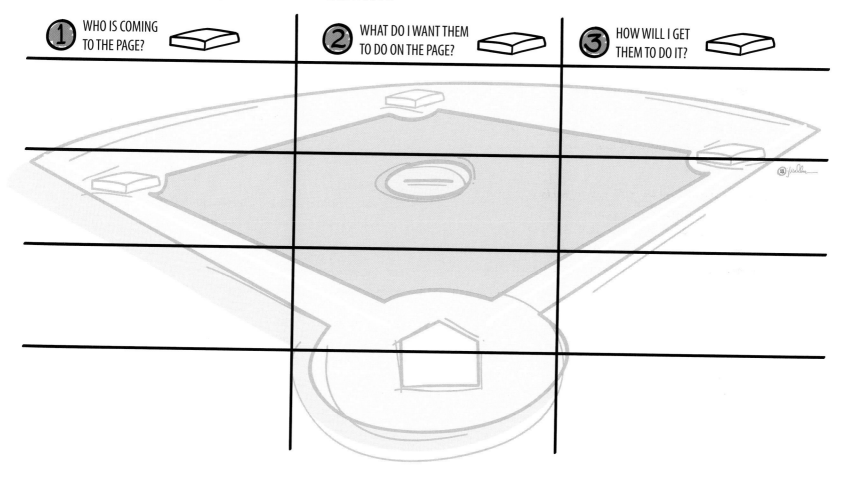

1 WHO IS COMING TO THE PAGE?

2 WHAT DO I WANT THEM TO DO ON THE PAGE?

3 HOW WILL I GET THEM TO DO IT?

Six Techniques to Get More Visitors to Your Web Site

Here is where we look at how to create a steady flow of traffic to your site and how to convert that traffic into business. These are six of the most important and easy-to-understand, tried-and-true techniques and strategies for generating more traffic to your site.

1. GET LISTED IN SEARCH ENGINES AND OPTIMIZE YOUR SITE

Search engine optimization (SEO) is all about how to get the search engines to notice your site and, ideally, to give you a good ranking. Then, when someone searches for what you're offering, your listing will be displayed in a high position in the search results.

❏ Identify the top five keywords and phrases for your site. The best are those with the most number of searches, have the least amount of competition, and draw targeted traffic that is ready, willing, and able to invest in your services. You can also search online for the Google Keyword Tool to help you identify the best keywords for your site.

❏ Build content-rich pages that your visitors want to see, that are legitimately filled with the same keywords and phrases they use to search for what you are offering.

❏ Submit your site to each search engine or have another site link directly to your site.

2. BOOST YOUR LINK POPULARITY

Your link popularity is tied to inbound links to your site. You need both quality and quantity here. Quality links are from sites that have a good ranking and serve the same target market as you, or offer related content.

❏ Identify five sites that are popular with lots of traffic and serve the same target market as you serve.

❏ Add the owner or webmaster of each site to your BYS list of 20, make friends, add value to their life and work, and offer to trade links with them (when you've built the proportionate amount of trust necessary for such a request). Make sure that you link to them first so they can see that you're intent on serving them.

3. LEVERAGE YOUR E-MAIL SIGNATURE

One of the most often overlooked methods of promoting your services is through your e-mail signature file, the information that you put at the close of your e-mail. It's a simple and effective way to tell people about what you have to offer and to encourage them to sign up for your newsletter or any other no-barrier-to-entry offer that you make. You can also consider asking a question and then provide the answer via a link to your site.

❏ Create a compelling e-mail signature and begin using it immediately.

4. PARTICIPATE IN ONLINE COMMUNITIES

Getting involved in the communities in which your target market hangs out gives you an opportunity to become a leader of the community by offering advice, support, and any other value. When you make a good name for yourself in a community made up of your target market, members of that community will be compelled to visit your web site to learn more about you and how you are able to serve them.

❑ Find the most active online communities that serve your target market and are focused on topics you know a lot about.

❑ As a member of the group, make intelligent, thoughtful posts that add value to the discussion topic. You might answer other members' questions or you might suggest helpful resources.

❑ Get involved in social media via Facebook, LinkedIn, Twitter, and other social networking hubs where your target market hangs out.

5. CROSS-PROMOTE THROUGH MARKETING PARTNERS

This is one of my absolute favorite online marketing strategies because it allows me to partner with, and promote, other people I think are fabulous while they do the same for me. We've talked about how important it is to get other people to talk about you so you can quickly build trust with new potential clients. Well, cross-promoting through marketing partners is the best way to do so. You can co-produce special promotions or have a contest with the prizes contributed by your partners (and then change roles so that you are the one offering the prize for her contest).

❑ Come up with several of your own unique ideas for cross-promotions and identify who might be a good marketing partner.

❑ Reach out, connect with, and share your ideas with the people you identified in the preceding exercise.

6. TAKE ADVANTAGE OF ONLINE PRESS RELEASES

Online press releases are one marketing tactic often underused, yet effective for increasing web traffic. They can improve your site's search engine ranking while, at the same time, enhance your credibility and increase exposure to media outlets.

❑ Write a press release about the most impressive result one of your clients achieved.

❑ Submit it to PRWeb.com. You can get tips at the site on how to craft a solid press release.

The Two Essential Principles of Visitor Conversion

You want to attract visitors to your web site and turn them into friends, then potential clients, and finally, current clients. You can generate all the traffic you want, but if that traffic does not want to stay or come back and get more information, advice, or resources from you in the future, it's not doing much good.

There are two essential principles of visitor conversion: enticement and consumption. Understand them, implement them, and profit from them, but never abuse them.

ENTICEMENT

Your web site is like your home. What's the first thing you do when someone comes to visit? You offer a drink and a bite to eat. You ask, "Are you hungry? Can I get you something to eat? How about a glass of water or some iced tea?" If you know your visitors well, you can offer them their favorite snack and beverage. In fact, when family or close friends come to visit, you make an extra trip to the supermarket to get all their favorites.

This is the principle of enticement. You offer something of value to your web site visitors as soon as they land on your site in exchange for their e-mail address and permission to follow up. They give it to you because they're interested in your enticement and they believe you'll deliver more good stuff in the days and months to come.

Be careful not to hide your enticing offers in the crevices of your web site. When you have a dinner party, do you hide the food around the house in strange places or set it just out of reach? Of course you don't. You put the hors d'oeuvres and munchies in the most obvious, accessible places possible. And sure enough, the places you put the hors d'oeuvres are exactly where everybody ends up hanging out! Have you ever been at a party where the host skimped on the hors d'oeuvres? Did you find that everybody started hanging around the kitchen as they got hungrier and hungrier? We're always searching for what we want and need, and your web site needs to speak to your visitors' needs and desires.

enticement

CONSUMPTION

The principle of consumption follows the principle of enticement. When your visitors have been enticed and have given you their e-mail address in exchange for a mini-course, white paper, special report, e-book, article, audio recording, coupon, or other free offer, you must follow up to help them consume the valuable information or experience they just received. Most people don't take advantage of all the opportunities available to them. It would probably be impossible to do so. An even smaller number of people follow up on all of the opportunities available to them through the Internet and e-mail, even the ones they've asked for. When someone does opt in to receive your free offer, he may not really consume it—really use it, learn from it, and benefit from it. It's your responsibility to help him do so by following up with an e-mail.

Does it sound like it would be a lot of work? Oh, no, my big-thinking friend, it's not. You can use an automatic e-mail responder system to set up a series of e-mail messages that are automatically sent to a new contact at any frequency you specify. You can send one a day, one a week, or one a month for a year—it's up to you. Your messages will check in with your new friend and begin to deliver the services you provide or other helpful resources.

The principle of consumption should follow the principle of enticement. It's just as you would ask your guest, the one you generously supplied with her favorite snack and beverage, "How is the tea? Is it cold enough? Would you like more ice? Is it helping quench your thirst?" Maybe you'd offer a suggestion, "You know . . . if you squeeze the lemon like so, it tastes even better!" You'll ask your new friends how they're doing with the information you gave them and you'll help them consume it. If you do this well, you'll increase your likability, and you'll create a more meaningful and lasting connection with your new friends, turning them from new friends into potential clients or maybe even into current clients.

consumption

How to Build Your Social Media Platform

Like all relationship and platform development, when it comes to social media or online social networking, you must be willing to make a long-term commitment to the cause. And, contrary to some expert advice, you should not outsource your social media marketing to an assistant or outside firm. Sure, get help with the technical aspects of organizing a Facebook Fan page, if you need it, but if you really want to build your social network online, you've got to show up to do it. I mean social is the operative word here. And, really . . . how hard is that? You just need to make the time for it. And, as you know, we need to make the time to do our marketing to earn clients.

Remember when we covered the 80/20 rule in Chapter 7—the Keep in Touch Strategy? The same applies with how you engage in social media channels. At least 80 percent of what you share and say needs to be about them and with them. Over time, you'll be able to turn your networking efforts into marketing initiatives that drive sales.

Your return on investment in social media networking is both quantitative and qualitative. You are likely to see more leads for new clients and increased profit and, at the same time, enhance your brand identity through positive and valuable interaction with and service to your community, industry, or field.

PULLING IT ALL TOGETHER

If you are serious about adding social media to your self-promotion strategy, you must start with a plan and schedule time in your day to devote to each of these platforms. Effective use of social media requires consistency and commitment. Results are not always apparent right away. Give your social media plan three to six months to start working.

Start using social media by developing your own daily, weekly, and monthly routine. Consider adding the following tasks to your routine.

DAILY:

- Post your personal tweets and updates a minimum of two or three times a day.

- Schedule 15 to 20 minutes of time in your calendar each day to post and monitor your social networks.

- Get involved in relevant discussions, conversations, and responding to direct messages, friend invitations, responding to @replies on Twitter, and so on.

- Read your Twitter stream, Facebook wall, and LinkedIn discussions for new, relevant information for you and to share with your social network.

TWICE PER WEEK:

- Write and post a new blog entry two or three times per week. If you are using article writing to promote your business, or doing an e-newsletter, simply reuse the same article in your blog. Blog content can also be used for your business-related posts and updates.

- Visit other industry-related blogs and add to the conversations.

ONGOING:

- Add new photos, links to videos you've produced and posted on YouTube, audio from radio interviews (such as Blog Talk Radio), and so forth.

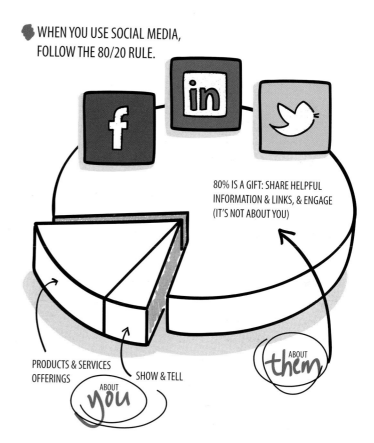

WHEN YOU USE SOCIAL MEDIA, FOLLOW THE 80/20 RULE.

80% IS A GIFT: SHARE HELPFUL INFORMATION & LINKS, & ENGAGE (IT'S NOT ABOUT YOU)

PRODUCTS & SERVICES OFFERINGS
SHOW & TELL

ABOUT you

ABOUT them

The Internet Is Your Friend

Creating web sites, driving traffic, social networking—sometimes it can all sound so exhausting. A little voice in your head whines, "Do I have to?" and you want to pull the covers over your head.

Actually, no, you don't, as I said at the outset of this chapter. Perhaps you have the kind of business that can flourish without an online strategy. For many of us, though, an online strategy is essential, and using the social media platforms to their fullest is one of the surest routes to success. Not only that, as I think you've already seen in each of the three parts of this chapter, it's not nearly as daunting as it might seem at first. Why? Because being social about what you love to do (that is, your business) is not hard.

In fact, it can be downright inspiring to connect with others and share what you know. After all, if you love to serve your target audience, what could be better than serving them better, faster, and easier. The Internet is your friend. Use it to make more friends. Oh yes, and to make more money.

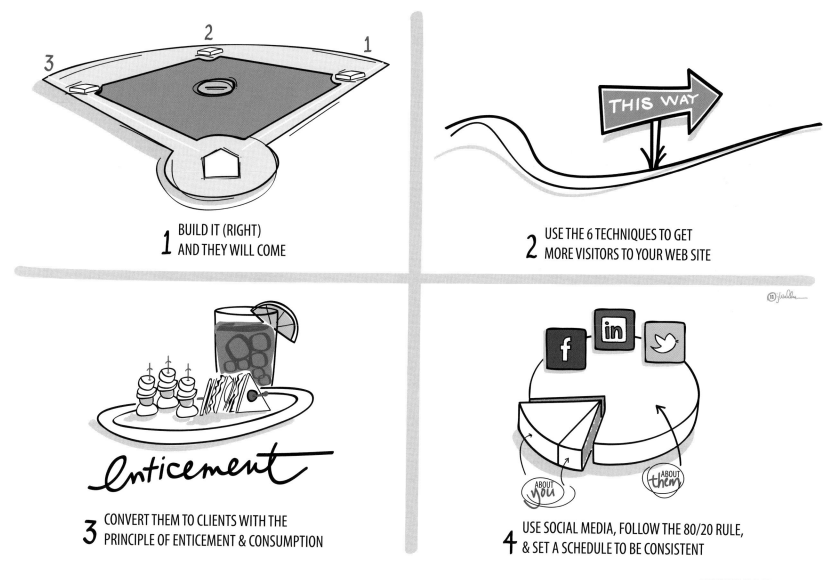

1 BUILD IT (RIGHT) AND THEY WILL COME

2 USE THE 6 TECHNIQUES TO GET MORE VISITORS TO YOUR WEB SITE

enticement

3 CONVERT THEM TO CLIENTS WITH THE PRINCIPLE OF ENTICEMENT & CONSUMPTION

4 USE SOCIAL MEDIA, FOLLOW THE 80/20 RULE, & SET A SCHEDULE TO BE CONSISTENT

THIS WAY

ABOUT you
ABOUT them

Final Thoughts

Congratulations! You made it through. The Book Yourself Solid system is provoking, challenging, sometimes scary, often exciting, and always powerful. The rewards you reap as a result of all your hard work will be well worth the time and effort you've devoted to this process. I hope you'll take the time now to acknowledge all that you've done because it's no small task. In fact, it's really big! We've covered a lot of ground, and you stuck with me, step-by-step, from beginning to end.

You now know who your ideal clients are and how to ensure that you're working only with those who most inspire and energize you. You've identified the target market you feel passionate about serving, as well as what their most urgent needs and compelling desires are, and what investable opportunities to offer to them. You've developed a personal brand that is memorable, has meaning for you, and is uniquely yours, and you know how to articulate whom you serve and how you serve them in a way that is intriguing rather than boring and bland.

You've begun thinking of yourself as the expert you are, and you're continuing to enhance your knowledge to better serve your market, and you understand the importance of your likability factor. You know how to develop a complete sales cycle that will allow you to build trust with those you want to serve. You've learned how to begin developing the brand-building products and programs that are a key part of that sales cycle, how to price your products and services, and how to have sincere and successful sales conversations with your potential clients.

You are networking with others in a way that is genuine and comfortable, and you've learned how to build a web site that will get results, how to reach out to others in a personal and effective way, how to generate a wealth of referrals, how to use speaking and writing to reach more of your potential clients, and then how to keep in touch with the multitude of potential clients you'll connect with when implementing all of the Book Yourself Solid core self-promotion strategies.

Everything you've learned is important, but even more important is to remember the philosophy that underlies the entire Book Yourself Solid system: There are people you are meant to serve, and they are out there waiting for you. When you find them, remember to give so much value that you think you've given too much, and then be sure to give more.

I mentioned at the beginning of our journey that the people who don't book themselves solid either don't know what to do or do know what to do but aren't doing it. You now know exactly what to do. There are no more excuses, no more reasons to procrastinate or drag your feet or hide in your office.

The question now is what are you going to do with what you've learned? Throughout the course of this book I've given you written exercises and Booked Solid Action Steps that can earn you more clients than you can handle. Have you been doing them throughout the book? If you have, fantastic, keep going. If you haven't, are you going to start doing them right now? Your success hinges on your continued action.

To that end, at MichaelPort.com, you can continue to get support and advice about all of the concepts I've laid out in this book. If you want more help, if you want to have your own Certified Book Yourself Solid Coach, if you want to work in a structured environment that will inspire you to action and keep you accountable so that you do book yourself solid, then join one of our highly acclaimed online learning programs, watch for a live event near you, or work directly with me in my personal mentoring program.

This may be the end of this book, but that doesn't have to mean the end of our work together. Your business is a generative and iterative process. You will be changing and evolving as you adapt to the ebb and flow of your growing booked-solid business, and I look forward to continuing to serve you in the best and most effective ways I can.

I sincerely thank you for spending this time with me by learning the Book Yourself Solid system. It means so much to me that you've taken the time out of your busy schedule to read my book and follow my advice. I am honored to serve you. I hope these principles, strategies, techniques, and tips make a true difference in your life and in the lives of those you serve.

I hope the Book Yourself Solid path helps you to look in the mirror every morning and have a mad, passionate love affair with yourself, do the work that you love to do, and book yourself solid while standing in the service of others and making a difference in their lives.

I love you very much (and not in a weird way).

Think Big,

Michael Port
www.MichaelPort.com
questions@michaelport.com
414-FOR-PORT

About the Authors and How to Reach Them

Photo: David Heisler

ABOUT MICHAEL PORT

Called "an uncommonly honest author" by the *Boston Globe* and a "marketing guru" by the *Wall Street Journal*, Michael Port is the author of four bestselling books, including the first edition of *Book Yourself Solid*, *Beyond Booked Solid*, *The Contrarian Effect*, and the *New York Times* best-seller, *The Think Big Manifesto*.

A television personality, Michael can be seen regularly on cable and network TV. He receives the highest overall speaker ratings at conferences around the world and offers inspiring, collaborative, and results-oriented mentoring programs for small business success.

At the end of the day, his most significant accomplishment and responsibility is probably just like yours—the job of being a devoted parent, son, friend, and citizen.

Michael speaks to companies and associations throughout the world on marketing and sales. For availability, please e-mail questions@michaelport.com.

3 WAYS TO GET MORE BOOK YOURSELF SOLID MOJO:

1. Participate in a Book Yourself Solid Training Course
2. Get involved with the Book Yourself Solid Mentoring Program
3. Become a Certified Book Yourself Solid Coach

They're like living, breathing, how-to manuals that will start your engine roaring and send you out the door with a complete system you can use to propel your business, your income, and your life.

Learn more at MichaelPort.com
Follow Michael on Twitter: @michaelport
Join Michael on Facebook: facebook.com/michaelport
E-mail Michael at: questions@michaelport.com
Call 414-FOR-PORT

Never hesitate to be in touch. We're here to serve you. And it's an honor to do so.

FULFILL YOUR DESTINY

Thousands of others have turned their passion for what they do into an abundant career that profoundly affects others. You can too.

ABOUT JOCELYN WALLACE

Jocelyn is founder of Red Eleven Group, LLC, a business strategy firm that helps entrepreneurial companies set their vision, create a plan that everyone understands, and go make it happen. Known and loved for her visual facilitation style, Jocelyn has a gift for pulling ideas from you and translating them visually onto large paper, whiteboards, or even your conference room windows!

A teacher-trainer at heart, Jocelyn uses visual thinking principles every day with her clients and has been a conference speaker on the topic at an international level.

Book Yourself Solid Illustrated is her second book.

Learn more at JocelynWallace.com and red11group.com
Follow Jocelyn on Twitter: @jocelynwallace_
Join Jocelyn on Facebook: facebook.com/red11group
E-mail Jocelyn at: questions@jocelynwallace.com
Call 855-887-1885

References

Bayan, Richard. 1984. *Words That Sell*. Chicago: McGraw-Hill Contemporary Books.

Boiler Room. 2000. Directed by Ben Younger. Las Vegas, NV: New Line Cinema.

Brogan, Kathryn S. 2004. *2005 Writer's Market*. Cincinnati: Writer's Digest Books.

Collins, Jim. 2001. *Good to Great: Why Some Companies Make the Leap and Others Don't*. New York: HarperCollins.

Covey, Dr. Stephen. 1989. *The 7 Habits of Highly Successful People*. New York: Simon & Schuster.

Crum, Thomas F. 1987. *The Magic of Conflict: Turning Your Life of Work into a Work of Art*. New York: Touchstone.

Curtis, Glade B., and Judith Schuler. 2004. *Your Pregnancy Week by Week*. Cambridge, MA: Perseus Book Group, First Da Capo Press.

Godin, Seth. 1999. *Permission Marketing*. New York: Simon & Schuster.

Levinson, Jay Conrad, and David Perry. 2005. *Guerrilla Marketing for Job Hunters*. Hoboken, NJ: John Wiley & Sons.

Peters, Tom. 1999. *The Professional Service Firm 50 (Reinventing Work)*. New York: Knopf.

Pink, Daniel. 2001. *Free Agent Nation*. New York: Warner Books.

Sanders, Tim. 2005. *The Likeability Factor: How to Boost Your L-Factor and Achieve Your Life's Dreams*. New York: Crown Publishers.

———. 2002. *Love Is the Killer App: How to Win Business and Influence Friends*. New York: Crown Publishers.

need tools?

bookyourselfsolidillustrated.com

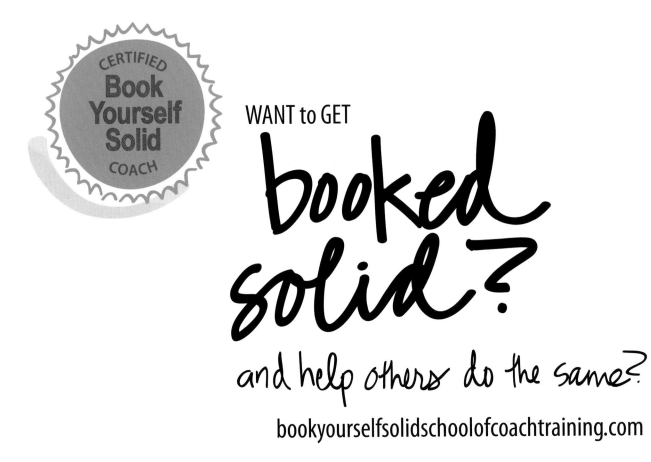

CERTIFIED
Book
Yourself
Solid
COACH

WANT to GET

booked
solid?

and help others do the same?

bookyourselfsolidschoolofcoachtraining.com

If you're interested getting booked solid while helping others do the same, become a Certified Book Yourself Solid Coach. To learn more visit www.BookYourselfSolidSchoolofCoachTraining. com for free weekly calls on how to be a successful coach.

QUESTIONS@MICHAELPORT.COM | 414-FOR-PORT

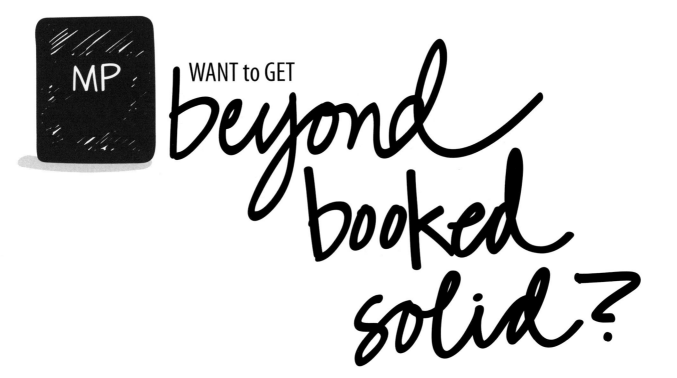

MP

WANT to GET

beyond
booked
solid?

thealliancewithmichael.com

When you are ready to fill your agenda with the most ideal clients, The Alliance with Michael Port can help you get booked solid. It's a mentoring and training program designed to grow your business in an intensive and enjoyable way. Give us your time and we'll give you the tools, training, and transformation you need.

QUESTIONS@MICHAELPORT.COM | 414-FOR-PORT

When you choose Michael or Jocelyn to speak at your event, you won't be getting vanilla sugar cookies. Instead, you'll get slightly irreverent, very funny, knowledgeable, compassionate, and passionate performers who hit their mark every time and leave their audiences a little smarter, much more alive, and thinking a heck of a lot bigger about who they are and what they offer the world.

QUESTIONS@MICHAELPORT.COM | 414-FOR-PORT
QUESTIONS@JOCELYNWALLACE.COM | 855-887-1885

WANT CORPORATE *training*?

With Michael and his coaches, your team will be able to generate a steady stream of leads and turn those leads into ongoing clients—easily. With Jocelyn, a pen, and a piece of paper, you'll turn your ideas into visuals so you can pitch and produce results faster and more effectively than ever before.

QUESTIONS@MICHAELPORT.COM | 414-FOR-PORT
QUESTIONS@JOCELYNWALLACE.COM | 855-887-1885